Caturmāsa

Celebrations of Death in Kathmandu, Nepal

Caturmāsa

Celebrations of Death in Kathmandu, Nepal

A.W. van den Hoek

Edited by
J. C. Heesterman, Bal Gopal Shrestha,
Han F. Vermeulen and Sjoerd M. Zanen

CNWS Publications, Leiden
2004

CNWS Publications
CNWS publishes books and journals which advance scholarly research in Asian, African and Amerindian Studies. CNWS Publications is part of the Research School of Asian, African and Amerindian Studies (CNWS) at Leiden University, The Netherlands.

All correspondence should be addressed to:
CNWS Publications
c/o Research School CNWS
Leiden University
PO Box 9515, 2300 RA Leiden
The Netherlands

Leiden: CNWS Publications.
(CNWS Publications, Vol. 133)
ISBN: 90-5789-098-4
Subject headings: Cultural anthropology; Newar rituals; Nepal

Printing: Ridderprint, Ridderkerk
Cover design: xpressie | visuele communicatie
Layout: xpressie | visuele communicatie

Photocredits: photograph of the author by Han F. Vermeulen (1996), photo 1 by Sjoerd M. Zanen (1979), photo 17 by Gautam Sayami (1991), all other photographs by Bert van den Hoek and Bal Gopal Shrestha.
Cover: Scene from Gāi yātrā in Kirtipur, Kathmandu, showing a lākhe dancer and a man holding a buffalo head, being the lākhe's share of the sacrifice (1992).
Backcover: Vārāhī dancer throwing festive food (samay baji) during the Bhadrakālī dance performance at the Nāsalcok courtyard in Hanumānḍhokā (1991). The author attending the Indrayaṇī (Lutim Ajimā) procession (1989).

Table of Contents

List of illustrations

A.W. van den Hoek (1951 - 2001)

Preface

Caturmāsa: Celebrations of Death in Kathmandu, Nepal contains the first part of a comprehensive study of Kathmandu's festival calendar by the late Bert van den Hoek. When he died in a hospital after a road-accident in Mumbai, India, he left behind, apart from a large number of challenging publications and a film, the as yet unpublished typescript presented here. His work was greatly valued by his peers, colleagues and friends, many of them Nepalese. We, therefore, felt that the present text – the first instalment of what was meant to be Bert van den Hoek's *magnum opus* – should be published as a contribution to our understanding of Nepalese culture.

Professionally, Bert's life followed a straight course. He was born as Albertus Wilhelmus van den Hoek in Apeldoorn, the Netherlands, on September 2, 1951. His call name was Bert.[1] As an adolescent at grammar school, the Stedelijk Gymnasium at Utrecht, he was already intrigued by geography, European classical history, Greek mythology and philosophy, and oriental studies. After graduation, in 1969, he travelled to Greece 'on a shoestring,' and a year later to India in the same way. Since then, he has never stopped travelling, usually in a west-eastern direction, and in a modest way, being most of the time short of funds. On the way, he developed an interest in many societies and in a great number of subjects, from anthropology and sociology to history, religion and linguistics. In the course of thirty years of scholarly dedication he published about countries and regions as different as Lebanon, the Netherlands, Southern Sudan, India and Nepal.

During his academic studies at the University of Leiden, the Netherlands – MA social anthropology in 1976; BA in Sanskrit and cultural history of South Asia in 1989 – Bert followed courses with Professor P.E. de Josselin de Jong on Southeast Asia, and with Professor J.C. Heesterman on South Asia. As a post-graduate student at the École des Hautes Études en Sciences Sociales in Paris (1977) Bert attended workshops by Professor Louis Dumont who, with *La civilisation indienne et nous* (1964) and *Homo Hierarchicus* (1966, 1970) had originally caught his imagination and awakened his interest in South Asian cultures. Reciprocally, Professor Dumont welcomed Bert's interest in Tamil Nadu (where he himself had also started his Indian studies), and valued his work.

Bert completed a number of field-studies, together with Sjoerd Zanen: research in Lebanon (1974), post-graduate research in Madurai, South India (1977), a consultancy in Southern Sudan (1978) and, as from 1979, PhD studies in Nepal. His Madurai study, *The Goddess of the Northern Gate: Cellattamman as the Divine Warrior of Madurai* (1979), published in France (CNRS), was to be the start of a research project on 'The Religious, Social and Political Significance of the Goddess Kālī (Devī, Durga) in Hindu-Buddhist Society'. This enterprise proved too ambitious, and was never finished as such.

During the 1980s Bert spent several years in the Netherlands, working at the Documentation Centre of South Asia at the University of Leiden. He served as editor of the *South Asia Newsletter*, published by the Universities of Leiden and Amsterdam, and was engaged in the organization of several conferences on Asian Studies (1989, 1990). In 1992, he resumed fieldwork in Nepal, with the competent assistance of Bal Gopal Shrestha. Nepalese studies became to him a vocation, a way of life, which he pursued either with or without a job or research grant. Being scientifically ambitious, he strove for a high level of achievement. He was planning a *magnum opus*, a comprehensive analysis of Newar festivals, rituals and myths, entitled *The Ritual Structure of Kathmandu*, and did not want to obtain his PhD degree with a book of lesser magnitude. In the meantime he published a number of articles (1992a,c,d, 1993a,b, 1994, 1996a,b,c), all of them in the mentioned fields. In 1992, Dr D.J. Nijland of the University of Leiden came to Nepal to shoot the celebrated ethnographic video-film *Sacrifice of Serpents: The Festival of Indrayani, Kathmandu, Nepal 1992-94*, based on the research of Van den Hoek and Shrestha (1997).[2] In the same period, Bert contributed to two other films made by Nijland. From 1994 till 1996, he worked at the Centre of Non-Western Studies (CNWS) in Leiden, where *Celebrations* was written.

Bert maintained warm relations with Tribhuvan University in Nepal and with the Centre for Nepal and Asian Studies (CNAS) to which he was affiliated until his death. Professor Kamal Prakash Malla of Tribhuvan University remembers him for his 'keen insight into the culture of Kathmandu Valley, particularly its festivals and ritual structure, (his work having always been) deep and penetrating, often ending in brilliant conclusions, synthesizing Indology with anthropological perspectives'. Bert was a member of several organizations in the Netherlands which promoted ties with Nepal and India, and he drafted Memoranda of Understanding, on the one hand for a cultural agreement between the Netherlands and Nepal, and on the other hand for co-operation between the University of Leiden and Tribhuvan University (signed in 1997). He was also actively engaged in cultural heritage conservation and raised funds for restoration works, i.c. the Vajrayogini temple in Sankhu, Nepal. These activities showed his deeply felt attachment to Nepal, which he came to consider as his second homeland. He realised that, with the current Dutch government policy of continuous cuts in university budgets, there was no future for him and his ambitious research interests in the Dutch academic world. Yet he persevered and persisted in his chosen direction, if not in Dutch academia, then in Nepal among his academic friends there.[3]

On November 28, 2001, Bert was expected to present his paper *Lingua Franca in Nepal: The Pre-Nationalist, the Nationalist, and the Ethnic Discourse* during a seminar in Pune, India. On November 27, coming from Nepal, on his way to the seminar, he was hit by a trailer in Mumbai (Bombay). He died there on December 1, 2001. During this last journey, in Lumbini, he underwent an initiation by His Holiness 17th Gyalwa Karmapa.

In his way of living and working Bert was unconventional. He was not particularly fond of formalities, and preferred to adapt to the life of the people he studied. This also meant that he did not try to impose pre-conceived 'models' on the material. More often than not some details captured his imagination, after which he started to collect, little by little, more information, at the same time developing personal relationships with his informants. He always started on the level of local informants' perceptions, the 'participant's view', and contrasted these with more formal Indological knowledge in a later phase of the research. He knew how to abstract from a mass of information a coherent picture, and so to separate essential from superfluous information. He then construed in an early phase of the research a logical picture, model or theory, and from that position started to work backwards, verifying the facts again. His method was comparative, in order to find significant features. In this way, he could accurately penetrate the core of a subject. The collection of facts and their analysis, theory-construction and -testing all went together, and as part of the process he then sought to share his ideas with ever more learned informants. In doing so, he aimed at a holistic picture, without, however, shirking the (meaningful) ambiguities in the data. It was a rewarding but also a rather exhausting way of investigation, which led to interesting results, but also to physical setbacks. In this way *Celebrations of Death* was composed. It may also explain that this text is only part – though a significant part – of what Bert had in mind.

The work is about meanings. It starts with the significance of the division of the city of Kathmandu in an Upper and a Lower part, which, the author claims, is basic to the rituals that are performed. The dichotomy refers to a battlefield that has been brought inside the city, in a ritualised form, because its unity rests in the last resort on managing society's agonistic inner tension. This image of the city as a sacrificial arena manifests itself even in the rituals of the state during the festival of Indra, in the presence of the king of Nepal. The features of the festival, which have often been described, do not consist of an amalgam of disparate aspects, but all point in the direction of a sacrificial contest – eventually the sacrifice of war, further elaborated in the Festival of Dasain and the 'campaign' of the masked divine dancers Pacalī Bhairava and Bhadrakālī who exchange warrior and sacrificial swords with the King.

The book is presented here, basically, as it was found in February 2002 on the computer of Arja Ruijgrok, a secretary in Leiden who had finished typing it for Bert on May 17, 1995. The editors have presented *Celebrations of Death in Kathmandu, Nepal* as an authentic whole. The body of the original text was preserved, although corrected and slightly shortened where repetitions occurred. However, two major modifications were applied. In the first place, an article by Van den Hoek, *Kathmandu as a Sacrificial Arena* (1993), was added to serve as an introduction to put the study in context. Rather than a static diagram, it offers a dynamic picture of the rituals performed in the 'sacrificial arena' of Kathmandu City. By paying attention to the shifting perspectives of the various participants and to changes over time, the article introduces the reader to the analytic description of the autumn festivals of Kathmandu.

Furthermore, the concluding chapter of the typescript contained an elaborate (and mostly repetitious) overview of the previous chapters. In some instances it offered interpretative considerations not presented before. The editors have sought to incorporate the latter in the main text. The concluding chapter itself they replaced with a short synthesis – entitled 'Concluding Remarks' – covering the main findings of the study.

Also added to the main text of *Celebrations* are a glossary, an index and two appendices, including a ritual calendar (Appendix I) and a table of contents of the intended second part of Van den Hoek's study to be entitled *Marches of the Goddesses* (Appendix II), so as to show how the work was meant to be completed.

The research on which this book is based was made possible by the Netherlands Organization for Scientific Research (NWO) in The Hague, the Research School of Asian, African and Amerindian Studies (CNWS) in Leiden, and the Centre for Nepal and Asian Studies (CNAS) in Kathmandu.

Bert would have wished to express his sincere thanks to all the people of Kahmandu who helped him. In the first place may be mentioned the Thakū jujus of Thane (upper) and Kvane (lower) parts of Kathmandu, Badriraj Malla and Jayram Malla respectively, their families and the members of the Jyāpu *guthis* associated with them. Equally thanks are due to the members of the Maru Indra guthi, Kilāgal Indra guthi, Brahmu Tvāḥ Indra guthi, Vaṃgaḥ Ākāśa Bhairava guthi, Kilāgal Devī pyākhaṃ guthi, Bākā Bhairava guthi, Halco Savābhaku guthi, Majipā Lākhe guthi, the Mahākālī dance groups of Bhaktapur and the patron of the Kumha Pyākhaṃ for supplying a wealth of information, as well as to the members of the Kumār and the Daitya dance groups (Khalaḥ) who made it possible to witness the preludes to the dances. In this connection also the late Laksmi Narayan Mali and Prithu Narayan Mali, Dhana Bahadur Mali and other members of the Gathu *sīguthi*, should be thanked for providing important background information on the divine drama of the Bhadrakālī dances.

Other persons who gave significant help are the chief officer of Hanumānaḍhokā, Tejratna Tamrakār, the main priest of Taleju, the late Keshav Man Karmācārya, the chief royal priest (*mūl purohit*), Rameshprasad Pandya, the main priest of Indrāyaṇī, Kedar Karmacārya, the main priest of Pacalī Bhairava, Labaman Karmācārya, the Buddhist priests, Badriratna Vajrācārya, the late Ratnakaji Vajrācārya, Sakalananda Vajrācārya and the mask maker, the prominent Nepalese traditional artist, Premman Citrakār.

Crucial support in terms of discussion and critical views was also provided by Professors Baldev Juju, Tejratan Kansakar, Prem Kumar Khatry, Kamal Praksah Malla, Tirtha Prasad Mishra, Nirmal Man Tuladhar, and Manik Lal Shrestha of Tribhuvan University, as well as by Bishnu Bhakta Gorkhali, Tirtha Narayan Mali, Pandit Gurushekhar Rajopādhyāy, Hari Prasad Shrestha, Rajendra Shrestha, Srilaksmi Shrestha, Udhav Shrestha, by Malla K. Sundar of the Nepalbhasa Academy, and by Suvarnaman Tuladhar.

Bert would also have wished to thank a few colleagues in Leiden who supported his studies in India and Nepal: Hanneke 't Hart, Loes van der Westrienen, T.E. Vetter and H.W. Bodewitz from the Kern Institute; Ilona Beumer, Dirk Kolff and Willem Vogelsang from the Research School CNWS; Jan Brouwer, Annebert Döbken, Roy Jordaan, Dirk Nijland, Jarich Oosten, Jos Platenkamp and Carla Risseeuw from the Department of Cultural Anthropology.

Special thanks are due to Professor Michael Allen for permission to include 'The Dying Gods: The Divine Dances of the Gathu' as chapter 7, first published in *Anthropology of Nepal: Peoples, Problems and Processes*, Kathmandu: Mandala Bookpoint, 1994; and to Professor Peter Nas and Brill Academic Publishers for permission to include 'Kathmandu as a Sacrificial Arena' as chapter 1, first published in *Urban Symbolism*, Leiden: E.J.Brill, 1993.

Finally, the editors wish to thank the Research School CNWS for facilitating this publication.

The Editors Leiden, November 2003

Chapter 1

Kathmandu as a Sacrificial Arena

Introduction

The rituals of the annual festival cycle of Kathmandu and of Nepal in general show a curious persistence in the face of political changes. Certain images and their configurations may go back well beyond Malla times and cannot easily be tracked down in history. A case in point is the two Thakū jujus, the 'ritual kings' that belong to the Upper and the Lower part of Kathmandu. Not to be confused with the ruling king of Nepal, they are a kind of *reges sacrificii*, who play the part of king within certain ritual contexts only. Their presence in urban ritual seems closely related to the ritual division of the city into an upper and a lower part, the origins of which remain equally obscure.

Lack of precise historical data is often compensated for by a profuse mythology, which, if it does not elucidate the past, may nevertheless account for some of the bewildering imagery encountered at present. Not one, but several images give expression to the city as a totality. An image of an all-encompassing spatial order exists side by side with an image of the city as divided into ritually opposed halves, roughly coinciding with North and South Kathmandu. Although they have often been treated as such, those two images of the city as a whole do not naturally or logically follow from one another. They reflect different perspectives, which, by their very contrast, help to unravel the complex urban symbolism of Kathmandu. Most Kathmandu images are moving in a complex cycle of ceremonies and ritual exchanges, and many of them would probably leave no trace in history if they could not be observed and recorded right now.

Sacred space and sacred motion

The number of divine images in the old city of Kathmandu, from the rough stones in front of every house to the exquisitely carved icons enshrined in temples, is said to surpass the number of human inhabitants. Yet the permanently visible images represent only a fraction of what the city has in stock. Some of the more hidden images always remain behind closed doors, but many are annually taken out in procession (*yātrā*). The yearly cycle of *yātrās* in the inner city shows a clockwise pattern both in time and in space. One month after the turn of the ritual year the cycle starts with the *yātrā* of the goddess Indrāyaṇī in northwest Kathmandu. Almost one year later it ends in the southeast with the *yātrā* of the god Pacalī Bhairava, which coincides with the great autumn festival of Dasain.

It proved also possible, however, to construct an immovable or at least static model of Kathmandu's sacred space strictly on the basis of permanent, mostly stone images. Stripped from the pageantry that periodically surrounds them and detached from the overall social context, a select group of sacred sites seems to offer a model for eternity. Gutschow and Bajracharya first brought it to light in their oft-quoted article 'Ritual as a Mediator of Space in Kathmandu' (1977). Their view of the sacred topography of Kathmandu Valley (Map 1) has found much following, an example being Robert I. Levy in his voluminous work on the city of Bhaktapur (1990). It is a view, which is largely congruent with the more exclusive views, which are handed down to this day by the Vajrācārya, the Buddhist ritual specialists of Kathmandu Valley. They constitute, in other words, a participants' point of view (de Josselin de Jong 1956, 1977) – albeit of course a partial and sophisticated one. In a highly stratified society like that of the Newars, it will however be hard to find participant views of any consequence that do not need further qualification.

In the particular vision of Kathmandu which the Vajrācārya hold, the city, the Valley and the furthest extentions of the old (Malla) kingdom of Nepal are each encircled by a ring of eight shrines, situated at the points of the compass. The shrines which thus demarcate the ordered space of the ancient kingdom at three different levels are all *pīṭha*, seats of power that belong to the *mātṛkās*, the so-called mother-goddesses. Offspring and spouses of the *mātṛkās* are more often than not disputable, and the goddesses rather seem to derive their power from the fact that they stand on their own. Female powers of that nature are known throughout South Asia in groups of five to ten, together with their attendants form a *gaṇa*, a host or troupe. Under the name *mātṛkā* they mostly consist of seven or eight members, with the number seven (*saptamātṛkā*) being current particularly in South India, and the number eight (*aṣṭamātṛkā*) being prevalent in Nepal. Most common to Nepal is the series of eight goddesses, which surround not only the capital Kathmandu, but a number of other towns and villages in the Valley as well (see Zanen 1986 and Shrestha 2002 for Sankhu). Ideally, the goddesses constitute a circle (*maṇḍala*) with each of the *mātṛkā* shrines situated at one of the eight cardinal directions.

In their *pīṭhas* the *mātṛkās* are represented either by stone statues or, more often, just by natural stones. As a rule they are also represented by brass images, which are kept in god-houses (*dyocheṃ*) inside towns or villages. Once a year those statues (*utsava mūrti*) are taken out in procession and placed at their respective *pīṭhas*, the immovable seats of power. Those ritual highlights, however, are absent in the model given by Gutschow and Bajracharya (1977). The *yātrās*, social events par excellence, appear to be quite irrelevant to the vision propounded by them and shared by the Vajrācārya specialists. It is not a matter of complementary views, one of which encompasses or elaborates the other, but rather of two visions of the same sacred space crossing each other. The notion of the *maṇḍalas* or sacred circles that surround the ordered space, does not require any motion – on the contrary, it is complete in itself.

The distribution of the *pīṭhas* is given in some detail by Gutschow and Bajracharya, and with it the connection between this macrocosmic pattern and, respectively, the three bodies of the Buddha (body, speech, mind) and the three corresponding *cakras* (nerve centres, lit. 'circles') of a human being. The Vajrācārya view Kathmandu city as being encompassed by *mātṛkā* shrines like an eight-petalled lotus. However, this macrocosmic-microcosmic equivalence bears little, if any, relation to the spatial reality of the city or, by extension, to that of the Valley and the Kingdom.

What the *maṇḍala* actually stands for can only become clear by looking closer to the *pīṭha pūjā*, the way in which the *mātṛkā* are to be worshipped according to the Vajrācārya guidelines. Putting it briefly, and confining ourselves to Kathmandu city, each of the *mātṛkās* surrounding it is thought to embody a human quality, or rather a defect, which must be surmounted by the individual in search of liberation. Starting in the north, the qualities embodied by the eight *mātṛkās* can be listed as follows: *rāga, dvesa, moha, ahaṃkāra, īrṣyā, darpa, māyā,* and *mada* (Badri Ratna Vajracharya, personal communication), translated approximately by: desire, hate, enchantment, selfishness, envy, pride, illusion, and intoxication.

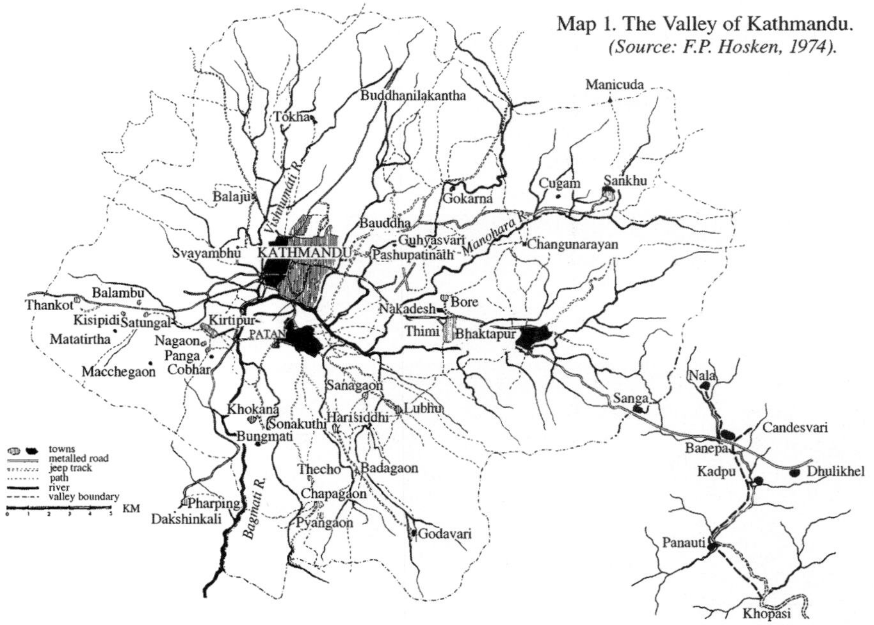

Map 1. The Valley of Kathmandu. *(Source: F.P. Hosken, 1974).*

Map 1.
The Valley of Kathmandu. (Adapted from F.P. Hosken, 1974).

The purpose of a *pīṭha pūjā*, a pilgrimage around the *pīṭhas* (the seats of the mātṛkās), is to free oneself from bondage, from the very chains that make up the self – which, in the Buddhist view, is an illusion. Short of liberation, the pilgrim may overcome envy and desire by degrees and thus proceed on his way to salvation.

Strictly speaking, the individual (*puruṣa*) does not exist in the Buddhist view and that is why, in contrast to the Hindu conception, the circle of *mātṛkās* is without a centre. In the predominantly Hindu town of Bhaktapur, the centre of the circle is automatically included as the ninth divinity who, moreover, encompasses the other eight divinities. The name of the group is not extended from eight to nine *mātṛkās* ('*navamātṛkā*') but to *navadurgā* instead, with the shift of terminology indicating a change of modality: the *aṣṭamātṛkā* are subordinate to the distinct concept of *navadurgā*.

In Kathmandu city both visions exist side by side and together make up one scheme in which the royal goddess Taleju occupies the centre (see Diagram). Apart

Photo 1.
Temple of Taleju Bhavanī at Hanumānḍhokā palace, Kathmandu (1979).

from her virgin manifestation, the living goddess Kumārī, and her god-house, Taleju has a huge temple inside the palace compound (Photo 1). The images of Taleju in there and the rituals performed are enveloped in secrecy by the Karmācārya officiants, a non-Brahmin caste of Hindu priests or ritual specialists. Unlike the *mātṛkās* belonging to the circle, the centre cannot be considered a *pīṭha* in itself. Being part of the palace compound it rather represents a magnificent *dyocheṃ*, a god-house. And indeed, we see that an emblem of the goddess, accompanied by one of Bhairava, the fearsome manifestation of Śiva, is carried once a year in procession to the *pīṭha* of Guhyeśvarī, east of the city, in a way that is parallel to the various local *yātrās*. The *pīṭha* of Guhyeśvarī, the importance of which is recognized at a supralocal level and confirmed by the Sanskrit great tradition, might be the ultimate seat of power of the royal goddess. Complete clarity is hard to obtain, the more so since in this case the secret bears on the royal power itself. Like the *mātṛkās* do, Taleju embodies the *śakti*, the divine energy which seems directly related here to the king. The king used to be initiated into the worship of the goddess Taleju, while the queen, as his earthly counterpart, was not allowed to enter the temple.

The names of the eight *mātṛkās* are in majority derived from those of the

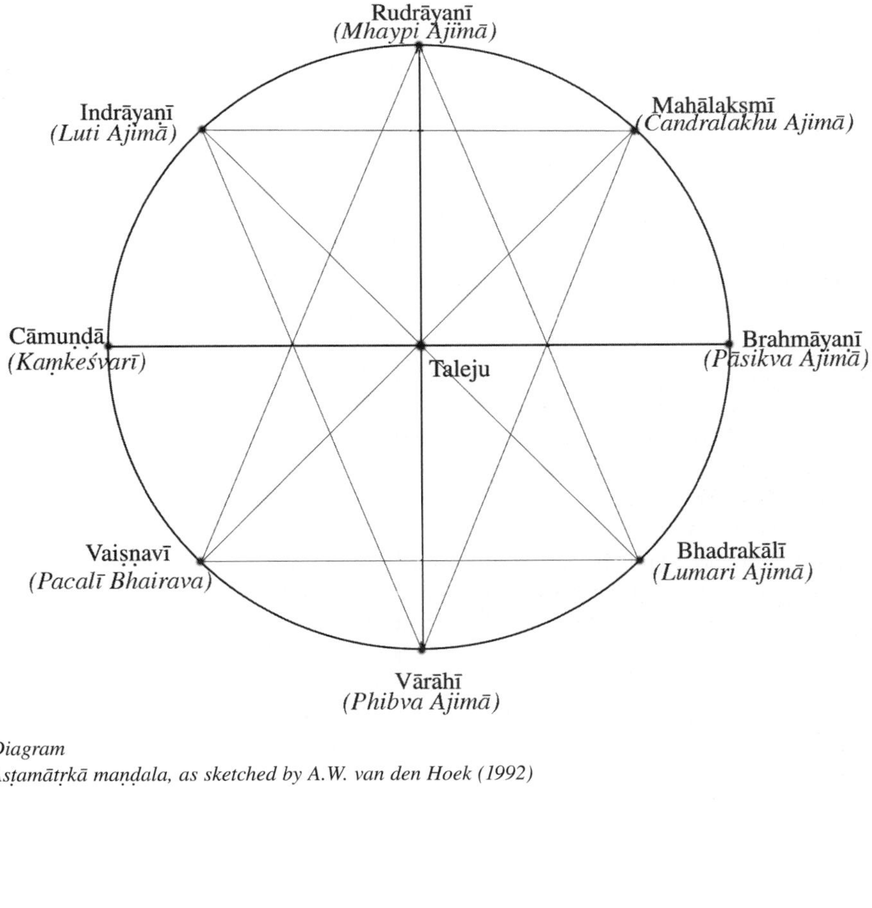

Diagram
Aṣṭamātṛkā maṇḍala, as sketched by A.W. van den Hoek (1992)

great gods of whom they represent the *śakti*, the essentially female power of action. But the ensemble of *śaktis* is not without secrecy either: every determination of the circle surrounding the city can be contested with regard to the names and the ultimate identities of the different divinities. Only when moving from the esoteric conceptions down to earth do the goddesses assume a more definite character and become part of the sociorítual composition of the city. At what might be called the highest level of perception, however, such as expounded by Gutschow and Bajracharya, the correspondence established is not between the *maṇḍala* of divinities and the spatial order of the city, but between the *maṇḍala* and the individual person – regardless of the point whether the individual is considered to be an illusion or not. However tempting it is to see in it the structure of the kingdom, the *maṇḍala* basically represents what is also the secondary meaning of the word itself: a mental diagram.

The more detached question may thus be asked whether the mental diagram has yet in some way influenced the city's spatial design. Although probably none of the *mātṛkā* shrines, which presently surround Kathmandu, came into being as the result of deliberate town planning, chronicles, ritual manuals and oral history undeniably evoke that impression. Tradition has it that the thirty-two wards (*ṭol*) of Kathmandu were before the Malla period divided into eight sets of four wards, each of which had its own king and, supposedly, its own *mātṛkā* shrine. The regular shifts of capitals and centres, of course, forestalled the realization of the perfect encompassment and the ultimate stasis that are inherent in the model. Yet one is led to believe that attempts have been made to make the model fit the unruly spatio-temporal conditions and, perhaps reversely, to make reality fit the model. The nature of the *pīṭha*, however, makes it impossible to easily relocate them: they are the true seats of *śakti*, the sources of divine power.

While dynasties broke up and capitals shifted, the *pīṭhas*, the stone-marked seats of divinities, most probably remained in place. This can be gathered from both past and present developments. Kathmandu's *pīṭhas*, theoretically located at the outer boundaries of town, have rapidly been incorporated in the sprawling city. One of the *pīṭhas* has become part of the palace gardens at Nārāyaṇahiti and can only be visited by the public on the king's birthday. Another one, ironically, has been surrounded by a bustling traffic circle. Indications are that such developments are not entirely new. The Cāmuṇḍeśvarī *pīṭha*, for example, is inside the buildings of the popular Newar daily *Sandhyā Times*. Because it is located well within the old city it cannot within living memory have belonged to a *maṇḍala* surrounding that very town. Evidently, it cannot be obliterated either. At the time of *pīṭha pūjā*, parts of the printing press are pushed aside to worship the stone slab representing Cāmuṇḍeśvarī, sunken in a cavity more than a meter below the present surface. It is easy to imagine that, were the capital to be shifted again, the site might be restored to a full-fledged *pīṭha*. Although, as a result of shifting patterns of settlement, *pīṭhas* have been subject to reinterpretation within their changing contexts, this has nowhere in the Valley led to an ideal pattern of eight goddesses surrounding a town according to the points of the compass.

It looks as if such a state can only be achieved by projecting it into times long gone, that is, by representing it as an original state. Indeed, if textual sources and archeological data were the only remaining evidence of Newar culture, one would easily be led to believe that the Kingdom of Nepal, and the Valley and the City of Kathmandu, were laid out in the form of three eight-petalled lotus flowers encompassing each other.

At present, but probably in the past as well, the predominant features of urban symbolism appear to be different from, and partly incompatible with the structural perfection which the Valley's ritual specialists – Vajrācārya, Karmācārya, and Brahmins alike – have in mind. Instead of the one and perfect vision on the city as a whole, several visions compete in shaping the cosmopolis, which Kathmandu really is – such in spite of, or even by the grace of its own contradictions. The unity of the city and the realm is not brought about by a fixed monolithic arrangement, but by a continuous movement that connects the parts with the whole, or by which the parts make up the whole.

The principal division in this regard is that between Thane and Kvane, the Upper and Lower part of the city (Map 2), and by extension, of the realm (Witzel 1992: 796). It is a ritual division that is not only manifests in Kathmandu, but in a number of other Newar towns as well. In contrast to the sacred topography with its eight or nine constituents, such a ritual division, manifested in almost every Newar town, has not been the subject of idealization. Nowhere in the manuals is it prescribed that cities should be composed of two ritually opposed halves, each of which constitutes a totality in itself, and nowhere do we find a standard for drawing the boundary.

Yet it can be gathered from scattered historical evidence and from the pattern as it exists today that the ritual division must be a persistent feature of urban structure and one of the most conservative features of Nepalese history (Regmi 1966: 554, Slusser 1982: 90-91, Toffin 1984: 186, Herdick 1986: 8, Levy 1990: 168-174). The *mātṛkās* prove to be prominent again but, naturally, the position they occupy in the dichotomy is different from the one accorded to them in the *maṇḍala*. While the *maṇḍala* stands by itself, the ritual divide is constantly re-enacted by the urban society at large. The yearly cycle of *yātrās*, the processions of the various local divinities, dominates this scene of motion.

The ritual divide

The two parts of the ritual dichotomy in Kathmandu city are nowadays designated by the simple terms Upper and Lower, in Newar *Thane* and *Kvane* (also spelled *Kone*). Each part used to have its distinctive fountain (*hiti*), as is borne out by the names of Thahiti quarter at the northern city boundary and Kohiti quarter at the southern one. In early medieval times the two parts were designated by the Sanskritic names Koligrāma and Dakṣiṇagrāma (Slusser 1982 I: 91). The difference in name has led

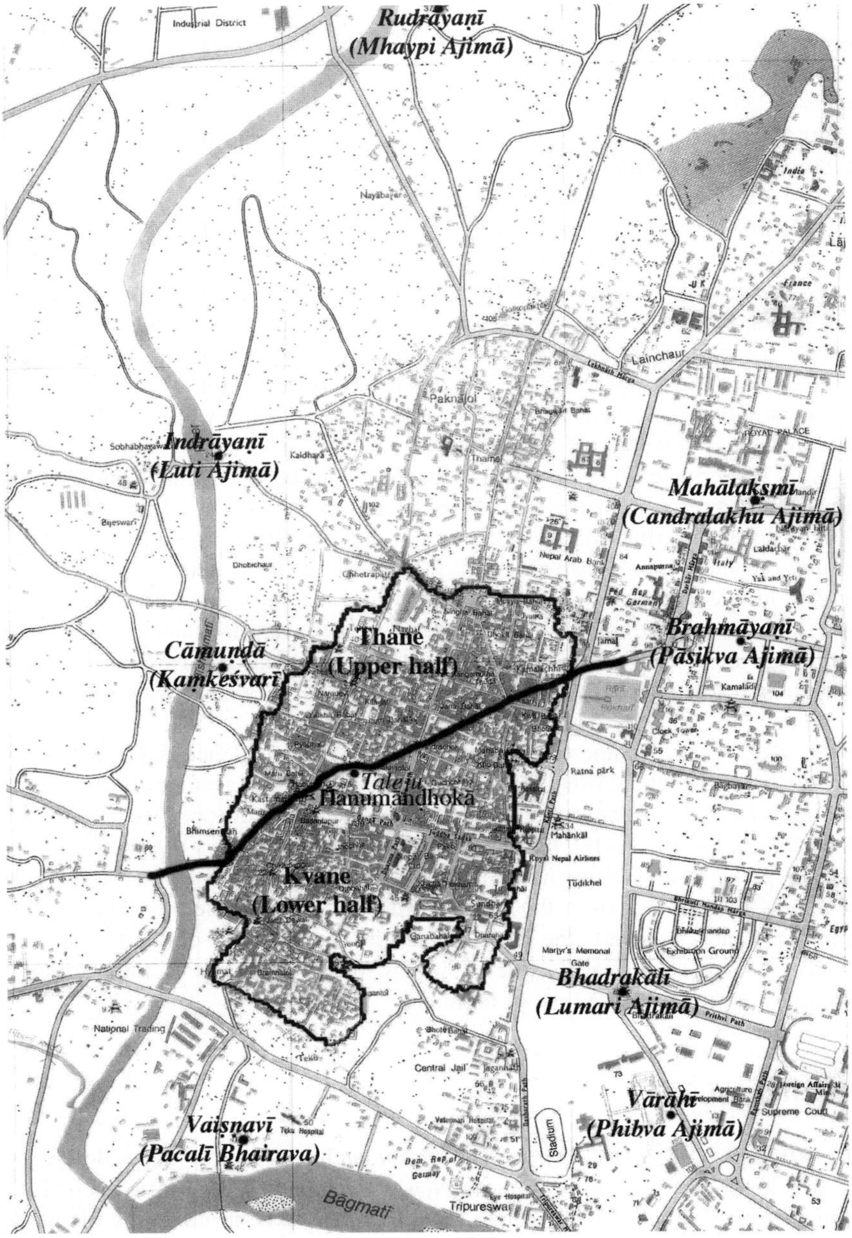

Map 2.
Kathmandu City, showing the location of the eight mother goddesses (aṣṭamātṛkā) shrines, the Thane-Kvane divide, and the temple of Taleju. (Adapted from Kathmandu City Map No. 1, H.M.G. Survey Department, Topographical Survey Branch, Kathmandu, Nepal, 1986).

some historians to believe that Kathmandu originally consisted of two separate towns, which merged in the course of history. As Levy (1990: 173-174) observes in his study of Bhaktapur, which shows a similar division into an Upper and a Lower town, such a hypothesis would imply that almost every Newar town came into being as a result of two separate entities growing together – which is unlikely, to say the least. Because there are no normative sources on which to fall back in this regard, the significance of the division must be derived from its actual manifestation, the rituals that are performed.

In Kathmandu a Thakū juju (New. king) is connected with each of the city halves. Whatever may have been the amount of 'kings' in pre-Malla Kathmandu, only two of those remain till the present day. These two kings no longer have any political power, but fulfill a ritual role only. Both carry the caste-name *Malla*, but in neither case the name is connected with the Malla dynasty which emerged in the thirteenth century. Instead, the Thakū jujus of North and South Kathmandu claim to stem from the preceding dynasty of Thakuri rulers, who held sway over different parts of Kathmandu Valley in the period between the end of the Licchavi dynasty in the ninth century and the emergence of the Malla dynasty. While the Licchavi and the Malla dynasties left behind a rich legacy of inscriptions, the Thakuri reign in-between left but a few traces. Yet important events, such as the introduction of a new era (*Nepal Saṃvat*) and the rise of Kathmandu city took place in this chronologically and dynastically obscure period of which the Thakū jujus claim to have been the protagonists. Their medieval roots cannot, however, account for their continued presence, which, we shall see, is closely linked with the persistent ritual divide of the city.

The Thakū jujus do not possess any political power and have no connections with the present kings of Nepal. They fulfil a purely ritual role, as lords of sacrifice, or, if one wishes to retain the royal connotation, as *reges sacrificii*. One of them is Thakū juju of the Upper city (Thane) with his residence near Thahiti, the other is Thakū juju of the Lower city (Kvane) with his residence near Kohiti. The first presides over rituals in the northern part of the town, the latter over those of the southern part.[2] It should be kept in mind, though, that the totality of Kathmandu's ritual structure is more complex than this division may seem to suggest.

The Thakū jujus ultimately trace their ancestry to the kings of Pharping, nowadays a small township in the south-western corner of the Valley. They consider themselves descendants of the legendary king Pacalī of Pharping. Here mythology enters the genealogy, for king Pacalī was not an ordinary human being but a form of Bhairava, the fearful manifestation of Śiva. Pacalī Bhairava still has an interesting *yātrā* in his town of origin, Pharping, in which the Thakū juju of Kathmandu Thane participates. The festival of Pacalī Bhairava in Kathmandu itself, however, of which the Kvane Thakū juju is in charge, is of much greater significance today. It takes place during the first five days of the celebrated festival of Mohanī (Nep. Dasain, Durgā *pūjā*).[3]

The Thakū juju of the North is intimately connected with the *pīṭha* and the *yātrā* of Indrāyaṇī, one of the eight *mātṛkās* (goddesses) of the *maṇḍala* scheme presented above. His residence contains the *dyocheṃ*, the 'god-house' where the brass procession statues of Indrāyaṇī and her *gaṇa* ('following', 'troupe') are kept (Photo 2).

The *dyochem̥* is accessible to devotees of pure caste. Once a year, during the festival of Indrāyaṇī (the second festival after the Caturmāsa), the statues of Indrāyaṇī and her *gaṇa* are taken out in procession to the *pīṭha* of the goddess on the banks of the Viṣṇumatī river west of the city and outside the city boundaries. Unlike the seats of most other *mātṛkās* of Kathmandu Valley, the Indrāyaṇī *pīṭha* is not an open-air shrine with slabs of natural stones, but a pagoda-type temple with stone icons of the deities.

The *gaṇa* of Indrāyaṇī remarkably includes the other *mātṛkās* of the sacred *maṇḍala* given above: the sacred topography turns out to be irrelevant at this level of ritual action where, in all cases known and in every single *pīṭha*, the *mātṛkās* have to be worshipped together. The *pīṭhas* are looked after by members of the ('untouchable') sweepers caste and are accessible to everybody.

For one night and one day the brass procession statues of the goddess and her *gaṇa* (represented by brass masks) are placed before their respective stone icons. The special task of the Thakū juju is to be Lord of the Sacrifice (*jajmān*) of a fire ritual (*homa*), which is performed in the night preceding the *yātrā* of the goddess Indrāyaṇī (see Van den Hoek and Shrestha 1992a). After receiving plenty of sacrifice the movable images are put in their palanquins again the next evening. Joined by several other local divinities with their own crowds and musicians, the procession of Indrāyaṇī moves back to town and stays for the night at Thahiti square. From there it is taken the next day all around the ancient city and, in some places, beyond the former city walls. With the exception of the goddess Bhadrakālī, the sister and southern counterpart of Indrāyaṇī, there is no other divinity in Kathmandu whose *yātrā* encloses such a vast domain.[4] A salient feature of the Indrāyaṇī *yātrā* is that it gains in strength across the boundary of the northern city half. From there on traditional orchestras as well as brass bands, employed by Thane sponsors, will add lustre to the goddess' passage through Kvane and the centre of town.

Indrāyaṇī has a perfect antipode in her sister Bhadrakālī, whose *pīṭha* is at the south-eastern point of the compass and whose *yātrā* reversely moves into the northern part of town. The *yātrā* of the goddess Bhadrakālī of Kvane forms a perfect simile of the Indrāyaṇī procession. Here it is the goddess of the southern part who conquers the north. Like Indrāyaṇī, this goddess figures as just one of the *mātṛkās* in the city's sacred topography. However, the *pīṭha* of Bhadrakālī again includes the other *mātṛkās*, among whom Indrāyaṇī herself. Both parties are complete in themselves and both of them circumambulate the whole city of Kathmandu, without however being identified with each other. On the contrary, they are conceived of as antagonists.

In Newar mythology, Bhadrakālī and Indrāyaṇī have been given additional – and probably primordial – Newar names, which strikingly resemble each other: *Luti Ajimā* ('Grandmother of the Golden Liquid') and *Lumari Ajimā* ('Grandmother of the Golden Bread') respectively. They are again nearly identical but yet distinct. Their relationship is seen as that between elder and younger sister (with the parentage remaining obscure) and their antagonism is attributed to an ill-omened invitation. Whether by misunderstanding or by bad faith, Indrāyaṇī was invited to a sacrificial party by her elder sister, but one day late, so that only left-overs were available for her

Photo 2.
The Thakū juju of Thane receiving the procession statue of Indrāyaṇī by touching it with a key, in his courtyard, after the completion of the procession of Indrāyaṇī (1988).

and her hungry children (who are, again, identified with the other seven *mātṛkās*, just short of including Bhadrakālī herself by her proper name). Indrāyaṇī was subsequently adopted by the king of Thane, and other castes took care of her children. The anger of Indrāyaṇī at the insult from her sister could only be appeased with an extraordinary sacrifice, a sacrifice of serpents (*sarpahoma*). The sacrifice of serpents into the sacrifical fire is performed to this day by the Thane Thakū juju, in the night preceding the start of her procession (*yātrā*). The children of Indrāyaṇī were adopted by members of the castes who presently take part in the festival. In addition, the Thane Thakū juju ordained that Indrāyaṇī's sacrifice, and her *yātrā*, from that time onwards would always precede that of Bhadrakālī by four months, making Indrāyaṇī the winner of what, under the surface, appears to be a sacrificial contest.

The pattern that comes to light now is far remote from the *maṇḍala*, the orderly scheme in which all goddesses occupy separate positions. In the ritual cycle of Kathmandu city, two of the *mātṛkās* prove to be predominant. While being called sisters and appearing to be doubles of one another, they are at the same time antagonists who run into each other's territory. One would, of course, expect the Thakū juju of Kvane to be the patron of Bhadrakālī, but here the system does not close. The Kvane juju is the patron of Pacalī Bhairava, and, even though Bhadrakālī is seen as Pacalī's consort, it turns out that during Pacalī's *yātrā* attention is focused on the god and his illegitimate lover, the Nāy girl. Their procession does not encircle the city or cross the ritual boundary, but only touches Hanumānḍhokā at the centre of the city, to be offered sacrifice from the palace. The royal Kumārī awaits them there in the dead of night and watches motionless, as if she is sitting there just to reconfirm the connection between the central power and its distant predecessor.

The divine network thus proves to be more complicated than the ritual divide between Thane and Kvane. However, the North-South division of the city is not only a matter of *jujus* and gods with their following. Although festivals provide the most impressive of urban images, the basic unit of urban social structure above the family level is not the caste (*jāt*) but the funeral association, the *sī-* or *sanāguthi*. Membership of these *guthis* is determined by both caste and locality. Here the dichotomy emerges again, for also funeral associations prove to be split into northern and southern *guthis*. The northern and the southern part of Kathmandu have separate cremation platforms (*ghāṭs*). In the *maṇḍala*, the sacred diagram of the *aṣṭamātṛkā*, a *śmaśāna* (cremation platform) is attributed to each of them. In fact only two of them have a cremation *ghāṭ*: Indrāyaṇī in the northern part of town and Kaṃkeśvarī in the southern part. Bhadrakālī is said to have possessed a cremation *ghāṭ* near her *pīṭha* as well, that is, before the government offices of Sinha Darbār were built over it in the last century. Another, still extant cremation *ghāṭ* is near the *pīṭha* of Pacalī Bhairava on the banks of the Bāgmatī river.

Although the performance of funerary rites is the main task of the *sī-* and *sanāguthis*, they are not completely defined by it. The members come together once a year for a sacrificial feast and they may also partake in festivals such as that of Indrāyaṇī. Cremation is since ancient times considered to be the last sacrifice (*antyeṣṭi*) that human beings make. As the activities of the *sī-* or *sanāguthis* also include other sacrifices, they could perhaps more suitably be termed sacrificial associations, the actions of which culminate in the last sacrifice. The ritual divide between Thane and Kvane, as it appears from the public festivals, is parallelled by a division in those associations. Taken together, the evidence suggests that the ritual divide, or North-South division of Kathamndu is, in the end, of a sacrificial nature.

The city as a sacrifical arena

The sacrificial nature of the North-South divide is also indicated by oral tradition. Particularly the Poḍe (New. Dyolā), traditionally fishermen and sweepers, but also guardians of the *pīṭhas* and public executioners, remember that real battles between North and South were fought in the bed of the Viṣṇumatī river. In his *Account of the Kingdom of Nepal* (1819) Francis B. Hamilton, though not being an eyewitness himself, reports on a 'vile custom' of the Newars of Kathmandu:

> At the end of May, and beginning of June, for fifteen days, a skirmish takes place between young men and boys, of the north and south ends of the city ... (which) on the evening of the fifteenth becomes more serious ... The fight (fought with

> stones) begins about an hour before sunset, and continues until darkness separates the combatants. In the one which we saw [that is, Colonel Crawford to whom Hamilton refers] four people were carried off much wounded and almost every other year one or two men are killed: yet the combat is not instigated by hatred, nor do the accidents that happen occasion any rancour. Formerly, however, a most cruel practice existed. If any unfortunate fellow was taken prisoner, he was immediately dragged to the top of a particular eminence [i.e. a divinity] in the rear of his conquerors, who put him to death with buffalo bones ... The origin of this custom is attributed to two causes. Some allege, that at one time Kathmandu was subject to two Rajas and that skirmishes first arose among their respective followers, and have ever since been continued. Others, with more probability, think that the combat is meant to commemorate a battle between a son of Mahadeva, and a Rakshas, or evil spirit. Colonel Crawford justly gives a preference to this opinion, for, if one of the parties obtained the victory, every thing favourable, seasonable rains, plentiful crops, and fine weather, is augured for the remainder of the year; the reverse is expected should the opposite party gain an advantage. (Hamilton 1819, repr. 1986: 43-45)

Remarkably, the scholarly debate today hardly deviates from the alternatives offered nearly two centuries ago. And what is more, the last sentence of the oft-quoted passage of Hamilton seems to have escaped notice. What it says, in an admittedly obscure way, is that one of the parties should win, but not which one. Good and evil are not ascribed to either the northern or the southern party but, strange as it may seem, to the battle itself and the ensuing victory of either party – making it irrelevant which of them wins. The description suggests that the very act of making a victim was central to this battle. Formerly, it is said, a prisoner was to be dragged alive to the top of a particular eminence, and killed – probably, as can be inferred from the buffalo bones, as part of a more elaborate sacrifice.

It is common knowledge in present-day Kathmandu that some of the *śaktis*, and *mātṛkās* in particular, require a human sacrifice, but it is generally assumed that this sacrifice is compensated for by 'buying off' (*niṣkṛti*) the human being with animal victims. Yet exceptions are made, such as in particular for Kaṃkeśvarī – undoubtedly involved in the ritual battle described by Hamilton – who is still believed to need and to get human sacrifice. Kaṃkeśvarī belongs to the *gaṇa* of Bhadrakālī and her festival is part of Bhadrakālī *yātrā*, the great manifestation of *śakti* by the southern part of town. Not only Hamilton's report but also a sufficient amount of local evidence indicates that this *śakti* had somehow to be nourished, or rather appeased, with human sacrifice. Considering the evidence from other parts of the Valley, such as the Navadurgā of Bhaktapur, Brahmāyaṇī of Pāṭan, Dakṣiṇakālī of Pharping, and many others as well, the mystery attached to human sacrifice does not concern its necessity, but its effectuation. How to select and procure a suitable victim is probably the most problematic aspect of human sacrifice, at least in South Asia.

Without any doubt the battlefield offered the best chances to make victims –

or to become one, as Heesterman (1985: 45-58) pointed out with regard to Vedic sacrifice. War, however, is something fought outside, with chances being that neither victory nor defeat is achieved. The crux of the North-South divisions of Newar cities, then, appears to be that the battlefield has been brought inside, albeit, as Hamilton described, in a regulated manner. Or, as one would put it nowadays, the battlefield has become ritualized, conditioned in such a way that it leads to the one or two victims required for the completion of sacrifice. Indications are that the victim could also be supplied by what we would call capital punishment, but this remains a matter to be further investigated.

The argument so far runs straight against functionalist explanations of war as a means to resolve or at least to redirect the internal tensions of a community or state, the sort of explanation that is also given by Levy (1990: 174) with regard to the ritual antagonism in Bhaktapur. The North-South or Upper-Lower divisions of Newar towns seem to contain a conception exactly opposite to this view: the battlefield has been brought inside – in a ritualized form, that is – because it delivers the fruits desired, and in that way, has a value of its own. Tellingly, king Jayaprakāśa Malla, who was the first to prohibit the ritual battle in the eighteenth century, revoked his decision from fear that he had thereby offended the gods. It was finally Jang Bāhadur Rāṇā who in 1849 banned the fights, or at least reduced the comprehensive scale on which these used to take place (Slusser 1982: 91).

Yet one might wonder at this point, after the *maṇḍala* of a static sacred topography has been replaced by the image of a sacrificial arena, what, in that case, brings about the unity of Kathmandu city – such unity that it can afford a division? In order to tackle this question, the centre and the seat of power will be re-examined, this time by starting from the margin.

The image of the city as a sacrificial arena is not confined to liminal cases or marginal castes, but also manifests itself at the highest level during Indra *yātrā*. It is the royal festival *par excellence*, dedicated on the one hand to Indra, the king of the gods, and on the other hand to the king of Nepal, who is towards the end of the festival empowered by the central *śakti* of the city and the country. Yet the context shows features of a sacrificial arena. The living goddess Kumārī does, in her huge procession chariot, make a round of the city along the established inner procession route, but her *yātrā* is split into two parts: one night for the southern half of town, and one night for the northern half. Belonging to the city as a whole, she thereby commits no transgression, but nevertheless reconfirms the division, with the king, as it were, like a sacrificial victim in-between. Just before giving the *ṭikā* mark to the king of Nepal, she makes a wild round of the heart of the city, as if, suddenly, the centre and the king transcend the ritual divide. In the heart of town, several temporary wooden poles represent Indra, the king of the gods with his image below or on top of it. The peculiar thing is, however, that the king of the gods is represented as a thief captured and bound by the populace of Kathmandu, as a victim and not as a victor (see chapter 5). Furthermore, a number of huge masks is brought down and exhibited in the streets, squirting rice beer from their mouths, and said to represent Hāthudyo, the God of

Liquor, another manifestation of Bhairava. The masks, which are all heads without body, are brought in connection with the legendary king Yalambar, whose valour forced him to join the battle in Kurukṣetra by choosing the side of the losing party, that of the Kauravas. For that transgression he was punished by Lord Kṛṣṇa, who beheaded him with such a force that his head flew all the way back to his capital Kathmandu. Such are the spoils of war.

It would seem then that the combined features of Indra *yātrā*, which will be described below, do not constitute an amalgam of disparate aspects, but all point to one direction, that of a sacrificial concours. This time, however, the victim does not spring from either part of the antagonistic divide in the city, but from its very heart. Lord Indra is bound to the wooden poles, or encaged like a victim is to the sacrificial pole. It can be gathered from the telling imagery of Indra *yātrā* what, at a hidden level, the blessing of the virgin goddess prepares the king for: not for an immediate sacrifice, but for what is considered the king's long-time duty: the sacrifice of war (see chapter 5).

The imagery is further elaborated during the great festival of Dasain, which is celebrated one month later, when the harvest is already collected or ripening in the fields, that is, at the appropriate time of going to war. The striking images of the captured king of the gods and the beheaded king of the country are absent now. Dasain, it seems, only leads to victory, which, symbolically, is the victory of the Goddess over the Demon Lord. Yet also here one must be aware of a fundamental ambiguity, for the Demon Lord is also considered a devotee of the Goddess. His position is thereby essentially analogous to that of the king in relation to his protective goddess. Transferred to a higher plane, that of the battle between different realms, an image arises which is again similar to that of the sacrificial battle between the two city segments: what matters is not the prevalence of the one or the other party, let alone its moral superiority, but the sacrifice of war itself.

One feature of urban symbolism, which extends over the greater cosmopolis, the Valley at large, seems to parallel the campaigns of the king: the divine dances by members of the Gardeners' (Gathu) caste. These divine dances will more fully described below (see chapters 5, 6 and 7). Here they will only be dealt with in so far as they form a final piece to the argument developed. In twelve-yearly cycles the Gathu caste of Gardeners carry out the masked dances that centre upon either Pacalī Bhairava or Bhadrakālī, followed by the divine host of attendants among whom are, once more, the *aṣṭamātṛkā*. Both in the Pacalī and the Bhadrakālī dances their first public performances is on the tenth and concluding day of Dasain (*Vijayā Daśamī*: the tenth day of victory), when they move from the Pacalī resp. the Bhadrakālī *pīṭha* to the old palace area in the centre of town. Depending on whose turn it is, either Pacalī or Bhadrakālī – familiarly called Āju and Ajimā, grandfather and grandmother – exchanges swords with the king of Nepal three times. The king's sword is brought from the ancient palace by a *khaḍga yātrā*, a sword-carrying procession, consisting of castes, which once constituted the Malla court. Two other unmasked divine dancers of the Tulādhar (Merchant) and the Śākya (Goldsmith) caste come along with the sword party, the first of whom embodies the god Kumāra and is said to protect the party against dangers from heaven, the second of whom embodies Daitya (in fact a demon) and is said to protect it against dangers from the underworld. At the same time they represent Thane and Kvane, a division which, it seems, never completely disappears. The Bhadrakālī dancers themselves, however, may well transcend the divide. On the day following the sword exchange they make a tour of the old city along the same route as the Kumārī *yātrā*, but without splitting it up into a northern and a southern part. Indications are that the exchange of swords with either Pacalī Bhairava or Bhadrakālī transfers power to the king of Nepal. It is told that king Pṛthvī Nārāyaṇa, the Shāhī conqueror of Nepal in the eighteenth century, was himself a form of Pacalī Bhairava – for otherwise he could not have succeeded in his conquest.

The exploits of the divine dancers during the rest of their year of existence affirm the idea of a campaign. Although they have a scheme of places to visit in the city and the Valley, they go, according to their own saying, only there where sacrifice awaits them. They drink the blood straight from the veins of the victims, together with liquor in great quantities, but state without winking that they are completely sober again after putting off the masks: it is not the human body but the god embodied who consumes the blood and the liquor.

Roaming through the town and the countryside, the *aṣṭamātṛkā* in the following of Bhairava and Bhadrakālī once more exhibit a different quality. In the sacred diagram, the *maṇḍala* which we started from, they were accorded fixed positions. In the ritual divide of Kathmandu they formed troupes, which, although nearly identical to each other, were also each other's antagonists in the ritual arena of the city. Finally, in the case of the Bhadrakālī dancers, they indeed seem to encompass the dichotomy of the city and, after being given sufficient offerings there, they strike out beyong the city in their insatiable quest for sacrifice. Finally, at the start of the rainy season, they perform their own last sacrifice by burning their divine masks. Again this war-like expedition is to a great extent a ritualized one. Although rumours have it that the Bhadrakālī dancers, like the Navadurgā of Bhaktapur, may take one or more victims at random – especially human ones –, they are invited and offered sacrifice on all known occasions. The ritualized context of their exploits is thus contrasted to those of the king himself, if indeed he goes to war. Even when empowered by the sword exchange with Bhadrakālī, the chances of the king will remain unsure. Indeed, the very exchange of his warrior sword with the sacrificial sword of Bhadrakālī seems again to indicate the ambiguity which we saw manifested in the ritualized antagonism between North and South Kathmandu. What matters is that they go to battle, not which of them wins. Likewise, at a level deeper than the quest for victory, the sword exchange prepares the king for sacrifice, irrespective of whether that will be his own or his adversary's. Here at least, in the sacrifice of genuine war, an image is evoked which is also accessible to the Western mind, much more so than the ominous division of an ancient city into parts that compete in gory sacrifice – albeit in a regulated manner.

Chapter 2

The Ritual Cycle of Kathmandu

It is virtually impossible to subdivide the ritual cycle of Kathmandu in such a way that it shows a beginning and an end. There is certainly a story contained in the chain of ritual events, but it is an unbroken one. Three-yearly, eight-yearly, and twelve-yearly festivals add to the complexity of the recurrent annual pattern. Every effort to arrange this state of affairs is to some extent artificial, the more so because rituals have different levels of meaning.

The annual ritual cycle has definite connections with the agricultural cycle in which the sowing, transplanting, and harvesting of the rice are central phases. Dasain, for example, which in other parts of South Asia is called Daśarā or Durgā pūjā and which in Newar is called Mohanī, can be considered a harvest festival. Yet its ritual features do not reflect an agricultural process, let alone that its main day, Vijayā Daśamī, could be ritually identified as the Harvest festival.

Generally speaking the ritual cycle cannot impose agricultural rules either. It is mostly determined by the lunar calendar, which, although 'corrected' every twenty-seven months, is diverging from the solar year and its seasons. The farmer, finally, will sow his rice at the start of the rainy season, a capricious moment without ritual demarcation. Hence there is no way to model the ritual cycle on the agricultural one.

Kathmandu Valley, one may remark, has since its most ancient history had an urban character with kingship as a central feature (see chapter 1). Rather than reflecting an agricultural cycle, rituals may serve to consolidate the state. Dasain may again be taken as an example, this time as a celebration of good over evil and of order over chaos, with the king at the apex of the order. There is truth in that view as well, but, as will become clear, not a full one either. Many forces are unleashed during Dasain, and sacrifice is the most crucial phenomenon. With disruption at its core, Dasain can hardly be considered a reflection of the statal order. Furthermore, the rituals at the central level do not prove to be predominant, or characteristic for the festival as a whole. Dasain is equally important at the level of the family and the ward as it is at the level of the city and the state.

The ritual order is more than a reflection on, or consolidation of the agricultural cycle, the state, or the family structure. It has a story and a logic of its own and constitutes a basic framework of orientation in itself. In a culture as ritualized as that of the Newars, ritual can in many respects be seen as prevalent in and over the social order. It is from that point of view that it can most fluently be presented and analyzed, not least because such an approach comes closest to the participants' point of view (a perspective introduced in Leiden by P.E. de Josselin de Jong 1956, 1977).

To be sure, 'Celebrations of Death' is not a participants' expression, but the span of time, which it covers is a recognizable unit. As such it is represented in a dual fashion. In the more Sanskritized view, it covers the four months' period in which Lord Viṣṇu takes his sleep, *Hari śayana*. This period is known as *Caumāsa*, the four months (Skt. *Caturmāsa*). It starts from Harisayanī Ekādaśī, the eleventh day after the start of Viṣṇu's sleep, when people transplant the *tulasī* herb (Ocimum Basilicum) sacred to Lord Viṣṇu. This takes place on the next day, twelfth, in the middle of the rainy season. Because the *tulasī* is sown exactly one month before, the ritual chain is considered to be unbroken in its details. Furthermore, the cultivation of *tulasī* parallels the growing of rice but, contrary to that, it is determined by *tithi*, the days of the lunar ritual calendar. The sleep of Viṣṇu ends with Haribodhini Ekādaśī, ten days after the turn of the ritual year, which is called Tihār in Nepali, Divālī in other parts of South Asia, and Svanti in Newari, or *Nepālbhāṣā*, the language of the Newar.

In the more common perception Svanti itself is the turning point, the start of a new year of the Nepal Era and the first occasion on which the newly harvested rice may be consumed. Likewise, the beginning of the ritual chain is not the falling asleep of Viṣṇu, but the first major festival after it, Gathāṃmugaḥ. On this occasion the rice transplantation should (ideally) be completed, ghosts must be expelled from the houses and the towns to the fields, and music and drama groups ritually resume their labour. In the more common vision of this festival period the *caturmāsa*, as defined by Viṣṇu's sleep, is shortened by almost one month. Because the start and end of the latter are not greatly celebrated occasions, the ritual period, which has been labelled 'Celebrations of Death' here shall be con-sidered in its narrower sense, as stretching from Gathāṃmugaḥ to Svanti (Tihār).

'Celebrations of Death' refers to a period, which is marked by the centrality of death and sacrifice.[1] It is a time in which the deceased of the previous year are collectively mourned and in which the gates of heaven open. From Vedic times up to the present day death has been conceived of as man's ultimate sacrifice. The sacrificial context of death will become amply clear from the following chapters. Death is also, perhaps by its very sacrificial nature, a cause for exuberant celebrations.

In the family sphere, celebrations have to start already eleven or twelve days after death, after the ceremony of *ghaḥsū*, the purification of the house. A feast should then be given for family members, neighbours, and members of the funeral association (*sī* or *sanā guthi*), which is in charge of the funeral procession. Since death pollution has scarcely been removed from the house, and since the sorrow of death is still strong, the feast is rather formal and not considered auspicious. Although invitees ought to partake in it, they will eat once again at home to 'add one layer to it'. The first real celebration is *latyā bhvay*, 'the feast after one and a half month', on the occasion of the first *śrāddha*, the recurrent rites in memory and for the nourishment of the deceased person. Depending on circumstances the *latyā bhvay* can also be celebrated immediately after the previous rites, on the twelfth or thirteenth day after death, and also in that case a fair number of guests will be invited to enjoy themselves. Other large-scale feasts will be given after six months, after one year, and finally two years after death.

The obligatory feasting of guests indicates already to what extent death is an event to be 'celebrated'. It is also a domain in which the private sphere passes into the public sphere. The funeral associations, which are bound to caste and locality, are at the basis of Newar social organization. They have their yearly community feasts, in which the sharing of sacrifice is central. Next to that are the massive celebrations of death, which will be dealt with below. The first festival of the cycle intimately associates death with aspect of sacrifice. In Newar society there are many suggestions of human sacrifice, especially with regard to the thirst for sacrifice of the *mātṛkās* or mother-goddesses. Real ritual homicide, if it existed, is shrouded in secrecy, and there is no festival, which shows significant features of human sacrifice so clearly as does Gathāṃmugaḥ.

Chapter 3

Gathāṃmugaḥ

The Expulsion of the Demons

Gathāṃmugaḥ, the etymology of which is unclear, is also called Ghaṇṭākarṇa, after one of the demonic characters in the Hitopadeśa. This collection of fables was already translated from Sanskrit into Newar at the end of the fourteenth century (Malla 1982: 35). The story most common in Kathmandu is that the mass-devouring Ghaṇṭākarṇa was led into a well or pithole by a frog. People then caught and killed him (Anderson 1971: 73). Frogs are still worshipped on account of this and other feats, but not on the day of Gathāṃmugaḥ. Asakaji Vajrācārya (1987: 50) presents the story more in line with the ritual events of that day by telling that Ghaṇṭākarṇa was first insulted all day long at a crossroads before being killed, dragged away, and burned to ashes.[1]

The picture of Ghaṇṭākarṇa in Kathmandu Valley is not overall negative, however. Sayami (1980: 5) and others draw attention to the fact that in other contexts than the story of Ghaṇṭākarṇa the figure of Gathāṃmugaḥ refers to a cultural rebel who revolted against the caste system and was therefore killed. In that view Gathāṃmugaḥ was a popular hero who stood up for the poor. In his last days he became mad and people had to raise funds to cremate him. According to Nirish Nepal (1985) this view of Gathāṃmugaḥ was prevalent before the twelfth century. There is, in fact, no authorita-tive story concerning either the history of Gathāṃmugaḥ or the ritual expulsion of the various reed images of this figure on Gathāṃmugaḥ Carhe (Skt. *caturdaśī*, fourteenth day), i.e. the day before the new moon of the month Srāvaṇa, July-August. It is a festival without ritual specialists and one which varies from place to place in the Valley.

Ghaṇṭākarṇa, 'bell-eared', is said to have been an atheist (*nāstika*) who put bells in his ears in order not to hear the gods. The expulsion of the reed-made demon idols, however, shows that Gathāṃmugaḥ himself has definite divine characteristics in the ritual context. The divinization seems to occur at least partly in the very act of his expulsion and ritual death. In the eastern part of the Valley it is accompanied by signs of mourning or the washing away of death pollution. The latter feature is also characteristic for the expulsion of the main Gathāṃmugaḥ of Kathmandu, that of Naradevī quarter, to which attention will be turned below.

The reed figures are generally addressed as *Āju*, which means grandfather in Newar but which is also used as a familiar term of address for the god Bhairava. They are also called *bhūdyo*, 'ghost-god', a designation, which marks the sacral ambivalence of the figures. The use of the term *bhūt*, finally, brings us to a completely different context: the agricultural one. At some day before the rice-sowing, in Kathmandu at *akṣayatṛtīyā* (the third day of the bright half of the month Baisakh, approx. April-May), the *bhūt* or *bhūtpret* are lured into the city by the strewing of special ghost-food, *bau*. In Gathāṃmugaḥ Carhe, when the rice has been transplanted and is considered strong enough to stand the ghosts, they are evicted from the city again. Gathāṃmugaḥ thus appears to be a multi-layered festival, albeit with one central ritual event: the expulsion of the ghosts from the inhabited areas.

The centrifugal process starts in the domestic sphere. One day before the festival one starts cleaning every nook and corner of the house. Adding another layer of meaning to the already mentioned ones: Gathāṃmugaḥ is in this context also called *sinājyā beṃkegu*, the purification of the house from the rice transplantation. During the latter work the impurities of land cultivation have penetrated the house. The process of cleaning continues on the festival day in conjunction with the casting out of the *bhūtpret* from the house, a ritual, which differs from place to place. In Kathmandu a nail is hammered above the door to keep the ghosts out. After the nail above the front door has been struck, nobody is supposed to go out anymore, for in Gathāṃmugaḥ night ghosts are still around who might infiltrate the house again. People also wear iron rings, which, after they have been brought in touch with a Gathāṃmugaḥ figure, protect them against evil spirits.

Just like the ghosts are lured into the inhabited space by the strewing of *bau* before the monsoon starts, they are now lured out of the houses by transferring *bau* from the houses to the crossroads and the Gathāṃmugaḥ effigies. These are erected from the early morning onwards at almost all crossroads of Kathmandu – Gutschow (1982: 147) has counted 46 of them. At first they consist of a tripod of reed stalks with branches of *khāyu-baḥsi* (Azedarachta Indica) attached to it. Children bring their cotton dolls to be hung from those branches: the dolls too are supposed to bring the evil spirits with them. The effigy of Gathāṃmugaḥ (Photo 3) is completed in the afternoon by the people of each quarter with reed and straw for the body, and a demonic mask painted by a member of the Citrakār (Painter) caste as a face. The reed idol is further provided with sexual organs made from a reed stalk and round-shaped fruits.

At sunset people start bringing the *bau*, the ghost-food, from their houses to the effigies. The *bau* mostly contains cooked or beaten rice with buffalo blood and intestines, and other ingredients like meat, black soyabeans, garlic and certain kinds of flowers, which are put in clay pots normally used for curd (see for details Pradhan 1986: 367-369). The *bau* is placed under the eaves of the roof opposite the front door at the place called *pikhālakhu* as well as in front of the local Gaṇeśa shrine and at different crossroads. After the placing of this *bau* one is supposed to close the house. As a final purification *ikāpaḥkā*, a mixture of yellow and brown mustard seeds is burned in the house on an earthen platter (*saliṃcā*) with charcoal. As mentioned above, a three-hooked nail (*pyākiṃ*) is then driven above the front door and nobody is supposed to go out anymore. Since most of the Gathāṃmugaḥ effigies are dragged away at dusk already, the *bau* comes mostly too late as a nourishment for the ghostly figures. The more logical sequence, in which all *bau* is placed or strewn around the figure before it departs, can be witnessed only in case of the main Gathāṃmugaḥ of Naradevī quarter. The latter effigy will stay in its place at the crossroads till two or three o'clock in the night.

The other Gathāṃmugaḥ effigies will be dragged away at dusk by impatient and clamorous youngsters, but not before the crucial ceremony has been performed. One person of Poḍe (Sweeper, Fisherman) caste should set fire to the effigy and subsequently take place on a straw heap in front of it to be dragged away together with the fiery mass. In former times the Poḍe were also executioners, and till the present day, remarkably, they are the guardians of several shrines around the city. Nowadays, however, it is hard to find a Poḍe willing to be identified with the demon effigy. And that is in fact what happens: the chosen person is called Ājude like the Gathāṃmugaḥ himself. He has to walk three times around the effigy with a burning torch, set fire to it and take place on the burning wheat stalks in front of it.

Before the actual ceremony the Ājude may collect money for his performance. Near-naked but with a demonically painted body and face he goes around the neighbourhood to raise money, in the company of boisterous youngsters. Few people dare to refuse putting some money in the held-out curd bowl of the Ājude

Photo 3.
An effigy of Gathāṃmugaḥ in Kathmandu (1991).

for fear of his curse. That is also the reason why poor people can still be found to fulfil the unenviable role. After the Ājude has walked around the effigy, set fire to it and taken place on the straw stalks in front of it, he is fed *dhau baji*, beaten rice with yoghurt, together with granulated sugar. That is the same food which was formerly given to a convict before being executed. It is also similar to the *sī jā*, the 'death-food' which the Gathu divine dancers take at the very end of their last performance, before falling stone-dead (see below, chapter 5). Thus, according to all signs, the Ājude is being identified with, and brought to death together with the Gathāṃmugaḥ effigy, which he first circumambulated like a funeral pyre – his own.

The chosen one then takes place next to the effigy which is rapidly drawn away with straw ropes in the direction of the Viṣṇumatī or, in the southern part of the city, the Bāgmatī river. The idea is that he is to be thrown into the river together with the effigy. In reality he is at risk of being scorched by the flames, and always manages to escape before he is burnt or immersed. A hot pursuit may be set in to catch the Ājude again, but to no avail: the effigy is not stopped but at high speed drawn to the river where it is immersed amidst loud cries of joy and victory.

In some cases there may, however, be another interruption because the Gathāṃmugaḥs of several localities meet each other on the way. Although in Kathmandu all of them are claimed to be male and provided with male organs, the male identity can be put on trial. Pradhan (1986: 366) describes the confrontation for the Gathāṃmugaḥ of Indrachowk and Kilāgal quarters. The two groups each try to put their effigy on top of the other to prove the masculinity of the one and the femininity of the other (see also Zanen 1986: 143 for Sankhu). Subsequently both of them pass the main Gathāṃmugaḥ of Naradevī who, however, is left undisturbed.

Attention will now be turned to this chief demon who is, in the participants' point of view, the leader of the legion, and to his celebration in Naradevī quarter. Although the setting up of the Gathāṃmugaḥ is a locality affair, the scene is dominated by the Jyāpu (Farmer) caste, and in some quarters like Vaṃgaḥ (Indrawchowk) and Neta (Naradevī) it is supervised by a Jyāpu *guthi*. In Neta quarter this is the Naradevī *guthi* which is also engaged in the *yātrā* of the goddess Naradevī and especially in the Svetakālī masked dances which will be treated later (see chapter 8). The departure of the Neta Gathāṃmugaḥ is surrounded by an elaborate ritual, most notably a fire sacrifice (*yajña* or *homa*) for which a Vajrācārya (the priestly Buddhist caste) ritual specialist is employed. Fire sacrifices during festivals are mostly performed on the eve of the *yātrā*, the procession of a divinity. The expulsion of Gathāṃmugaḥ cannot be called a *yātrā*, yet the *homa* indicates the ambivalence of this act and of the divine-demonic character of at least this particular Gathāṃmugaḥ.

The problem in reporting the rituals at Naradevī is that both the *homa* and the expulsion of Gathāṃmugaḥ are secret. Whoever sees the exit of the demon 'will die vomiting blood', it is said. *Guthi* members clear the streets from those people who may not know or believe this. Thus, although the final part of the demon's extrusion could be witnessed from a hideout by the author, the description of the crucial part has to be based on partly contradictory information obtained in interviews. The secrecy contributes to the mystery surrounding the main demon to be banned from the city. Pradhan (1986: 369, 370) was told that the goddess Svetakālī and the other members of the troupe of divine dancers 'come out from the temple, costumed and dressed and shaking with rage. The goddess herself cremates the effigy and rides on it while her attendants drag it to the river'. This view of the mystery, which Pradhan was unable to verify, is perhaps the most widespread one. In fact the Naradevī Gathāṃmugaḥ is without a human representative when it is dragged to the river. The secret seems to be that in this particular case nobody is there. This is, as the Vajrācārya officiant confirmed, because the leader – unlike his followers – is complete in himself. Therefore it is the sole effigy, which is not complemented by, in the Vajrācārya's words, a human sacrifice.

The leader of the legion is, according to the *gubhāju* (the Vajrācārya officiant) the god-demon Pātāla Bhairava, who once rose up from the underworld (*pātāla*) to conquer the three worlds, heaven, earth and underworld. Unfortunately for him, he was not only driven by a lust for power but also by an immeasurable sexual craving. The latter quality made him desire the goddess Svetakālī herself. However, the goddess caught and bound him at the crossroads and insulted him the whole day before she killed him. From that time onwards the Naradevī Gathāṃmugaḥ – of which the others are said to be copies – is dragged from his crossroads to the Viṣṇumatī river, taking with him all *bhūtpret* still remaining in the city.

It is true that the whole troupe of dancers are to attend the *homa*, albeit not costumed. The Svetakālī dancer himself is the *jajmān* (*yajamāna*), the Lord of the Sacrifice. All dancers leave their hair permanently uncut as a sign of their sacrality, that is of their being *dhāmīs* ('sorcerers'). Svetakālī is the main *dhāmī*, who is also receiving worship from the people when the dancer is not playing the part of the goddess. This *dhāmī* does not take place on the effigy of Gathāṃmugaḥ, but remains with the *homa* until its completion, that is the distribution of *prasāda* (blessed remains of the sacrifice), particularly the black soot used for a mark on the forehead (*ṭikā*). Other dancers and *guthi* members may join the procession, which drags Gathāṃmugaḥ to the river. They carry torches, which are lit by a wick (*itāḥ*), which is kindled from the sacrificial fire. The torches cannot set alight the effigy, which has no straw in front of it and is itself of non-inflammable reed. This Gathāṃmugaḥ is carried to the river undamaged, albeit accompanied by the fires of the burning wheat straw torches. Yet the connection between the *homa* and the expulsion of the effigy is there, as the act of expulsion appears to be the tail end of the fire sacrifice itself.

The fire sacrifice, which takes place inside the temple behind closed doors, is said to be identical with the one carried out during the festival of Pāhāṃ Carhe in spring. The latter *homa*, however, is also secret. In both cases 165 items are offered into the fire, among which are 40 varieties of paddy, and, for the rest, mostly other grains, beans and fruits. The non-vegetarian part consists of 108 pieces of lungs, which are according to the *gubhāju* from a buffalo sacrifice but according to the Jyāpu from a (he-)sheep sacrifice which takes place in the temple in the morning.

The 108 pieces of lungs are standard in many *homas*, but here they are, according to the *gubhāju*, representing the lungs of the demon, *daitya* during Pāhāṃ Carhe and Gathāṃmugaḥ during the festival of the latter. The *homa* during Pāhāṃ Carhe precedes the *yātrā* (procession) of the procession statues as usual, the *homa* during Gathāṃmugaḥ precedes and encompasses the expulsion of the demon. In both cases, however, the procession statues are brought down from the adjoining god-house and put into the temple in front of their fixed representations to attend the *homa*. The *gaṇa*, the divine troupe of *aṣṭamātṛkā*, Gaṇeśa (Lord of the *gaṇa*), Bhairava, Siṃhinī, and Vyāghinī (the lion- and tiger-shaped guardian deities) is thus represented thrice: by the fixed stone or stone-with-metal statues, the bronze procession statues and masks, and the troupe of dancers.

Before the Gathāṃmugaḥ is drawn away, the *gubhāju* sends with the Jyāpu a *kotaḥ pūjā*, a brass plate with items of worship (like rice, flowers, red powder) common for any divinity, but here destined for the demon effigy. By that time, however, all outsiders have already been sent away. Till the last possible moment people come to place or to throw *bau* around this particular Gathāṃmugaḥ. Among them is also a group of members of the Vaṃgaḥ *guthi* who strew *bau* from a *khāsi*, a large brass vessel. According to the *gubhāju* they do so in order to test the strength of the Naradevī Gathāṃmugaḥ, but this view seems to be rather fanciful. The *guthi* also strews *bau* in front of the Naradevī temple and at other crossroads and sacred sites surrounding Vaṃgaḥ. Here we find the only straight parallel with the *bau holegu*, the strewing of ghost food during the day of *akṣayatṛtīyā* to invite the ghosts.

After the *kotaḥ pūjā* is completed, the effigy is noisily dragged away, but in the company of *guthi* members only. People along the route who may still be awake close their shutters from fear of the sight. The effigy is drawn with a thick straw rope straight to the Viṣṇumatī and thrown from the bridge into the river. On their return the group members wash their hands, legs, and eyes at the Tamsipākhā stone tap. This ritual washing purifies them from the death pollution they have incurred by the disposal of Gathāṃmugaḥ. Only then they can return to the Naradevī temple to receive the *prasāda* of the *homa* from the *gubhāju*. Purification is not required for the participants in an animal sacrifice, but only for those people who attend the cremation of a human being. In case of Gathāṃmugaḥ it is the violent death of a divinity, which makes the ablution necessary. The expulsion of the demon leader may thus be situated on the thin dividing line between sacrifice and funeral rites.

The context of the coming into being of Gathāṃmugaḥ is sacrificial. He is not a demon or divinity who is either feared or worshipped at any other time of the year. The sole purpose of erecting the effigies is to sacrifice them. The same holds true for the role of the Ājude who in most cases takes place on the effigy as a human substitute or embodiment. His apparent role as a sacrificial victim is an almost perfect illustration of Girard's (1972) scapegoat theory. Effigy and human embodiment are divinized or 'demonized' by the very act of their violent eviction. What remains is only the removal of the pollution, which this violent act brings about. Afterwards the people celebrate the death of the demon with a feast behind closed doors.

The divinization of the Gathāṃmugaḥ of other quarters than Naradevī is somewhat less explicit, but it appears from their being addressed as Āju and from their masks which strikingly resemble the face of the fearsome god Bhairava. As shown elsewhere (see below, chapter 7), the death of temporary forms of Bhairava occurs in other instances as well, such as in Bhaktapur's Gāi yātrā and in the death of the Gathu divine dancers. There are numerous myths about battles between gods and demons as well as ritual enactments of those battles, foremost in Dasain. In Gathāṃmugaḥ, however, it is an enemy from within who is expelled by human beings. As shall be seen in the next chapter the theme of the eviction of the enemy-within finds a continuation in the festival of death par excellence: Gāi yātrā.

Chapter 4

Gāi yātrā

The Day of Entry to Heaven

Two or three days after Gathāṃmugaḥ Carhe the month of Guṃlā (July-August) starts, which, as a whole, is sacred to the Newar Buddhists. The higher Buddhist castes congregate every morning at the *stūpa* of Svayambhū west of town, where the Urāy caste then plays the characteristic Guṃlā music *bājaṃ* (see for details Lewis 1984: 349-364). The most important day is the full moon in the middle of Guṃlā, popularly called Gunhi Punhi, when the victory of Lord Buddha over his opponent Māra is celebrated. Gunhi Punhi, which is on the eve of the Gāi yātrā or Sāyāḥ festival, is of great importance for Hindus too.

However, the distinction between Buddhists and Hindus is at no time of the year so marked as it is during the month of Guṃlā. In the week around Gunhi Punhi the higher Buddhist castes (the distinction between Buddhists and Hindus is blurred at the level of the Jyāpu or Farmer) put their statues, ancient manuscripts and other treasures on show in houses and in *bāhāls* and *bahīs*, the monasteries inhabited by the married monks of the Śākya and Vajrācārya castes. The latter, and also the Buddhist castes of merchants and artisans which are together called Urāy, do not participate in the massive celebration of death, which is called 'cow procession' (Nepali *Gāi yātrā* or Newarī *Sāyāḥ*). The first and most important day of Sāyāḥ is the day after Gunhi Punhi, which is also the first day of the dark half of the lunar month, Sāpāru (New. *sā*: cow + *pāru*: the first day of a lunar fortnight).

The non-participation of the Buddhist castes in Sāpāru does not appear to be based on Buddhist belief, or rather the rejection of the belief in an eternal soul or *ātman*. In the predominantly Buddhist town of Pāṭan they have their celebration of death on the day following Sāpāru, and in Kathmandu during the festival of Indra yātrā. However, the more outspoken Buddhists consider the streetcarnival of clowns, travestites and burlesque shows during Sāpāru as the manifestations of Māra, Death as well as the master of illusion and the challenger of Lord Buddha (Deep 1978: 59). Remarkably, and rather unfortunately, the carnival atmosphere in Kathmandu is not as heated as it is in towns like Bhaktapur, Sankhu and also Kirtipur. An investigation into the meaning of Gāi yātrā in fact requires a full-scale comparative study of the ways in which it is celebrated throughout the Valley - something beyond the scope of the present work. The performances in the other towns will be briefly touched upon though, in so far as they illuminate the celebration in Kathmandu, which, in recent times, has lost almost all of its theatrical and burlesque performances. Gāi yātrā is most elaborately celebrated in Bhaktapur, where it is a festival of the same magnitude as Indra yātrā is in Kathmandu.

Gunhi Punhi seems to pave the way for the next day of Sāpāru when Yama, Lord of Death, opens the gate of his kingdom for those deceased during the past year.

The full moon day contains renewals and purifications of various sorts. It is, for one thing, the climax for pilgrimages into the high mountains, to holy sites like the lakes of Gosāinkuṇḍa, Pāṃcapokharī and the mountain shrine of Muktināth. It is arduous and dangerous to reach those places along the slippery trails in the midst of the monsoon. Whoever dies on the way will immediately obtain release (*mokṣa*) or be admitted to heaven (*svarga*). It is hard not to see a link between this opportunity and the following day of Sāpāru, when Yama will be judging the fate of the dead souls.

For those who do not set out for the Himalayas and particularly the most sacred site of Gosāinkuṇḍa (at the altitude of nearly 4,800 metres) there are alternatives for purification. Through underground channels the lake of Gosāinkuṇḍa, where Lord Śiva took a rest after he swallowed the poison that came forth from the churning of the ocean, is believed to be connected to Manicur lake at an altitude of about 2,400 metres, above the town of Sankhu in the north-east corner of the Valley. Many devotees, and also faith-healers of mostly Tamang origin (*jhāṃkri*), start to climb the trail in the early morning to make the trip up and down to Manicur lake. Further down, in the heart of Pāṭan town, the pond of the Kumbheśvara temple dedicated to Lord Śiva is also believed to be in straight connection with Gosāinkuṇḍa. On Gunhi Punhi an enshrined cavity is opened to the public where water is bubbling up in a stone basin. The cold water from this spring is distributed among the devotees as being the holy water coming from Gosāinkuṇḍa.

In all those sacred places Brahmins are ready to provide the devotees with a *rakṣābandhan*, a gold-coloured thread which is wrapped around the left (women) or the right (men) wrist, together with the swift uttering of a *mantra*. The *rakṣābandhan*, which protects its wearer against evil, can be worn until the turn of the year at the time of Tihār or, alternatively, can be offered to one of the statues of Indra during Indra yātrā in Kathmandu. The Brahmins themselves have ceremonially renewed their sacred thread (*janai*) on that very morning. The full moon of Guṃlā is for that reason also called Janai Pūrṇimā. On this day a particular kind of hot soup, consisting of nine kinds of beans, is eaten in Newar houses to ward off stomach diseases. After the name of this dish, *kvāti*, the full moon day is also nicknamed Kvāti Punhi (Deep 1978: 2-56).

The next day, Sāpāru, is the greatest celebration of death in the Valley and the start of the most joyous festival. It is, remarkably, a festival during which no sacrifices are brought to the gods. Indeed, it seems that death still carries with it the ancient connota-tion of being the ultimate sacrifice. The deaths of the past year, in other words, have been the sacrifices made, and it is just the feast, which remains. During the first two years after the death of a member, the family holds monthly memorial feasts for the deceased (*śrāddha*) to appease and nourish the ancestors, and it may be questioned with good reason what the festival of Gāi yātrā has to add to this. Or, the other way around, it may be asked what is the function of the monthly (and later yearly) family propitiations of the ancestors after the Lord of Death has in one way or the other already accommodated them. The two ways of celebration cannot be reconciled with each other at one and the same level.

On Sāpāru, in Kathmandu, all families in which a death has occurred the past year, send out decorated boys with a picture of a cow covering their heads. Sometimes these cow masks – a piece of cotton or paper with a colourful cow head painted on it – are attached to a rough palanquin carried by young boys (Photo 4). On the way other bereaved families nourish the boys with sweetmeats and fruits. Ideally,

Photo 4.
A boy carrying a picture of a deceased person together with a decorated and painted cow head (sākhvāḥ) during Gāi yātrā (or Sāpāru) (1992).

a live cow should be sent in the procession (Photo 5), but there are few families who can afford or are disposed to do so. For those the boys with cow masks represent the cow or cows which are to help the deceased ones crossing the wild and bloody river Vaitaraṇī. The Vaitaraṇī has to be crossed in order to reach the gates of Yama's realm. Additional figures may be added to the cow figures according to what a family can afford. Most popular are children dressed up as *ṛṣis* (seers), *saṃnyāsins* (world renouncers) or as gods such as Śiva, Pārvatī, Kṛṣṇa or Rāma and Sītā. Also in accordance with the available means, those small processions can be preceded by traditional orchestras like the Jyāpu *dhimay* (see below, chapter 6) or by blaring brassbands. It goes nearly unnoticed, but the joyous procession is always followed by the chief mourner and others in the white dress of mourning: it is the only festival of the year in which the mourners are expected to partake.

In Kathmandu each family sends out a procession on their own behalf, without waiting for others to join them, such in contrast to the magnificent long processions in towns like Bhaktapur, Sankhu, Pāṭan and Kirtipur. All individual processions in Kathmandu do, however, follow the same procession route, which is, with some extensions, the one also followed by the goddess Kumārī during Indra yātrā (see below, chapter 5 and the map of Gutschow 1982: 125) and which is commonly but misleadingly called *pradakṣiṇapatha*. The *pradakṣiṇapatha* in the literal sense of the word is not crossing the city but circumambulating it (Slusser 1982 II: map 7, and, slightly different, Gutschow 1982: 123). This path will be followed in another celebration of death during the next great festival, Indra yātrā. At the end of the Sāpāru procession in Kathmandu, when the city has been crossed up and down, the individual families hang the cow masks on the temples of local divinities, mostly in the *tvāḥ* (ward) Gaṇeśa.

Sāpāru in Bhaktapur is much more spectacular and contains such a myriad of musical and theatrical events that even the description in the voluminous monograph on Bhaktapur by Levy cannot do justice to it (Levy 1990: 442-452). The dead are mostly represented by long conic bamboo structures dressed up in man or woman's clothes, mostly with a portrait of the deceased in front and with the cow mask and horns on top, protected by a fixed umbrella. The huge structures rest on poles which have to be carried in front and behind by at least four persons. More modest are the horned baskets, which are drawn over the head of one carrier. Alternatively large earthen cows on a palanquin are brought in.

Photo 5.
Procession of real cow and boys carrying painted cow heads, during Gāi yātrā (1992).

All representations join the procession at the site where it passes them nearmost, irrespective of caste and gender, although the very lowest castes like Poḍe and Cyāme are, as in Kathmandu, excluded from it,[1] while the Buddhist castes abstain of their own accord. The representations are preceded by clowns, bushmen, travestites, masked dancers, children and youngsters dressed as *saṃnyāsins* or gods or *nāgas* and *nāginis* (divine snakes) (Photo 6), orchestras, and most prominently, by often large groups of stick fighters, who carry out a wild dance typical of Bhaktapur and also Sankhu (Zanen 1986: 143). The procession is closed by long structures representing the goddess Mahākālī and the god Bhairava, the first one dressed in *sārī*, the second one with only a straw covering. While the other structures will be dismantled at home, Bhairava and Mahākālī will, together with the representations of the dead of Taumadhi quarter, be disposed of at the cremation ground bordering the Hanumante river. Their expulsion and immersion resembles the eviction of Gathāṃmugaḥ and raises the question whether the whole festival does not contain an aspect of expelling the dead. The two tail figures are brought in by the *guthi* that is in charge of the Bhairava yātrā, but all other representations have, together with all show, to be arranged by the bereaved families themselves.

In the small town of Sankhu the Sāpāru celebration resembles that of Bhaktapur but is somewhat less exuberant. The procession follows a *pradakṣiṇapatha* around the city centre, which is larger than the procession routes of several divinities. All castes (including Poḍe) can join the procession as per *tvāḥ* (ward) where it passes, but the lower castes generally do not bring in the long structures (*tāhāsā*) or the inverted baskets (*dhākacā*). Instead they send decorated boys or, if they are rich, earthen statues which can later be placed in local *bhajan pāṭīs* (shelters for playing religious music). All people who can afford so may send live cows, which should afterwards be given to a Brahmin.

In Pāṭan the Sāpāru procession is more organized and divided into two groups. The morning group passes the four ancient *stupas*, which were supposedly built by emperor Aśoka on the four cardinal sides of the town. Yet Buddhists abstain from the pro-cession, which mostly consists of Jyāpu, who cannot be classified as either Hindu or Buddhist. The afternoon group contains the Brahmins and higher Hindu castes, who follow a different route starting from the house of the organizer or rather, the sponsor. For he has to send in the procession a Kṛṣṇa figure (represented by a Rājopādhāya Brahmin), accom-panied by figures decorated as Rādhā, Rukminī, Balarām, and the Gopinīs, as well as another Rājopādhyāya as priest for the *pūjās* offered to Kṛṣṇa, and a group of religious singers (*bhajan*) as accompaniment. This group precedes the procession of decorated children with cow masks and some live cows, who represent the dead. If no patron can be found among the bereaved families, Sāpāru is organized by the Kṛṣṇa Bhajan Maṇḍala from the Kṛṣṇa temple on the palace square.

Also in Kirtipur the procession starts from the house of a patron who in this case has to provide for a troupe (*gaṇa*) of masked dancers with the accompanying music. Typical for Kirtipur is the representation of the dead by two decorated men

Photo 6.
Young boys dressed as nāgas and nāginis (divine snakes) on the day of Gāi yātrā in Bhaktapur (1991).

carrying a yoke-like oxen, with cow masks on their turbaned heads. A multitude of clowns and bizarre figures accompanies the procession, which is one of the most dramatic and exotic ones of the Valley. It continues into the night when buffalo legs are distributed by the *lāykū* (the palace, but nowadays the village development committee) to the different *dāphā* musical groups, which in daytime have gone around the city. Two buffalo heads and legs are given to the two *lākhe*, red-masked demonic figures one of which stands for the Upper part of town and the other for the Lower part of town. Fights are likely to break out over the division of the buffalo limbs and between the parties which follow the *lākhe* figures, but not so when the ceremony was witnessed in 1993. The receivers of the limbs are required to swim with them across the central pond of the town and the two *lākhe* have to do so with the heads – assisted by somebody of their company. In 1993 only a few persons dared to swim across the heavily polluted water of the pond, and the two *lākhe* abstained.

The Kirtipur drama on the day of Sāpāru deserves a separate study, but here the main question is more general: why are such exuberant scenes performed all through the Valley? Is it to direct the dead family members from the world they know or is it to please the Lord of Death? The Buddhists may not be far from the truth if they see in all extravaganza the instruments of Māra. Pomp and circumstance, music, dance, sexuality, and intoxication are also the classical attributes of Mṛtyu, Death. Among those attributes the weapons can be recognized with which Mṛtyu, Death, tried, in vain, to beat Prajāpati in a contest related succinctly in the Jaiminīya Brāhmaṇa (Heesterman 1985: 32-34; 1993: 53-58).[2]

What we see in Gāi yātrā is almost certainly a celebration of death in the most literal sense of the word, or, put differently, a feast to recognize the Lord of Death by indulging in his own attributes. Thus the survivors conclude the sacrifice of death with a great and lusty celebration, which surpasses the feasts given after most other sacrifices. Such a view does not, however, preclude the other side of the picture, which is intensely solemn. The celebrants organize the festival to make sure that the deceased ones cross the river Vaitaraṇī to Yama's realm with the help of cows, which are said to have immediate access to Yama's gates.

The latter view, of course, cannot account for all the extravaganza of Gāi yātrā: a sober procession of cows would be sufficient.[3] The sober aspect of the festival exists in the mourners, who solemnly follow the gay procession. Both views are necessary: if the stick-fighters with their dance appease the Lord of Death, the vigorous and almost demoniacal cow masks assure that the dead may cross the river to their destination. The purpose of both the festive and the solemn aspects of Gāi yātrā then seems to be that the souls of the dead definitely leave this world. It is perhaps as much a sign to the deceased ones as it is to Death himself, and in that respect it can again be seen as an eviction of an enemy from within – of the dead who pose a threat to the living ones.

Here another question, which has already been touched upon may now be answered. If the deceased are in Sāpāru accommodated in yonder world, why are the *śrāddhas* to nourish the dead continued after that? Or what does Gāi yātrā have to add to the monthly *śrāddhas* which already assure the position of the dead one as an ancestor? This seemingly contradictory state of affairs must be seen at two levels. The monthly *śrāddhas* are a family affair, even though the family has to organize regular feasts for a larger group of people. Death, however, is not a matter of sole concern for the family, but also for the society at large. Such a perspective may already appear from the social organization, which is founded not so much on caste in the large sense of the word, but on local death societies (*sī* or *sanāguthi*), which are caste- and locality-bound, and which may be compared to medieval European fraternities.

Yet neither caste nor sī and *sanā guthi* stand for the society at large. What we see in Gāi yātrā is a participation independent from caste and community. Gāi yātrā represents the social aspect of coping with death. Every wandering soul constitutes a danger for the society at large, and it is in Gāi yātrā that all concerned show their earnest effort to bring the dead across, to their destination in the other world. Obviously all communication is not broken off by this large-scale ceremonial farewell, but the dead ones are now considered to be accommodated at a safe distance. The society at large does not celebrate this for one day only, but for one week filled with dance, music and satire. Many people from Kathmandu make trips to Bhaktapur to see there the most joyous and magnificent celebrations. Likewise people from outside visit Pāṭan on the day after Sāpāru, when the mostly Buddhist inhabitants celebrate their own festival of death, Matayāḥ.

Matayāḥ literally means the procession of light, and the giving of oil-lamps or wicks to the countless Buddhist *caityas*, is the most important act of the festival. The devotees form an unbroken chain, which meanders through the small streets, alleys and courtyards of Pāṭan town. It is the Buddhist festival of the dead: each bereaved family should send at least one member to join the procession, which takes about eight (Deep 1978: 63) or fifteen (Gellner 1992: 88) hours to complete. But Hindus too may join the procession, which, as a matter of fact, also includes the Kumbheśvara temple dedicated to Lord Śiva.

Strikingly, Matayāḥ contains many clownesk elements in the form of mask bearers, bushmen, *khyāḥ* (a benevolent kind of ghost) and other disguised as well as richly costumed participants. The justification of all those Gāi yātrā-like features is not that different; here the *victory* of Lord Buddha over the hordes of Māra is celebrated, so in its own way it is also an overcoming of Death.

The sequence of Sāpāru and Matayāḥ gives many inhabitants of the Valley the occasion to witness the carnival twice. The cows and cow masks, however, are absent in Matayāḥ, and the joyfulness is balanced with the hardship of completing the whole prescribed route on a hot summer day. Some of the participants perform this feat while prostrating for each and every shrine or *caitya*, of which there are said to be more than 1,300 (Deep 1978: 61) on the way. A different yet similar Buddhist celebration of death takes place in Kathmandu during the city's greatest festival of Indra yātrā, as we shall see in the next chapter. Again, grief and joy are inseparable aspects of the celebration.

Chapter 5

Indra yātrā

The Captive King of the Gods

Introduction

Comparatively little is known about the accretion of ritual in Nepal. On the one hand the Kathmandu Valley preserves archaic features, on the other hand its ritual configuration has been subject to innovations, inventions and additions up to the present day. The question of ritual accretion is especially pertinent with regard to Indra yātrā. Numerous authors have tried to tackle the problem whether Indra yātrā constitutes a mixture of disparate elements brought together under the heading of Kathmandu city's greatest festival, or whether there is an underlying unity or purport in the festival as a whole.

Few or none have addressed the question how the process of ritual accretion actually works. Is it possible for new elements to be inserted just like that into a previously existing ritual complex? In general, such an assumption implies that there is a virtually empty space before the addition comes in, or at least a contextually free interval. Such a state of affairs is unlikely to exist if it concerns major additions to the ritual cycle, such as the Kumārī yātrā in the greater context of Indra yātrā. In that and similar cases the addition is more likely to change the overall context of the festival. Indeed, when Newars speak about Indra yātrā without specification, they generally mean the first day of the Kumārī yātrā, which is also the only official holiday in the sequence of eight festival days. If this shift in meaning, from Indra yātrā to 'Kumārī Indra yātrā' as the *pātro* (printed almanac) has it, demonstrably occurred in recent times, it makes the process of accretion all the more interesting. If, on the other hand, it is not so clearly traceable, the first approach to the festival must be an attempt to view it in its totality, including both the supposedly archaic and the supposedly new components.

Two of the most extensive descriptions of Indra yātrā, one by Pradhan (1986: 378-419) and one by Toffin (1992: 73-92) take different viewpoints. Pradhan's point of departure is that 'Unlike the textual tradition which mentions the rituals relating to Indra's banner (*Indradhvaja*) as the major focus of the festival (cf. Gonda 1967; Raghavan 1979: 117-155), the Newars accord centrality to a series of deities and rituals: to Indra in his role as a thief; to Bhairava as the god of alcohol (Hāthudyo); and to Kumārī, Gaṇeśa and Bhairava in their human representations. In addition to the worship of these deities, there are religious dances (*dyo pyākhã*) which depict battles between gods and demons, and street plays (*khyāla/dabu pyākhã*) which comment on social themes. Finally, there are circumambulations of the city boundary and the festival route within the city on behalf of the recently dead' (Pradhan 1986: 378). Pradhan goes on with the question whether Indra yātrā is one festival or a conglomeration of festivals, which he immediately, in anticipation of the description to follow, answers in favour of the relative independence of the major components.

Toffin shares the view of Indra yātrā as a multi-faceted festival but, restricting himself to the cult of Indra proper, concludes that 'Indra jātrā of the Kathmandu Valley is mainly derived from Hindu textual tradition. The local ("folk") aspects of the rituals, such as those observed in the village of Pyangaon, are no less based on themes prevalent in this Hindu high tradition than the central, in other words kingly, ones' (Toffin 1992: 74). Both authors have a similar view on the royal function of Indra yātrā: it is a festival, which supports the natural and cosmic order with the king at its centre, as a mediator between man and cosmos.

The sacrificial pole

The focal point in this view is the erection of a long (50 to 60 feet) pole at Kathmandu's Darbār (palace) square at an auspicious moment in the morning of the twelfth day of the bright half of Bhādra (in August/September). The ceremony, which was up to 1956 attended by the king and his government, is the official start of Indra yātrā. The long pole itself is called *yaḥsiṃ* (New.) or *liṅga* (Skt.), like the somewhat smaller but similar poles which are erected in Kathmandu and elsewhere on the eve of many *yātrā*s like Indrāyaṇī yātrā, Pacalī Bhairava yātrā, Kaṃkeśvarī yātrā, Manamaiju yātrā and so on, all through the year at locations near a temple. On none of those occasions, however, does the pole occupy such a focal position as it does in Indra yātrā, with the exception of the pole erected in Bhaktapur's Bisket yātrā at the start of the solar New Year, on the fourteenth of April. The latter pole comes from the same forest as the one for Indra yātrā in Kathmandu and it is felled according to the same procedures, including a goat sacrifice on the spot. There is no conclusive evidence, however, that the central *yaḥsiṃ* of the Indra yātrā was copied from the one of Bhaktapur.

The *sāl* trees are taken from the Nālā forest east of Bhaktapur, which is nicknamed Yaḥsiṃ Guṃ, 'forest of the sacrificial post'. The word *yaḥsiṃ* is probably derived from *yala*, sacrificial post, and *siṃ*, wood (D. Vajracharya 1968, quoted in Slusser I: 97). It is equal in meaning to Sanskrit *yūpa*, but the *yaḥsiṃ* in present-day Nepal is, as far as I know, never used to fasten sacrificial animals, but represents the secondary meaning of *yūpa*: 'a column erected in honour of victory' (Monier-Williams 1988: 856). Following Gonda (1967) and Kuiper (1983: 241-246) both Pradhan (1986: 392) and Toffin (1992: 81) recognize in the *yaḥsiṃ* the *axis mundi*, the pillar that connects heaven and earth.

Toffin elaborates the connection between Indra yātrā and similar ceremonies in classical India further by concentrating on the *yaḥsiṃ* and the banner, which is attached to it. According to the Viṣṇudharmottara (II, CLV) Indra's banner was created by Indra himself with the help of Viṣṇu to frighten the demons (*asuras*) and to give victory to the gods. Kings who raise a similar banner every year will overcome their enemies and bring prosperity to their people. The ancient festival of Indramaha was celebrated at exactly the same time of the year as the present Indra yātrā. The banner of Indra appears to be a sort of emblem of the king on earth. On the basis of the similarities between textual traditions (including the ādiparvan of the Mahābhārata and the Atharvaveda) and Indra yātrā, Toffin draws the conclusion that the Nepalese festival is unquestionably based upon ancient Indian beliefs and rituals. In both cases the aim of the rite is to consolidate and preserve the power of the king (Toffin 1992: 78-80).

Unlike the *yaḥsiṃs* in other *yātrās* of Kathmandu, the Indra yātrā pole is freshly acquired every year and afterwards disposed off. Formerly a goat was let loose in the Yaḥsiṃ Guṃ near Nālā in order to indicate the tree to be felled for the purpose. Such a procedure also existed for other *yaḥsiṃs* and for acquiring wood for fire-sacrifices such as that of Luti Ajimā (Indrāyaṇī). Nowadays, for selecting the tree the goat has been replaced by a contractor, and the Kathmandu Mānandhar (Oilpressers) who formerly came to ritually cut down the tree, have been replaced by *pipā*, army recruits. Yet a *pūjā* for the tree and for Bandevī – the forest goddess – is still carried out by Mr. Ravindra Satyal, the Parvatīyā (non-Newar, Nepali speaking) Brahmin in charge of Indra's worship. On that occasion the national anthem is played twice, once for the king and once for Indra. Then a goat is sacrificed and the tree is cut down at an auspicious moment and with the consent of the Department of Forestry.[1]

From Dvitīyā, the day (the second of the bright half of Bhadra) when the tree is felled, up to Kāyāṣṭamī (the eighth day of the brignt half of the month Bhādra), the pole is on the way from Nālā village to Bhotāhiṭī quarter in Kathman-du, carried again by *pipā*. Only the last part of the route is still under the care of the Mānandhar and carried out by volunteers. The pole gets a *lasakusa* (welcoming worship) at Bhotāhiṭī from the Mānandhar of Casān quarter. Formerly all nine quarters where Mānandhar live were participating in the ceremonies surrounding the *yaḥsiṃ*, including its raising. They stopped doing so because, according to some of them, king Mahendra – successor to king Tribhuvan in 1956 – just sent his horse to witness the ceremony instead of coming himself. In 1993 even the king's horse came late for the ceremony, just after the pole had been erected. Raising the pole is again done by *pipā*, but under the supervision of the *nāyaḥ* (the eldest) of the Casān Mānandhar.

Before the pole is erected, a small *homa* (fire-sacrifice) is performed by the Brahmin in front of the pit where the *yaḥsiṃ* comes to stand. It consists of 32 grains and a betelnut, which are offered into the fire. During the eight days of Indra yātrā the Brahmin also has to perform a morning worship (*nitya pūjā*) and an evening worship (*ārati*: the showing of a light) to the pole and the small Indra statue, which is placed at its feet. Remarkably this Indra statue is only placed there after all official fanfare accompanying the pole-raising has finished, and by one of the Newar castes (Putuvār) of the Valley. Likewise, the much-discussed banner of Indra is also raised after the dignitaries and the general public have left the place. The official spectacle is thus confined to the raising of the naked pole (bereft of its bark by the general public, which ascribes medicinal qualities to it). The dignitaries who are present, the official carrying the royal sword, the royal astrologer, the main court priest, the royal guru, the chief of Hanumānḍhokā (the ancient palace), the chief of the Guthi Saṃsthān (the government office in charge of religious endowments), all leave after the pole has been fixed by the army recruits.

The raising of the *yaḥsiṃ* on the twelfth day of the bright half of the month Bhadra is spectacular because of the length of the pole and the surrounding activities: music, dance, and canon shots (Photo 7). The pole is not completely bare: to the top of it the Putuvār have already bound some green branches and a bamboo stick with a *bhvagatyā* (a large green citrus fruit which is red within) and a red flag. The *yaḥsiṃ* is erected just in front of the monstrous-looking Kāla Bhairava statue, which was installed at the Hanumānḍhokā palace square in the seventeenth century by king Prātap Malla. The *pipā* erect it with large thick ropes and bamboo props, under the sound of canon shots. To add further lustre to the occasion three groups of musicians are in attendance: the *pañcaibājā* of the (Parvatīyā) Damāi caste, the antiquated army band belonging to the royal guru (*baḍā guruju*) and an army brass band. The Newar contribution to the show is confined to the members of the Devī *pyākhaṃ*, a masked dance group from Kilāgal quarter in Kathmandu. The dances are a shortened version of the real performances which the troupe gives on Kāyāṣṭamī and on several days during Indra yātrā. After the pole is fixed in its place, the dignitaries and the musicians make three rounds of it before leaving the site. Around the *yaḥsiṃ* eight small poles are erected representing the *aṣṭamātṛkā*, the eight mother-goddesses which are also surrounding the town.

Then the scene is taken over by the Putuvār of the Pulāṃ Guhyeśvarī *guthi*, the association in charge of the temple of Old Guhyeśvarī north-west of Kathmandu. The special task of the Putuvār is to blow a long type of trumpet (*kāhāḥ*) during funeral processions. That instrument, however, is not used on the occasion of Indra yātrā and it is unclear how or why the Putuvār came to be in charge of placing the statue and raising the victorious banner of Indra. Before bringing the statue and the banner from the palace the Putuvār make a fence around the *mātṛkā* poles, for which they use the bamboo props of the pole-raising. After cleaning the area within the fence they hoist the banner, which has auspicious symbols painted on it. Although the banner is called Indradhvaja in Sanskritized language (*haripatā* in Newar), it can no more be seen as a sign of the victorious Indra once his statue has also been placed below the pole. The very small statue shows Indra mounted on his elephant but locked up in an iron cage. It is Indra as the thief-god (*khuṃdyo*) who has, according to the story, been caught in the act of stealing a *pārijāta* flower from a garden in the Maru quarter of Kathmandu. He was taken to the court by a farmer and then exposed to the public for one week, until his mother, for whom he had been stealing the flower, came to exonerate him. Indra had to promise dew and winter fogs before he was released.

The act of thieving is not alien to the nature of the gods and to that of Indra in particular, as Toffin (1992: 86) demonstrates, but the submission and humiliation of the king of the gods have perhaps no precedent. Other images of Indra, placed on high scaffolds at four places in the inner city, enhance the impression of the god who

Photo 7.
The ceremonial Yaḥsiṃ or Indra pole erected in the compound of Hanumānḍhokā (1992).

is not a winner but a loser, not a victor but a victim. In those images the king of the gods has outstretched arms wound with pieces of rope to indicate his being imprisoned. A most remarkable feature of the Indra images is that they are no object of worship throughout the rest of the year. In other words, Indra is highlighted only as a captive god. His position below the great sacrificial pole at Hanumāṇḍhokā may indicate what Indra was destined for if his mother had not come to his rescue: to be executed, or as Nepali (1965: 359) has it in his version of the story, to be buried alive.

Can that be the background of the role of the death-associated Putuvār with the main *yaḥsiṃ*? The Putuvār will attend to the small Indra statue all through the festival week, staying in the adjacent Indrapura temple (dedicated to Śiva). Eight days after its erection the pole is brought down, again by army recruits and without any ceremony. They draw the pole through the southern part of town to the Bāgmatī river at Tekudobān *tīrtha* and leave it there without immersing it in the river. The *yaḥsiṃ* is mostly brought down in the evening of the fourth of the next month (Āśvin Kṛṣṇa Cathurthi), just after the conclusion of the Kumārī yātrā and Kumārī's blessing of the king of Nepal. In 1993, however, the *sāit* (the auspicious moment) fell on the next day at 5:25 in the morning, and public attention was less intense than in other years.

At the bank of the Bāgmatī river the same Brahmin who performed the *homa* before the *yaḥsiṃ* was erected, now does a farewell *pūjā*. According to him the *pūjā* (of red and yellow powder mixed with some rice) is similar to the *pūjā* performed after a body is cremated and the ashes are immersed (Nep. *selāunu*), that is, among the Parvatīyā (Nepali-speaking) people. There are many stories about what happens to the 'dead body' of the *yaḥsiṃ*. Formerly, the pole was probably taken by Mānandhar to be used for their oil-presses; this might explain the prominent role of the Mānandhar in transporting and raising the *yaḥsiṃ*. In 1993 it was collected by members of a Rāṇā religious association to repair a temple under their custody – they are doing so for several years already. This last transaction does not illuminate the meaning of this particular *yaḥsiṃ*, however. Other *yaḥsiṃ*s are erected on the eve of a *yātrā* and brought down – without a funeral though – after the conclusion of the procession. The only procession which takes place two days after the erection of the Indra pole is Kumārī yātrā, while her concluding procession takes place in the evening before the pole's lowering and symbolical death. To avoid the connection and to speak about Indra yātrā and Kumārī yātrā as two separate festivals, is thus nearly impossible. Before turning to the Kumārī yātrā, however, attention must be paid to a number of events that precede or occur on the same day as the raising of the *yaḥsiṃ*. Other Indra images[2] as well as bodiless heads of Bhairava (or Āju or Hāthudyo) are exhibited as part of the eight-days festivities.

Captive and beheaded gods

The impression of the captive god is enforced by other statues of Indra, which are brought out the evening before the raising of the *yaḥsiṃ*. Except for one, they are raised on high platforms supported by one or four poles (Photos 8 and 9). From the ground only the upper body can be seen, which is in a crucified position.[3] It is only in Nāsalcok, within the confines of the ancient Hanumānḍhokā palace, that Indra is positioned on the ground, that is, on the slightly elevated stage (*dabū*) of the palace courtyard. Here the gilt bronze statue is sitting in lotus seat (*padmāsana*) but still with his arms stretched horizontally in both directions. The other painted or gilt statues of Indra are high up and served by people on the platform. Small offerings can be made in a basket that goes up and down with a rope. One can release here the *rakṣābandhan* that was tied around the wrist in Gunhi Punhi (see above, chapter 4). Most prominent however, especially on the full moon day, is the lighting of 108 wicks in memory of the deceased.

It is usual for divinities in Kathmandu Valley to have a fixed representation in a temple as well as a procession image in a *dyocheṃ*, a god-house – both of which are worshipped throughout the year. Sometimes, as in the case of Seto Matsyendranath, the temple image itself is taken in procession. Indra, however, has neither a temple nor a *dyocheṃ*. The Indra statues raised during the festivals are kept in the *dyocheṃ*s of other gods: Maru Gaṇeśa, Ākāśa Bhairava, Kilāgal Gaṇeśa and Naradevī. The Jyāpu (Farmer) *guthi*s who are in charge of those *dyocheṃ*s and the *yātrā*s of the respective divinities, also take care of bringing out the statue of Indra, which is mostly left aside or put in a storeroom for the rest of the year. In contrast with the other gods, Indra receives no regular worship but is just exposed, 'pilloried' as Slusser (I: 268) has it, for the period of eight days. Although the statue is brought out and placed on its high scaffold (*khaḥ*) that is not considered a *yātrā* by itself. Indra yātrā becomes a *yātrā* through the procession of the goddess Kumārī, who passes the four main Indradyos. The display of these Indras is a purely Jyāpu (Farmer) affair, with the exception of a small *pūjā* which is given to the Indra of Indrachowk (Vaṃgaḥ) by a Newar (Rājopādhyāya) Brahmin at his house.

Apart from the big *yaḥsiṃ* at Hanumānḍhokā, the Indradyo in Nāsalchowk and the four *yāpu* Indras in the inner town, several smaller *yaḥsiṃ*s are erected in different quarters of town: at Thamel, Thahiti, Yathkā, Tyauda, Vatu, Tebāhāl, Bhimsensthān, as well as additional poles at Naradevī and Vaṃgaḥ. They are put up by smaller *guthi*s of Malla, Prādhan, Mānandhar and others. Some of them are so inconspicuous that they are hardly noticed by the general public. Much more significant in the total pattern is the display of bodiless heads of Bhairava in his manifestation as Hāthudyo, the god of the spouting beer (*thu* < *thvaṃ*, the local rice beer). Like the erection of the *yaḥsiṃ*, the display of Hāthudyo is not limited to Indra yātrā. On a more limited scale it also occurs in for example the Pacalī Bhairava yātrā (see next chapter) and the festival of Pāhāṃ Carhe, the marches of the goddesses in spring, but it occupies a central position only in Indra yātrā.

The foremost Hāthudyo is Ākāśa Bhairava of Vaṃgaḥ, on the same square where also one of the four Indradyo is situated. The big blue head of Bhairava, with its open mouth and protruding eyes, is worshipped throughout the year on the second floor of the Ākāśa Bhairava temple. Through the wooden lattice work of the second

Photo 8.
The captive god Indra, displayed on a scaffold in the Kilāgal quarter of Kathmandu (1992).

Photo 9.
The captive god Indra, displayed on a scaffold in the Maru quarter of Kathmandu (1992).

floor the god overlooks the square and can himself be seen from there. In the dead of the night before the raising of the Indra pole, between Ekādaśī and Dvādaśī, the magnificent head is lowered through the bottom of the second floor and put on a platform in front of the building. From there the eastward looking head is facing the high-raised Indradyo, which, like other Indradyos, is facing west – the assumed direction of Indra's release from Kathmandu in the mythical account of his captivity.

Ākāśa Bhairava has his own story, in which he is also on the losing side, albeit by his own choice. He is identified with the mythical Kirāta king Yalambar, who joined the Mahābhārata battle of Kurukṣetra on the losing side, that of the Kauravas. For that unfortunate choice he was punished by Lord Kṛṣṇa, who cut off his head with such a force that it flew all the way back to Kathmandu. In Indrachowk the beheaded god faces the captive god, but the beheaded one, whose mythical act comes close to a self-sacrifice, is much more revered. And what is more, Ākāśa Bhairava has something to give to his devotees. As a Hāthudyo, he gets at set times a tube in his mouth, from which rice-beer spouts for the comfort of the crowd. According to the *guthi* members some *ghee*, milk, yoghurt and honey are mixed in the beer to turn it into *pañcāmṛta*, the mixture of five holy ingredients. The *hāthu hāyekegu* (the spouting of beer) is at certain times preceded by a sheep or a goat sacrifice in front of the platform and is accompanied by the Jyāpu's *dhimay* music and the distribution of *samay baji*, a mixture of beaten or puffed rice, roast meat, soyabeans and ginger, which is customarily taken (with alcohol) after a sacrifice or the worship of a deity.[4]

The Ākāśa Bhairava *guthi* is an example of a multifunctional Jyāpu *guthi*. It is centred upon the worship of Ākāśa Bhairava or Yambādyo (Skt. *yalambar*) but is also a *vaḥlāḥ guthi*, a *guthi*, which initiates young boys into Jyāpuhood and more especially the *dhimay* music (Toffin 1994). For this *vaḥlāḥ* ceremony the batch of boys goes for three subsequent years to a temple and spends there two nights under the guidance of their parents. After having spent those two nights in the temple for three years, the boys are fully fledged members of the Jyāpu caste and their *tvāḥ*. Because also the Mānandhar (Oilpresser) caste used to have its *vaḥlāḥ* groups (till the present day at Svayambhū and before also at other shrines) it is perhaps appropriate to speak of *vaḥlāḥ* as 'a custom observed by Buddhist laymen' (Manandhar 1986: 240). It would then be parallel to the initiation into monkhood, which the higher Buddhist castes (not considered laymen but *bhikṣu*, monks) undergo. Gellner (1992: 200) places the monastic initiation at the same footing as the 'loincloth worship', a *rite de passage* within the family among higher Hindu castes and also among Jyāpu. However, the Jyāpu of Kathmandu and north of it (Manamaiju) happen to have both the loincloth ceremony indoors and the *vaḥlāḥ* ceremony outdoors.

As Toffin emphasizes, the *vaḥlāḥ* ceremony among the Jyāpu of Kathmandu prepares them for the *dhimay* music. A *dhimay* is a two-headed drum, which is beaten on one side with a cane (rolled up as a spiral) and on the other side with the hand; by extension the term is used for the typical *yātrā* music as a whole. The orchestra includes, in the case of the Ākāśa Bhairava one, a pipe instrument called *pvaṃgā* (which the boys learn to play six years after their *vaḥlāḥ*), *tāḥ* cymbals, a large two-headed drum called *daṃgaḥ* and a *kaṃypvī* (a disk struck to the beat of the drums). The Ākāśa Bhairava *guthi* organizes the *dhimay* musical performances and is also a Nāsaḥ *guthi*, an association which worships Nāsaḥdyo, the god of music and dance. It is also the Ākāśa Bhairava *guthi* which supervises the Gathāṃmugaḥ of Vaṃgaḥ and throws *bau* (ghost-food) to invite (just before the start of the mansoon) and to expel (Gathāṃmugaḥ) the *bhūtpret* (see chapter 3). Similar large Jyāpu *guthis* exist in other quarters and can contain, as in Kilāgal, *guthis* within the *guthi*, which have more specialized functions. All *guthis* in charge of a divinity get a compensation from the state office for religious endowments, the *Guthi* Saṃsthān, but this is never sufficient to carry out the job. In addition to that subsidy, most *guthis* still own some land, but since the land reforms of the 1960s less and less income can be gathered from lands given in tenancy.

The 'godhead' which comes next in importance to Ākāśa Bhairava is Svet (Seto) Bhairava, a gigantic gilt head on Hanumānḍhokā square. Svet Bhairava is a typical example of ritual accretion: the head was commissioned by king Raṇa Bāhadur Śhāha in 1795 after the Shāhī conquest of Kathmandu Valley (1769). The wooden lattice in front of the image is only opened fully during the eight days of Indra yātrā, and partially the day before (Ekādaśī) as well as two other days of the year. The Hāthu *guthi*, which takes care of the worship of Svet Bhairava is neither caste- nor locality-bound. The members seem to have been chosen among the higher Buddhist castes of the southern, middle and northern part of town: two Śākya (Goldsmiths) from Ombahāl, two Tāmrakār (Copperworkers) from Maru and two Tulādhar (Merchants) from Asan. Ingredients for sacrifices are provided by the Guthi Saṃsthān as are the ingredients for the hāthu *hāyegu* from Bhairava's mouth and the *samay baji* distributed with it.

The hāthu *guthi* is only constituted for the worship of Svet Bhairava. For the musical accompaniment an appeal is made to the Ākāśa Bhairava *dhimay*, who come to play at the time of sacrifices. On Ekādaśī, the eve of raising the Indra pole, a goat is sacrificed for the half-opened lattice window and a *gubhāju* (a Vajrācārya priest) is employed to perform a small vegetarian fire-sacrifice. On Dvādaśī, the day of the pole-raising, a Citrakār (Painter) *guthi* paints the eyes (a symbolical 'eye-opening') of the image. A duck, a goat, and a buffalo are sacrificed below the head towards evening, when also the *hāthu hayegu* starts among the enthusiastic crowd. The cult of Svet Bhairava at Hanumānḍhokā, installed by the present Shāhī rulers but with a completely Newar cast and script, is thus a beautiful example of how the new rulers were integrated in the old ritual, of *Graecia capta Romam cepit*. Or, as Toffin remarks with regard to Indra yātrā as a royal festival: 'From a sociological point of view, such a dialectic between state centralization and local ethnic assertion is one of the most interesting and pervasive aspects of the modern Indra jātrā' (Toffin 1992: 75).

Smaller and bigger heads of Bhairava, which can be of wood, metal or (mostly) painted earthen ware are on display in other places of town, served by *guthis* and sometimes even families. One of the bigger heads is Bākā Bhairava, exhibited in

Vaṃgaḥ at the corner of the street leading from Indrachowk to Vatu, nearly within sight of Ākāśa Bhairava. Its name is according to the *guthi* members derived from 'Bākā', the centre of town. The blue head, which resembles in its features the nearby Ākāśa Bhairava, is said to be made like an (earthen) jar itself, covered with copper, silver ornaments, and a big crown. The *guthi* in charge of this Hāthudyo consists of seventy-three Mānandhar (Oilpressers) of Vatu 'Bākādeśa', who bring out the head since times immemorial.[5] Once (up to sixty years ago) they also constituted a *vaḥlāḥ guthi* that went to the Bhadrakālī temple for the boys' ceremony. They have no *dhimay* but *dāphā*, another type of music (common to a number of castes including Jyāpu), which includes large drums, pipes, and cymbals. The *guthi* nearly stopped bringing out their Bhairava for lack of resources, but then constructed a new house with the *dyocheṃ* of Bhairava on the topfloor, and the rest of the house given in rent to cover the *guthi*'s expenses. Whether it is for lack of money or for some other reason, this Hāthudyo receives no animal sacrifice nor is there a priest involved in the worship.

Another Hāthudyo on the Hanumānḍhokā palace square is served by a *guthi* consisting of three Vajrācārya priests only. There is reason to assume that this god's head, which is called Svatantra Bhairava, independent Bhairava, is relatively recent too. The head is kept in the *dyocheṃ* of Bhagavatī from Nuwākoṭ, who was brought there by Pṛthvī Nārāyaṇa Shāh, the conqueror of Kathmandu Valley. This king himself is often compared to Bhairava because of his power to conquer the Valley. Bhairava clearly is a god of war as much as he is a god of death (see also Toffin 1993b: 60). Both aspects are combined in the worship of the several heads which spout beer, liquor or *pañcāmṛta* as *prasāda* of a sacrifice that may be considered their own. The head of the sacrifice of war contains the holy fermented beverage. A parallel may be drawn with several severed heads of Vedic mythology, such as those of Namuci and Dadhyanc, which also contain the secret of fermented drinks (*sūrā* or *madhu*). In Vedic mythology, however, Indra is the classical headcutter in what was originally an agonistic pattern of sacrifice, with two parties (*deva*s and *asura*s) contesting for the spoils of it, te head in particular (Heesterman 1985: 47-48).

The scenario of Kathmandu's greatest sacrificial feast offers no parallel to Indra as the victorious slayer. The captive king of the gods who has to promise rich dew for the farmlands in return for his release, is not the hero of the festival, but rather its anti-hero. The sacrificial theme may still be traced in the story that Indra is caught, exposed and deemed to be sentenced. But at the critical moment his mother comes to beg freedom for the victim, who is thus not slain but set free. (Only during the eight days of Indra yātrā he is exposed as a victim enchained to the *yūpa*, the sacrificial pole.) The captive god contrasts with the beheaded one: it is only to the latter that sacrifices are brought. Thus the divine stage is set in the morning of the twelfth when the Indra pole is raised, and the mortals make up for one of the greatest celebrations of death, *upākhu vanegu*, the festive circumambulation of the entire city in memory of the deceased of the past year.

Circumambulation of the city

Gāi yātrā has its most spectacular celebration in Bhaktapur, but the festival is celebrated all over the Valley. *Upākhu vanegu* as the most festive celebration of death for Kathmandu is, however, confined to that city and the villages of Hadigaon and Deopāṭan in the eastern neighbourhood (Slusser 1982 II: maps 5 and 6). It is sometimes considered the Buddhist counterpart of Gāi yātrā (like Matayāḥ in Pāṭan), but it is celebrated by both Buddhists and Hindus. As will be seen further on, the Buddhist population of Kathmandu has one more special celebration of death during Indra yātrā. *Upākhu vanegu* is a clock-wise circumambulation of the city in the true sense of the word. In the procession the route along the old city walls (long demolished) is followed, keeping to the left all areas that do not properly belong to the city: untouchable quarters, fields as well as newly built suburbs (see Slusser 1982 II: map 7).

The stage for Indra yātrā with its captive and beheaded gods has been set in the morning, but the procession does not pass those divine landmarks in the inner town. Instead it has its own decorated pathway, which is marked with enormous heaps of beautifully arranged *samay baji*, the food usually distributed after the completion of sacrifice or worship. The mountains of *samay baji*, of which there are twenty-one along the route, are mostly situated in front of temples, shrines, and images which are brought out for the occasion. They are crowned with large fishes or buffalo heads but also the latter serve only as decoration: they do not this time originate from sacrifice, but are just bought from the meat market. Like other celebrations of death, *upākhu vanegu* follows the pattern of a sacrificial feast for which the sacrifice itself has already been completed. The display of the divine victims in the centre of town is providing a setting, but the procession in memory of the dead has to be seen in its own right: as celebrating the ultimate sacrifice of the deceased ones.

The mourners who circumambulate the town put small earthen bowls (*pālācā*) with lights on the streets and at every shrine or image of a divinity. Children, also those belonging to impure castes excluded from the procession, try to collect *pālācā* and money offerings by exposing pictures of deities along the road. For the larger part of the population who do not mourn a relative, *upākhu vanegu* may vary from a nice evening stroll to a wild feast. The rich decorations and the various music groups on the way (from traditional *dāphā* to popmusic blared by loudspeakers) make it a terrific experience, especially for (male) youngsters who dance till the depth of night in their make-shift discos. After midnight the heaps of *samay baji* are, together with beer and liquor, divided among the participants or ward members.

Upākhu vanegu, although still following the long demolished city walls, also shows its accretions, the most conspicuous of which is not the popmusic, but an up-and-down excursion to the temple of Kaṃkeśvarī along the Viṣṇumatī, outside the city walls. The extension did not lead to a greater circumambulation of town, for that would include quarters of the lowest castes like Poḍe and Cyāme. Below the surface of joy and grief an effort can again be recognized to banish the ghosts of the deceased from the pure space of the city. By ritually demarcating the boundaries both the ghosts and the impure castes are relegated to where they belong: outside of town. The great feast can likewise be seen as a sign to the deceased to stay away as well as a tribute to Death as the ultimate recipient of sacrifice.

Kumārī yātrā

The institution of the so-called living goddess Kumārī has attracted much attention and so has the Kumārī yātrā as one of the most popular festivals of Kathmandu city. The cult of Kumārī as the human embodiment of a goddess (Taleju Bhavānī represented by the royal Kumārī or Rājkumārī of Kathmandu) has been described for the different Kumārīs of the Valley by Michael Allen (1975). He notes that the institution of the royal Kumārī of Kathmandu is often ascribed to the last Malla king of Kathmandu before the Gorkhā conquest, Jayaprakāśa Malla. The king used to play dice with the royal goddess Taleju, the *śakti* (lit.: 'power') of the realm, until his daughter intruded on them. Thereupon the goddess became angry and predicted in a dream that the Malla king's reign would soon vanish. The king would never get a sight of the goddess again. Instead, a prepuberal girl of Śākya caste would embody her. In other stories king Jayaprakāśa made sexual avances towards the goddess who, as a result, never appeared to him again. In both cases the realm of the king was doomed but his downfall could temporarily be averted by worshipping the human embodiment of Taleju and installing her *rath yātrā* (chariot procession).

Yet most authors (Nepali 1965: 366; Allen 1975: 5, 6; Slusser 1982: 312) agree that the cult of Kumārī can be traced further in history than the tragical figure of Jayaprakāśa Malla on whom the popular stories concentrate. The last Malla king certainly aggrandized the cult: he built the *Kumārīcheṃ*, the richly decorated house of the royal Kumārī on the Hanumānḍhokā palace square, in 1757. A popular story has it that Jayaprakāśa also started the so-called *nānicāyāḥ*, the *yātrā* of Kumārī through the centre of town on the last day of Indra yātrā. According to the story he did so at the wish of his *nānicā*, his concubine, who lived in Kilāgal quarter and could not witness the larger processions of Kumārī through the southern and northern half of the city. *Nānicāya* is the only procession of Kumārī which passes all statues of Indradyo just before the end of the festival; this singular feature is hard to reconcile with the trivial origin accorded to it in the story.

Wright's chronicle (1972: 227) credits Jayaprakāśa Malla with instituting the *rath yātrā* (chariot ride) as a whole, as does Hasrat (1970: 90). Hasrat, however, also has it that 'he (Pṛthivī Nārāyaṇa, the conqueror of Kathmandu in 1768) was succeeded by his son Pratāpsiṃha Śhāha who established the Indra yātrā which continues for 8 days and commences on the 12th day of the light half of August and (ends) under the 4th dark half of September' (Hasrat 1970: 93). It does not become clear from the chronicles what exactly the respective kings established or instituted and what kind of popular event preceded their royal acts. Both Allen (1975: 3) and Slusser (1982: 312) quote Petech (1958: 95, 97) who identified two manuscripts from the late thirteenth century, which according to Slusser are concerned with choosing, ornamenting, and worshipping Kumārī. The distribution of Kumārīs in time and space indeed precludes that the Royal Kumārī of Kathmandu originated from Jayaprakāśa's dreams.[6] Wright's Vaṃśāvalī briefly mentions that king Guṇakāmadeva (of the twelfth century) 'instituted Indra jātrā by erecting images of Kumārīs' (Wright 1972: 155). Images of Kumārī are not found in present-day Indra yātrā, but the reference may indicate that a Kumārī worship took place in the context of Indra yātrā before the *rath yātrā* started. In the end the institution of the *rath yātrā* may not have meant more than the replacement of Kumārī's usual palanquin by a three-tiered pagoda-like chariot.

All in all, it is hard to reconstruct a sequence of accretion with regard to the components of Indra yātrā. The presence of Kumārī in Indra yātrā may, in a different form than the *rath yātrā*, go further back than assumed. The raising of the Indradhvaja at Hanumānḍhokā may, as a central feature, have been borrowed from Bhaktapur's Bisket yātrā, and so on. The captive and beheaded gods of the previous section do not receive any attention in history; they may nevertheless constitute one of the eldest layers.

Nowadays, the royal presence is only required at the start and at the conclusion of Kumārī yātrā. The start of Kumārī yātrā on the fourteenth of the bright half of the month Bhādra was also the occasion on which king Pṛthivī Nārāyaṇa Śhāha captured Kathmandu – but this is not adduced as a reason for making this day the only official holiday in the sequence. For the start of the *yātrā* various dignitaries are invited or obliged to come to the old palace, from the ministers in His Majesty's government and the opposition leaders to the corps diplomatique present in Nepal. But after the king has paid his tribute (in the form of a golden coin) to Kumārī and received flower *prasāda* in return, the procession that follows is an entirely Newar affair: the king and the dignitaries do not come down from the balcony of the palace on this occasion.

In the *yātrā*, Kumārī (Photo 10) is accompanied by two other living gods as her attendants: two young boys embodying Bhairava and Gaṇeśa precede her chariot in their own one-tiered chariots. Bhairava and Gaṇeśa are the common attendants of the *gaṇa*, the group of eight or nine *mātṛkā* goddesses which is worshipped throughout the Valley. They also appear in masked dances of the goddesses and, as two young boys again, in some of the ritual feedings (*marahjā*) of children. In the latter case, which can be witnessed for example on Gathāṃmugaḥ Carhe in the nearby forgotten Cāmuṇḍeśvarī/Kumārī *pīṭha* at Banghemudā, nine young girls sitting in a row embody the Kumārīs, with two young boys embodying Bhairava and Gaṇeśa sitting on each end of the row.

The worship and *yātrā* of the royal Kumārī have been elaborately described by Allen (1975: 8-18), Pradhan (1986: 402-405) and others such as Nepali (1965: 366-369) and Anderson (1971: 131-135). The procession route of the divine girl and her attendants is said to have the form of a sword like the old city itself. It is, however, broken up in two parts which together look like a double-bladed axe with the royal palace at the intersection. Elsewhere I have focused attention on the ritual divide existing in Kathmandu between the Upper, northern part of town (Thane) and the Lower, southern part (Kvane) (see above, chapter 1). The dividing line is most often seen as the diagonal leading from the northern palace gate in a north-eastern direction towards Asan square; all areas above it belong to Thane, the areas below it to Kvane (see Map 2). The line is, however, shifting according to the viewpoint from which the divide is seen.

From the viewpoint of the participants in Indrāyaṇī yātrā, this goddess belongs to the northern part of town while her sister and antagonist Bhadrakālī belongs to the southern part. In the eyes of her own people, the latter goddess belongs to the centre of town, the area, which is called Dathu. The core of the city can thus be

Photo 10.
The living goddess Kumāri in her three-tiered chariot during Kumāri's procession (1992).

viewed as much larger than just the palace and the street, which constitutes the Thane-Kvane dividing line, but its extension depends on context. The greatest extension of the Dathu area can be found in a map, which Gutschow drew with Manabajra Bajracarya as his chief informant (Gutschow 1982: 115). The city may, in historical terms, have grown from such a core area, yet the Thane-Kvane division is not of a historical but of a ritual nature, as it is in other towns such as Bhaktapur and Kirtipur. *Guthi*s, divinities, *yātrā*s, and sacrifices are marked as belonging to Thane or Kvane and often relate to each other in antagonistic terms.

According to Hamilton's account of the Kingdom of Nepal (1819) stone fights took place in the bed of the Viṣṇumatī river, the stakes of which appear to have been the appropriation of a human victim for sacrifice (Hamilton 1819/1986: 43-45). The Thane-Kvane divide is, as I argued above, in essence a sacrificial one, with the two parts of the city partaking as two sides in the sacrificial arena.

Kumārī cannot be reckoned to belong to either Thane of Kvane, yet her *yātrā* is neatly divided into a southern Kvane part for the first evening of her procession and a northern Thane part for the second subsequent evening. Most interesting is Kumārī's come-back on the fourth day (*caturthi*) after the full moon, when she makes a wild round of what is contextually the central scene: the path marked by the captive and beheaded royal gods. At the end of this short last round, heaps of *samay baji* are distributed when the virgin goddess passes Hanumānḍhokā. The human embodiment of the royal goddess Taleju is circumambulating the core of the arena just before she is to give the mark of blessing (*ṭikā*) on the forehead of the king to confirm his reign. It can be gathered from the telling imagery of Indra yātrā what, at a hidden level, the blessing of the goddess prepares the king for: not for an immediate sacrifice, but for what is considered the king's long-time duty: the sacrifice of war – which may involve, though, his (sacrificial) death.

This sacrificial pattern, with the king at its core, will be continued during the next festival of Dasain, the proper time of going to war. While the virgin incarnation Kumārī does not accept blood sacrifice, the goddess Taleju herself has to be placated with numerous sacrifices during Dasain. In that respect, Indra yātrā is a prelude to Dasain: it paves the way for the royal sacrifices to come and it consecrates the main Lord of the Sacrifice, the king of Nepal. For the latter act the king is not dependent on a Brahmin, but on the living goddess Kumārī, who is served by the tantric Karmācārya and Vajrācārya priests. The actual ruler of the realm is the goddess Taleju, the divine counterpart of the king. The human queen is not entitled to participate in the cult of Taleju.

Indra yātrā does not in any way consolidate the social and cosmic order, on the contrary, it sets the stage for the still greater sacrificial disorder of Dasain. Yet there is a change of aspect: while in Indra yātrā both the king of the gods and the human king are marked as victims inside the city, the great sacrifices of Dasain prepare for victory in the outside world – albeit not without ambivalence, as we shall see below.

The procession of the mourners

The sacrificial stage of Indra yātrā contains one more celebration of death, just after Kumārī completes her first round of the southern part of town. This time it is a more specifically Buddhist affair. A procession of Buddhist mourners then follows the masked figure of a *ḍākiṇī* (Skt.) or *dāgiṃ* (New.), a demoness (Photo 11). The story behind this strange phenomenon is a sequel to the myth of the captive Indra, in which Indra's mother is identified as a *ḍākiṇī*. In return for the release of her son she promised to take the souls of those who died that year straight to heaven, to be joined with their families. The souls of the dead had to cling together in a row following Indra's mother. However, either accidentally or wilfully, the line broke up some miles west of Kathmandu at the site of the lake Indradaha and the souls fell down. It is in memory of those lost souls, and to assure a better fate for the souls of the past year, that families – this time including women – follow the path of the *dāgiṃ*.

The responsibility of bringing out the *dāgiṃ* rests with one family of Tāmrakār (Copperworker) in which the duty passes from father to son. Likewise the task of impersonating the *dāgiṃ* belongs to one family of Jyāpu living near Naradevī. In the Tāmrakār's house in Maru (where Indra was once caught for stealing flowers) the serene white mask of the *dāgiṃ* is kept, and it is from there that the procession starts. The Jyāpu is received there with some drinks and snacks and then dressed in shiny clothing (*tās*) of an orange colour. The masked performer has not, as is

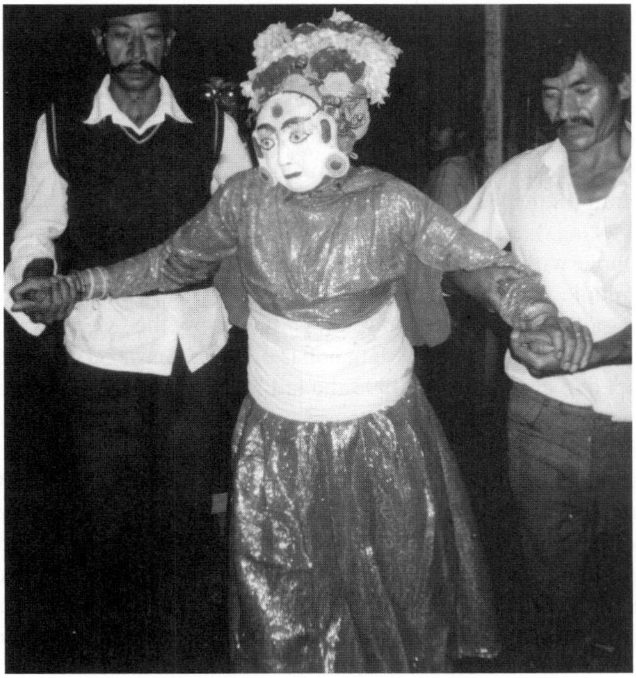

Photo 11.
Masked figure of the dāgiṃ, a demoness whom Kathmandu mourners identify as Indra's mother (1992).

otherwise usual, received a special training or initiation to perform his task. Once his mask and crown have been put on his head, he receives a small *pūjā* from the lady of the house in front of the door.

As soon as this worship is completed, the mourners who are assembled in the small alley next to the house start throwing grains (paddy, husked rice, wheat, barley, black soyabeans, popped rice), flower petals, and pieces of banana over the masked figure. This *pūjā* of the mourners will continue all along the route followed by the *dāgiṃ* – the same route which Kumārī follows in the two subsequent days of her *yātrā*. The *dāgiṃ* with her quick, robot-like steps is preceded by a Jyāpu *dhimay* musical group with a swinging *dhunyāmunyā* – a long pole decorated with yak tails and flags usually carried by *dhimay* players from the northern and central part of town. The Tāmrakār patron has a piece of land for the purpose of sponsoring the *dāgiṃ* procession, but the Maru Jyāpu come of their own accord. Apart from the wild throwing of grains the procession is remarkably sober.

All grains which are left over after the route is completed are disposed of in the Bhutisāḥ, a cavity next to the Kaṣṭhamaṇḍapa in the centre of town which is dedicated to the *bhūtpret*, the ghosts or wandering souls. Few if any devotees then make the pilgrim-age to Indradaha, the lake where the souls of the deceased were lost according to the story. For the others the well in Maruhiti, the Maru ward, believed to be in direct connection with the lake of the lost souls, fulfils the same function. Although the procession is again said to help the dead relatives in getting a place in heaven, indications are that this particular *yātrā* is directed at guiding the souls who have lost the way and are at risk of wandering around. The mourners who try to keep pace with the rushing *dāgiṃ* in a solid group, appear to be a straight reflection of the fear to lose the connection.

The small mysterious procession of the *baumata*, the lights for the ancestors, reinforces this impression. It starts from the Kaṣṭhamaṇḍapa when the *dāgiṃ* has completed her round and follows the same route. The *baumata* is made of reedstalks in the form of a *nāga* (Satya Nāga), a snake or according to others a fish. The head of it is like a three-tiered temple with three lights (on *saliṃcā*, earthen dishes) at the bottom floor, two at the middle floor and one at the top floor. This front structure, crowned by a bunch of green leaves and flowers, is made by the Mānandhar (Oilpressers) of Lāykūsāḥ. The tail is made by Mānandhar of other quarters, some of whom have, however, stopped to contribute; in 1993 the tail had five strips with three lights each. The *baumata* is swiftly carried and followed by merrymaking youngsters full of vulgar slogans and sexual abuse.

The reason for carrying the *baumata* is to guide those souls or mourners who have lost track of the *dāgiṃ*, it is said. At the completion of its round through the city the *baumata* is disposed of at the place from where it started. The procession of the *dāgiṃ* and that of the *baumata* appear especially directed at tracking down the lost souls, those that have missed the connection to the other world. They are the tailpiece of the processions for the deceased, but they are not yet the end of the play with sacrifice and death that permeates the festivals of the fall. The cycle will only be closed with the auspicious reception of Death at the turn of the ritual year (chapter 9). In Indra yātrā the victim is highlighted in all its ambivalence, whether it is the captive king of the gods, the beheaded hero, or the human king. The theme gets a special elaboration in divine dances performed during Indra yātrā, which have as a central figure Daitya, the demon who has to be defeated and yet belongs to the inner circle of the divine company.

The Devī Pyākhaṃ and other divine dances

Several *pyākhaṃ* (dance dramas) of the Valley celebrate the victory of the goddess over her demon enemy. In the twelve-yearly special performance of the Naradevī masked dances Daitya is unmistakenly slain by the goddess. Even there ambivalence is not absent: at first Daitya is a member of the *gaṇa*, the divine troupe, who falls in love with the goddess Kumārī. The love is mutual, and it is only by a change in personality (to the grown up Caṇḍeśvarī) and a magical spell that the hostility can be created which is a prerequisite for the slaying of Daitya.[7] Daitya is the victim, but at a more hidden level he is the hero and the counterpart of the goddess. In the twelve-yearly Gathu *pyākhaṃ* Daitya is not acted out by a dancer, but represented by a wooden mask which is hit with a sword by the goddess Bhadrakālī, and supposedly killed. But the whole *gaṇa* of gods dies at the end of the season, and in the cremation scene the wooden Daitya head is most tellingly hidden in the mask of Bhadrakālī herself. As an indissoluble duality the two of them are laid on the funeral pyre.

In the Devī *pyākhaṃ* of the Kilāgal ward, which is yearly performed during Indra yātrā, Daitya is the most desirable role. He is again defeated by Kumārī, but, as it is told, not killed: Daitya belongs as much to the *gaṇa* as the other members do, and he is as much revered as the other masked dancers are. Nevertheless, his special function, his privilege one would nearly say, is to be vanquished by the goddess Kumārī. While it is the goddess herself who, according to the textual tradition, is brought into existence by the other gods to slay the unconquerable demon adversary, the divine dances of Kathmandu suggest the opposite: Daitya is staged to give the goddess her indispensable counterpart and victim.

In the Devī *pyākhaṃ* of Sankhu (a small town in the north-east of the Valley), which constitutes a close parallel to that of Kilāgal in Kathmandu, the part of Daitya is surprisingly not fulfilled on the stage, but it is highlighted in the accompanying songs. The reason given for the omission is that the goddess Devī (Kumārī) is so powerful that the actor, once possessed by her, might actually slay the performer of Daitya. The story goes that the Sankhu Devī *pyākhaṃ* was invited to Kathmandu to perform their dance at Hanumānḍhokā. At the moment that the goddess and her divine company struck their swords at the ground in a gesture of killing Daitya, the Daitya performer of the Kathmandu Devī *pyākhaṃ* fell dead. The Sankhu Devī dancers have never been invited since (Shrestha 1996: 255, 2002: 396).

Like in all masked dances, the members of the Devī *pyākhaṃ* of Kilāgal undergo a gradual process of divinization which leads up to their first performance. With the exception of Daitya who has to be young, the dancers may continue their part as long as they are able and willing. Yet they have to start their activities every year with a sacrifice to Nāsaḥdyo at the first Sunday or Thursday after Gathāṃmugaḥ. Not only the dancers, but also the musicians and the *nāyaḥs* (the elders) of the group are consecrated by performing sacrifice to the god of music and dance. At Kāyāṣṭamī, four days before the start of Indra yātrā, they have another sacrifice of a buffalo and a goat at their Nāsaḥdyo shrine, which precedes their first performance in the middle of that night.

The Devī *pyākhaṃ guthi* is one of the many *guthi*s which the Kilāgal Jyāpu have and which partly overlap. Some of the dance *guthi*'s members also belong to the *pulukisi guthi*. *Pulukisi* is a bamboo-made elephant, covered by cloth over its body and with a big elephant mask on its head. Moved by two people inside, the elephant roams around Kathmandu during Indra yātrā in search of his master Indra, whose vehicle is the elephant Airāvata. During the rest of the year the white elephant mask is, together with the image of Indradyo, kept in the Kilāgal Gaṇeśa *dyocheṃ*, which again has its own *guthi*. The masks and the instruments of the Devī *pyākhaṃ*, however, are not kept in the *dyocheṃ* but in the house of the *kaji*, the hereditary leader of the dance.

The organization of the dance is complex; it consists of several elders or leaders (*nāyaḥ*) according to the different components of the performance. There is of course a *nāyaḥ* for the dance and a *nāyaḥ* for the songs, but there are also *nāyaḥ*s for the music and separately, for the most important musical instruments, the drum (*khiṃ*) and the long pipes (*pvaṃgā*). All of them are chosen according to their talents, and so are the dancers. For the desirable role of the Daitya there were, in 1993, two equally good performers who took turns. What makes the role of Daitya so strikingly attractive is that he is the only dancer who wears no mask, but only an impressive silver crown. Surrounded by masked assailants, his bare and serene face brings his royal divinity closer to humanity.

After their long and lonesome appearance in the late night of Kāyāṣṭamī, the first public performance of the dance troupe is in the evening when Kumārī passes through the southern part of town (i.e the evening of the second day after raising the Indra pole). The stage (*dabū*) is at Jaisideval and the show starts just after Kumārī has passed the crossroads there amidst tumultuous crowds. In the esoteric night programme the performance is very long, consisting of nine parts of which the fight (*yuddha*) is only one, but on the *yātrā* evening the *yuddha* is the highlight. It is preceded by dances of the three divinities Caṇḍī, Bhairava and Kumārī, first together and then separately. After that Daitya enters the stage and is attacked by the green-masked Bhairava who is, however, unable to beat him. Therefore Kumārī has to take over and assumes a long fight with Daitya, with both of the opponents holding a sword and Daitya a small shield as well. Daitya is several times brought down before he makes his final backwards salto.

This highlight is followed by comic performances of three minor figures:

betāl (ghost), *kavaṃcā* (skeleton), and *khyāḥ* (a hairy ghost) as well as an appearance of the complete divine host, which then marches home with small dances to greet all gods on the way (*dyo lhāyegu*). According to the complete programme the victory over Daitya is followed by a scene in which Kumārī, *betāl*, and *khyāḥ* pretend to drink blood. The sequence is at least suggestive of a scenario in which Daitya's blood is drunk. In the Naradevī and Gathu *pyākhaṃ*, which were briefly mentioned above, drinking the blood of a sacrificial victim is part of the procedure, but it is never brought in direct relation with the part of Daitya. The killing of the latter is demonstrated in the Naradevī *pyākhaṃ* by two separate figures (Fox-face and Dog-face) who, after Daitya has been carried off, enter the stage with the head and limbs of the slain demon. Yet the killing of a buffalo, which happens in the Naradevī and the Gathu *pyākhaṃ* as well as in the Savābhaku dance treated below, always carries the connotation of slaying a demon. In the dances of Indra yātrā it is clearly the enemy from within who is brought down, with all its concomitant ambivalence.

A Disappeard Dance: Kumha Pyākhaṃ

One of the most remarkable dance performances of Indra yātrā has unfortunately disappeared since 1991. It was an unmasked dance which contained a party of unarmed gods and a party of demons armed with swords and shields. Strikingly both parties did not only fight against, but also among each other. The reason why it disappeared is that the glittering clothes (*tās*) of the dancers were too worn out to be shown on stage. Once, it is told, their glitter so impressed the Rāṇā rulers that they were asked to put off their crowns, as the Rāṇās feared that the dancers were outmatching their own decorations. The last set of costumes was given by king Birendra at the occasion of his marriage in 1972. From the Religious Endowments Department (*Guthi Saṃsthān*) the *guthi* used to receive only an inflation-hit sum of money, not even enough to pay half of the amount necessary for the obligatory buffalo sacrifice to the god Nāsaḥdyo at the start of the season. In his responsibility as patron of the *pyākhaṃ* Mr. Mangaldas Pradhān talked to the minister of culture Mr. Govinda Raj Jośī, who waved away his request for support. His son, up to 1991 a Daitya performer, tells enthusiastically how the fight between the Daityas was the most dramatic part: it was unsure which side would win. This elaborate play was only performed on stage (customarily at Ḍhokābahāl), while for the rest, like the other dance groups in Indra yātrā, they accepted invitations and presented themselves every evening at Hanumānḍhokā. In its heydays the dance group included twelve *deva*s (gods), seven *daityas*, two *dvārapālas* (doorkeepers), and two *lākhe* – only the latter two ghosts were masked.

The dance is called *kumhā* or *kumha* pyākhaṃ, either after the majority of the performers, Kumhā (Potters) or – after the *deva* who defeats the main *daitya* – Kumāra, *Kumha*. The main *daitya* is Tripurāsura, and the dance group itself prefers to call their *pyākhaṃ* '*Tripurāsura vadha* (=killing) *pyākhaṃ*'. Alternatively it is also known as *Khā pyākhaṃ* after the locality (Khābāhāl) where the performers come from. Although the majority of the dancers and musicians are of the Kumhā (Prajāpati, Potter) caste, the patron and a number of participants from his family are of the higher Pradhan caste.

The common career of a member of the *pyākhaṃ* was to start as a small unarmed deva and to end up as an adolescent or grown-up *daitya*. The *deva*s had names like Kumāra, Varuṇa, Indra, Brahma, Viṣṇu, Maheśvara, but the *daitya*s were, apart from their hero, unnamed. The principal characteristic of the *daitya*s was, again, that they were ultimately defeated, but the setting appears completely different from the various Devī dances: it reflects the classical opposition between the *deva*s and *asura*s, who are not so alien to each other and also fight among themselves, but eventually show up as two parties one of which is bound to lose.

Ākāśa Bhairava (Savābhaku), Majipā Lākhe and other dances

A different pattern is manifested in yet another indispensable Indra yātrā dance, that of Ākāśa Bhairava. In this case the three protagonists, Bhairava, Caṇḍī, and Kumārī come from outside the city to beat the enemy within. It is a fearsome group of dancers, who are together called Savābhaku (of unclear etymology) and whose dance is also called *dhiṃnāle siṃtāṃ* after the sound of the music. The dance group consists of members of the Putuvār caste from Halcok, north-west of Kathmandu. The *pyākhaṃ guthi* is also the *sī guthi*, the funeral association which is in charge of the funerals of caste members in Halcok. The dancers are thirsty for the sacrifice of buffaloes of which they drink the blood. Formerly a bullfight was staged for them in Hanumānḍhokā palace, in which the three dancers killed the buffalo let loose on them in the royal centre.[8] This buffalo was at the same time the main demon (*asura*), which they had to kill during their eight-day visit to the capital.

They have another opponent in the figure of the *lākhe* demon-dancer from Majipā in Kathmandu Kvane. Kathmandu Thane does not have its own *lākhe*, but the Savābhaku group makes up for that deficiency. Staying overnight in Kilāgal in Kathmandu Thane, they are in many people's view representing the Upper part of town. Real fights between the following of the two sides used to occur until recently a treaty was concluded in which the two parties agreed to avoid each other. Savābhaku thus has an enemy in the masked demon of the opposite half of town and a victim in the centre, the two of which are linked in a story rendered by Pradhan (1986: 399, 400).

The *lākhe*, nowadays impersonated by a member of the Ranjitkār (Dyer) caste, was formerly a *rākṣaka* (demon) who was caught having an illicit relationship with a Ranjitkār girl in Majipā, and brought before the king. In return for his promise of better behaviour, he was put in charge of the prison, where, it so happened, every night a prisoner was devoured by somebody unknown. The *lākhe* found out that the king's own son and daughter were guilty of eating prisoners, but when he tried to seize them they took refuge in the temple of Ākāśa Bhairava in Halcok. The latter refused to hand over the two, and a bitter fight ensued between the *lākhe* and Ākāśa Bhairava without either side being able to win. This story, which has no reference to the buffalo fight and sacrifice in the palace, makes Ākāśa Bhairava the protector of man-eating royalty.

The Ākāśa Bhairava or Savābhaku dance with its bullfight may well be a very ancient feature of the festival (Slusser 1982 I: 238). Several masked dancers who come to Kathmandu from Bhaktapur for the period of Indra yātrā are most likely to be an accretion since the time Kathmandu became the capital of a unified Nepal under Śhāha rule. In Bhaktapur these dance groups, with the goddess Mahākālī in the leading part, have their main performances during Gāi yātrā. Strikingly absent in those Bhaktapur performances is the figure of Daitya, which is in the case of the greatest Mahākālī *pyākhaṃ* (of the Darbār square in Bhaktapur) especially added for Indra yātrā in Kathmandu. The Bhaktapur Darbār *pyākhaṃ* has a sparkling show, which has also been presented in Germany and Japan. All dance groups including the six (if they all come) Mahākālī *pyākhaṃ* from Bhaktapur can participate in a tournament for dance groups held in Nāsalcok, Hanumānḍhokā. Furthermore they receive the very modest sum of Rs. 4,000 if they appear every evening at the gate of the palace to add luster to the Indra yātrā celebrations. To stand a better chance in the competition, the Mahākālī *pyākhaṃ* of Bhaktapur Darbār square adds not one but three *daitya*s to its team on the occasion of the tournament. From this commercially oriented approach it also becomes clear how crucial it is during Indra yātrā to bring out a victim, an enemy from within who is sure to be brought down.

Conclusion

The *ṭikā* (the mark on the forehead, made from red powder, rice and curd) which the king receives from Kumārī just after *nānicāyāḥ* (the last ride of the goddess) also signals the end of Indra yātrā.[9] As soon as the auspicious moment (*sāit*) is there, the long Indra *yaḥsiṃ* will be lowered, and subsequently the Indradyo on the high platforms. It is the release of the captive king of the gods, which only in case of the *yaḥsiṃ* has a funeral aspect. The king of Nepal is also considered divine, being an embodiment of Lord Viṣṇu. As I have shown elsewhere (Van den Hoek 1990), the divinity of the king rests on his capacity of being the Lord of Sacrifice (*jajmān*) of the realm. Lingat (1967: 262) emphasizes the king's prerogative of punishment (*daṇḍa*) and execution as a religious function, including his identification with Daṇḍa as a god emanated from Brahma. The punitive capacity of the king can thus be seen as derivative from his quality as chief sacrificer. In the execution of punishment the king is not affected with impurity, just as the sacrificer does not incur impurity by the slaying of the victim.

Heesterman (1978) points out the contradictions inherent to the notion of kingship in ancient India. The king is supposed to uphold the *dharma*, but he is also called the eater of his people and, in the celebrated *dharmaśāstra* of Manu, he is compared to a butcher who keeps a hundred slaughterhouses. The single criterion that transcends the conflicting qualities of a king is that he must be an *abhiṣikta*, which means that he becomes a royal *dīkṣita*, a consecrated sacrificer. Like the king in ancient India, the king of Nepal can also be considered the principal celebrant of sacrifice – which ultimately is conceived of as his own. The reign of the king can thus be seen as a protracted sacrifice, in which his life is constantly at stake. Although the king can find (animal) substitutes for himself in regulated sacrifices, his prerogative of going to war – the sacrifice of battle – inevitably puts his own life at stake. The bodiless heads of Bhairava during Indra yātrā are the grim reminder of that ultimate sacrifice – which is also the source of the king's divinity.[10] The huge mask of Ākāśa Bhairava is the last divinity of Indra yātrā to be brought back – amidst secret rites—from his scaffold to the second floor in the temple.

Underlying the composite character of the Indra yātrā is the unifying notion of sacrifical death. If this festival is celebrated in Kathmandu as a 'royal festival' (Toffin 1992), this is because the king is the exemplar of sacrifice, being both sacrificer and victim. Although the kings appear to have furthered the notion of a royal festival[11], the interesting point is that the royal ceremonies are embedded in popular Newar ritual. As we shall see in the following festival of Dasain, on the other hand, the conquering Gurkhā dynasty (since 1768) asserted itself by additions that stand apart from Newar ritual and consequently are of little interest to their Newar subjects (cf. below, chapter 8).

Chapter 6

The Start of Dasain

Pacalī Bhairava yātrā

Introduction

The festivals of the fall in Kathmandu constitute a string of ritual events, which is broken up in time but continuous in purport. The question what originally belonged to the one or the other festival and what is a shift, an adaptation or an accretion, is hardly relevant to the meaning of the ritual cycle as a whole. There is a gap of eleven days between the end of Indra yātrā and the start of Dasain, yet it is as if an invisible thread is spun between them. Indra yātrā ends with the hoisting up of Ākāśa Bhairava to his place on the upper storey of the temple, and Dasain – in its public aspect – starts with the descent of another god of liquor Pacalī Bhairava. In contrast to Ākāśa Bhairava, however, the liquor-filled jar which represents Pacalī Bhairava is taken on a true *yātrā* through the southern part of town. Along the way four other Hāthudyo are brought out, two of which will spout rice-beer during the yātrā of Pacalī.

The spectacle of Indra yātrā takes place almost entirely in the central and northern parts of town. Only a few Indradyo or Hāthudyo are on display in the southern part, which is linked to the overall context by the Kumārī yātrā and the different processions for the dead. It is as if the Kvane part of town makes up for that deficiency in the Pacalī Bhairava yātrā, which takes place at the start of Dasain, but can easily be seen as an extension of Indra yātrā. Again a mythical king stands at the origin of the particular manifestation of Bhairava and he, again, is a gallant loser. But while the story of Yalambar's beheading linked Ākāśa Bhairava and other Hāthudyo with the All-India epic, the Mahābhārata, the story of Pacalī is more tragicomic and restricted to the Valley.

Once upon a time Pacalī was the king of Pharping, a small town on the south-western edge of the Valley, on the ancient route from India to Tibet. He was a great *tāntrik*, an expert in magic, who went every morning to Benares for his bath. At night he secretly loved a girl from the Nāy (Butcher) caste at Teku, the area where the present Pacalī temple is located. In one version of the story his way out from the girl's sleeping room was blocked one morning because *sārī*s were hung to dry from the door. Gods cannot pass below *sārī*s (lady's clothing). At dawn he was discovered and beaten by the girl's relatives and he ran away searching for a hide-out. At last he found a bush of *kanhāysvāṃ* (the green leaves of which are now offered to Pacalī during his *yātrā*) to conceal himself. At that place, close to the Bāgmatī river and the Teku cremation *ghāṭ*s, he is nowadays worshipped as Pacalī Bhairava. According to some, Pacalī wrapped himself in a *pulu*, a reed mat used to encase a dead body (Manandhar 1986: 154), before going into hiding. This *pulu* is identified with the reed canopy which is attached above the jar representing Pacalī during his *yātrā*.

Other versions have it that the Nāy girl wondered about Pacalī's magical powers and asked him to show his true identity. Pacalī agreed on the condition that the girl would later throw some grains of rice over him to turn him back into human form. But when Pacalī revealed his awesome form of Bhairava the girl was terrified and ran away forgetting about her part. Pacalī followed her in vain and finally buried himself at the site of the present shrine and turned into stone. Having been unable to bury his full body in the ground, one piece of stone – mostly viewed as his buttocks – remains

Photo 12.
The fiercesome god, Pacalī Bhairava, displayed on a copper jar containing beer, during his procession (1992).

visible and is worshipped till the present day. In both versions Pacalī shows his divinity: either by revealing his true form, or by his inability – even though in human form – to pass below *sārīs*. In either case he gets the worst of it and is forced to hide or, as some say, pounded into the ground by his persecutors. The Nāy girl and the son she bore by Pacalī are nowadays partaking in the *yātrā* as Nāy Ajimā and Nāy Gaṇeśa.

Pacalī Bhairava's openair shrine is called a *pīṭha*, a seat of divine power. *Pīṭha*s almost invariably belong to female deities and more particularly to the *mātṛkās*, the mother goddesses, whose shrines surround the city. In each of the *pīṭha*s surrounding town, the *gaṇa* (the host) of the *aṣṭamātṛkā*, the eight mother-goddesses, with their attendants Bhairava and Gaṇeśa is represented as a whole. The demi-circle of natural stones in the Pacalī Bhairava *pīṭha* also includes the *aṣṭamātṛkā* but the central divinity is Pacalī himself. The stone which represents his buttocks or, according to some, his *liṅga* (phallus) is in the middle of a square brass plate which covers the space bordered by the ring of other gods. According to Wright (1972: 214) it was king Prātap Malla who 'caused the *jalharī* (or stone on which the emblem of Śiva is fixed) and the greater part of the emblem of Pañchliṅga Bhairava to be covered up, because people from the plains of India, seeing the jalharī, used to laugh at the Nepalese for sacrificing animals to Mahādeva'. At least nowadays, animals are not killed inside the sunken space of the *pīṭha* but for Pacalī's attendant and vehicle, the *betāl* (ghost), who is represented by a naked copper corpse lying in front of the *pīṭha*.

From the viewpoint of the ritual dichotomy of Kathmandu, Pacalī Bhairava unequivocally belongs to the lower part of town, Kvane. Both city halves have their "king", who do not possess any political power (and have no connections with the present kings of Nepal) but who fulfil a purely ritual role, as lords of sacrifice or, if one wishes to retain the royal connotation, as *reges sacrificii* (see above, chapter 1). These two kings carry the title of Thakū juju and the caste-name Malla, but no connection is made with the Malla dynasty that ruled Nepal from the thirteenth to the eighteenth century. Instead, the Thakū jujus claim to stem from the rulers who held sway over Kathmandu between the end of the Licchavi dynasty in the ninth century and the emergence of the Malla dynasty. As we have seen above (chapter 1), one of them is Thakū juju of the upper city (Thane) with his residence near Thahiti, the other is Thakū juju of the lower city (Kvane, Kone) with his residence near Kohiti.

The Thakū jujus ultimately trace their origin to the legendary king Pacalī of Pharping, and the Thakū juju of Kvane is the patron of the Pacalī Bhairava yātrā in Kathmandu. The Thakū juju of Kvane is the patron of the Indrāyaṇī yātrā which takes place with the first new moon after the turn of the year. Pacalī Bhairava still has a less important but interesting *yātrā* in Pharping itself, ten days before that of Kathmandu and as part of the larger Pharping yātrā. Here the Thakū juju of Pharping, who by marriage relationships came to be the Thakū juju of Kathmandu Thane as well, is the patron of the whole festival.

Dr. Kamal P. Malla, himself belonging to the same ancestry, has written a historical study on his forefathers back to the time of the arrival of Pacalī in Kathmandu. According to Dr. Malla (1980), kings in the medieval time were called the incarnation of Bhairava rather than of Nārāyaṇa (Viṣṇu). In the most ancient chronicle, the Gopālarājavaṃśāvalī (end of the fourteenth century) king Śivadeva of the Thakuri dynasty, who ruled from 1097 to 1115, is called an incarnation of Bhairava from Kāmarūpa (Assam). There is a difference of sixty-seven years between his rule and that of Guṇakāmadeva, who, according to the nineteenth-century chronicles, founded Kathmandu and settled Pacalī Bhairava at its southern end (Hasrat 1970: 46; Wright 1877: 154, 155). Because those kings maintained a special relationship with Pharping as a centre of tantric learning and Bhairava worship, there may well be a historical base for calling Pacalī Bhairava the king of Pharping as the myth has it (Malla 1980: 1-12).

Dr. Malla considers the name Pacalī as a distortion of Pañcaliṅga, Pañcaliṅgeśvara or Pañcamukhī Liṅgeśvara, but he also quotes Gautam Vajra Vajrācārya, in whose view Pacalī derives from the *pāṃcālikas* of southern Kathmandu who saw this Bhairava as the god of their territory (Vajrācārya 1976: 183). Mary Slusser too argues that 'Pacalī Bhairava may originally have been the deity of a Licchavi *pāñcālī* of Dakṣiṇakoligrāma, from whence his name, rather than from five (*pañca*) *liṅgas*, as is frequently thought' (Slusser 1982 I: 239). A *pāñcālī* was a local administrative unit in the time of the Licchavi dynasty (fourth to nineth century) and in the subsequent transitional period; Dakṣiṇakoligrāma was in that time the name of the present Kvane part of Kathmandu. The oldest inscription, however, to which all authors refer, is a copperplate first reported by Regmi (1966: part 3, app A., inscr. 27: 18-21), which dates from the fourteenth century. It refers to 'Pañcali Bhahrāha' and is attached to Kaṣṭhamaṇḍapa, the great wooden resthouse on the Maru side of the palace square, from which Kathmandu derives its name.

In Pharping the ruined Pacalī Bhairava *dyocheṃ* is near the equally ruined *lāykū* (palace) but surprisingly, the *yātrā* is in the hands of the towns lowest castes: Jugi, Poḍe and Nāy. The role of the Jugi may be viewed in the light of their background as descendants of the tantric Kapālika *yogis* (Boullier 1993). The Pharping Thakū juju is present at the Pacalī Bhairava yātrā, but does not have to fulfil any function. As in Kathmandu, the Pacalī *kvaṃ* (jar) was formerly made of earth, but because of its vulnerability a copper one was offered by the palace in recent times.

The Pacalī *kvaṃ* is taken out when it is already filled with liquor and theoretically it may go wherever it directs its carriers. The first stop is at the Ghoragaṇeśa temple, in front of which a buffalo is sacrificed with the Pacalī jar as a witness. Afterwards the intestines are cleaned, filled with air and put as an ornament over the Pacalī jar. It is joined there by the copper jar of Sveta Bhairava, who also has an open-air shrine where a goat was sacrificed just before. Sveta Bhairava is quietly carried by members of the Shrestha caste but Pacalī may go into every house which he likes, even up to the third (kitchen) floor. Part of his wild play he carries out in front of the *dyocheṃ* of Sveta Bhairava, who is curiously called Pacalī's wife. The representation of Pacalī at Pharping as a jar filled with liquor is the main similarity with the *yātrā* in Kathmandu, which is on the whole much more elaborate.

The social setting

Twelve Jyāpu families of Kvane take turns in being guardian of the *pīṭha* for one year and host to the Pacalī jar in the subsequent year. When a new king ascends the throne or when the old jar becomes too much battered (as happened in 1994) it is replaced by a new one for which 100 kg of copper and 300 grams of gold are said to be necessary. The new jar has to undergo all rites de passage (both male and female) from birth to initiation. On the jar the image of Pacalī is depicted with a prominent head but also with his six hands, his garland of skulls, and the *betāl* (ghost) under his feet.

The twelve members of the Jyāpu *guthi* among whom the care of Pacalī circulates organize a feast on Ghaṭasthāpanā ('Establishing the Jar'), the first of the ten days of Dasain. In other houses, from the palace to the humblest dwelling, a garden of *naḥlāsvāṃ* is sown (see also below chapter 8, section 1). According to Manandhar (1986: 123) *naḥlāsvāṃ* (Nep. *jamarā*) derives from *navarātri* (the nine nights of Dasain) and the Newar word for flower, *svāṃ*. Mostly barley and maize seeds are sown in the room of worship or another place where no sunlight can penetrate. The white sprouts are harvested on Vijayā Daśamī, the tenth day of Dasain, and worn in the hair above the ears as a sign of the great day of victory. The Jyāpu Pacalī Bhairava *guthi* is one of the exceptions to this pattern. Instead of sowing the *naḥlāsvāṃ* at Ghaṭasthāpanā they collect two months before (on the first of the summer month of Śrāvaṇa) the seeds of the plant sacred to Pacalī Bhairava, the *kanhāysvāṃ*. After the seed collection at a site with an Āju (Bhairava) stone near Budhanilakantha in the north of the Valley, they plant it the next day in a garden in Lagan quarter in South Kathmandu. In the celebration of Dasain the green plant sacred to Pacalī replaces for them the common white grain sprouts.

The feast on Ghaṭasthāpanā is given by the *pāḥlā* (*pāḥlāmha*), the keeper of the Pacalī Bhairava *kvaṃ* during the preceding year. Pacalī is kept there together with a silver-ornamented *pātra* (bowl), the representation of Nāy Ajimā, the lover of Pacalī in the myth related above. The Pacalī jar will be taken on the evening of the feast to the house of a Citrakār (Painter), to be repainted for the *yātrā*. Just before it is going there, a secret ceremony is conducted in which the jar is emptied of the remains of the previous year (beer, liquor, eggs, and *samay baji*). Those will be deposited into the Bāgmatī river after Pacalī is taken out, when public attention will be directed towards him. Yet it is told that some people who know may take a nightly bath at the time, a little downstream from the place of disposal in order to catch the *prasāda* in the river water.

The empty Pacalī *kvaṃ* is swiftly carried to a house that was traditionally a Citrakār home, but which is now inhabited by Jyāpu. Evidently, the original location has an importance of its own, which exceeds the current occupants of the house. In the time that a Citrakār was still living there, he would be the *pāḥlāmha* of Pacalī during the next three days, but presently he comes only on the fourth day to do the painting work. When the Pacalī *kvaṃ* was still an earthen one, the Citrakār had more work in painting Pacalī's image on it. Nowadays he accentuates with black, white, and red colour the eyes of Pacalī as well as the eyes of the skulls in his hands, those in the garland around his neck, and also the eyes belonging to the *betāl* below Pacalī. The Citrakār of Kohiti ward take yearly turns in the 'eye-opening' rite of Pacalī and also in painting various other deities such as the wooden statues of Bhimsen and Vajrayoginī (in Sankhu) and the masks of the Gathu dancers. They also paint the *pulu*, the reed mat which is used as a canopy for Pacalī, with signs of the sun, the moon and a *khaḍga* (sword). In the case of Pacalī they are because of their duty the first who can offer new liquor into the Pacalī jar. As will be seen later, the vessel of the god has to be totally filled up with liquor and *samay baji*.

The Jyāpu Pacalī Bhairava *guthi* is the mainstay of the festival, whether it concerns organizing, carrying the idols, music making, and housing the Pacalī and the bowl, representing his lover Ajimā, before and after the festival. Next in importance is the Gathu (Gardener) *guthi*, by whose music the idol of Pacalī – whether the jar is still light or filled to the brim – is said to move to and from the *pīṭha*. A Nāy (Butcher) *guthi* is celebrating its own Gaṇeśa festival during the time of the Pacalī Bhairava yātrā. Because Gaṇeśa is said to be the son of Pacalī, the two festivals intersect, and the Nāy Gaṇeśa precedes Ajimā and Pacalī in their *yātrā* to Hanumānḍhokā. Several other *guthi*s fulfil very minor roles such as filling the oillights surrounding the *pīṭha*, and as such will be left out of the discussion of the festival here.

There are, however, important individuals besides the Thakū juju, who will already figure in the invitation *pūjā* to be treated next. They are the Karmācārya who also officiates at the *homa* reading his text, and the figure of the Kaḥmi (Carpenter) who seems to act as a double of the Thakū juju. The movements are between the *dyocheṃ*s (the yearly changing abode at the Jyāpu guardian's place) of Pacalī, the Citrakār's house, the Thakū juju's residence, all in town, and the sunken space of the *pīṭha* south of town, near the cremation *ghāṭ*s along the Bāgmatī river. The highlight of the *yātrā* is the march towards the centre, the ancient palace of Hanumānḍhokā.

Nimantraṇa: the invitation pūjā

Other gods in the surroundings of the *pīṭha* of Pacalī are informed about the impending *yātrā* of the god in a *nimantraṇa pūjā*, an invitation worship, which takes place in the evening of the third day the day before Pacalī is moved from the Citrakār's house. The Thakū juju, his Karmācārya ritual specialist and his mysterious counterpart, the Kaḥmi (Carpenter), participate in this elaborate *pūjā*. The Kaḥmi, whose caste title is *Sthāpit*, is not an assistant to the Thakū juju, but appears to be his double. He is a *jajmān* like the *juju*, and, at the fire-sacrifice the following night, brings in his own animal to be sacrificed. Neither the Thakū juju nor the Sthāpit himself knows why or since when the Carpenter family fulfils this task as the ritual double of the *juju* and his family. In both families the ingredients for the *nimantraṇa pūjā* are prepared by the women in the house. The Karmācārya, in his own words, 'mixes up' those two *pūjās* as he has to be *ācāju* (priest) for both of them.

One of the most characteristic items in the worship of divinities are the *gvaḥjā*, conical portions of rice flour, moulded in the form of a *caitya* or divinity. They serve as temporary receptacles of the divinities, which are worshipped, a function which they share with earthen jars, *kalaśa*. In the nimantraṇa *pūjā* also another type of *gvaḥjā* is used, the *kavaṃcā* (lit: little ghost) made of leafplates (male) and leafbowls (female) on which cooked rice with soyabeans is put. The *kavaṃcā* are used to appropriate the *bhūtpret* and other ghostly beings. No matter how edible the *gvaḥjā* may seem, they are in no case used as *prasāda* (blessed food) of the worship but just left on the spot after the function is finished.

Three Jyāpu carry two brass plates (*kotaḥ*) with *pūjā* items and the baskets with *gvaḥjā* to the deities invited in the vicinity of the Pacalī Bhairava shrine. Gaṇeśa is the first to receive an elaborate *pūjā* of rice, coloured flags, a string of cloth, sweetmeats, *kanhāysvāṃ* and several flowers. Before the two *jajmān*'s make their offerings, their *kotaḥ pūjā* is consecrated by the *ācāju*, who asks them to lay their hands on the brass plate while he is uttering a *mantra*. At the conclusion the Thakū juju and the Sthāpit receive a flower and a *ṭikā* as *prasāda* from Gaṇeśa.

Less elaborate *pūjās* will be done at other shrines and sacred spots in the neighbourhood of the Pacalī *pīṭha*. These include one more Gaṇeśa shrine and a Mahādeva shrine, but also the pithole for the *yaḥsiṃ*, the festival pole, in spite of the fact that it has not been raised since a few years.

Close to the *pīṭha* is another *mātṛkā* shrine, which is overshadowed in importance by the gaṇa of the *pīṭha* itself, but not forgotten in the *nimantraṇa pūjā*. A string of green branches of *kanhāysvāṃ* is attached to the row of mother goddesses, as will later be done at the *pīṭha*. The westward facing Pacalī *pīṭha* is an open air shrine sheltered only by a giant peepul tree, but the pāṭī or *sataḥ* (resthouses) which surround the shrine and the small square with the fire pit (*homakuṇḍa*) in front of it, give the impression of an enclosed space. In this courtyard *pūjā*s are done for Sveta Bhairava and the *āsana* (seat) where the Pacalī jar will be placed for some hours preceding the fire-sacrifice. A small Nāga shrine in the wall, which surrounds the sunken space containing the *homakuṇḍa*, also receives a short *nimantraṇa pūjā*. One striking feature of the compound receives no attention at all: below the peepul tree on the edge of the *pīṭha* an eternal fire is kept burning in a large metal *makaḥ*, a fire-pot. This fire stands by itself and bears no relationship to any of the *pūjā*s and the *homa* that accompany the Pacalī Bhairava yātrā, nor does it have a place in the myth of origin of the shrine. It is one of several eternal fires in the Valley (see Van den Hoek 1992: 553).

The divine host in the *pīṭha* itself offers a beautiful example of syncretism, for it contains not only a stone representation of Buddha but also one of Daitya, the sworn enemy of the gods. Next to Daitya in the south-east corner is the stone representation of Ajimā, the slayer of the demon, suggesting again the complementarity between the goddess and her chosen victim. All gods in the *pīṭha* are in the *pūjā* connected by a string of *kanhāysvāṃ* and provided with small and big *gvaḥjā* as well as *kavaṃcās*. The highlight of the elaborate *pūjā* is the pouring of liquid over the *pīṭha* gods by the Sthāpit. For that purpose the *ācāju* adds milk, *ghee* and honey to three pitchers (*tāhāṃpha*) filled with water. The Sthāpit sprinkles the contents over the *gaṇa* and Pacalī himself: the liquid is poured through the hole in the metal floor in which the stone representation of Pacalī has been encased. He repeats this *abhiṣeka* thrice; in the last pouring three big citrus fruits (*taḥsi*) are placed on the neck of the pitchers and rolled onto the Pacalī hole from where they are removed again after a little while. This act is specific for the *pūjā* of Pacalī but, like so many ritual acts, its significance remains unclear. The *taḥsi* fruit appears most prominently in a very different context: in the family feast of Svanti at the turn of the ritual year (see chapter 9).

The Pacalī *nimantraṇa* ends as usual with the distribution of flowers and blessing marks to the *jajmāns* and the other people present. On the way back to the Thakū juju's residence the group calls at the temple of the goddess Macalī on the edge of the city. Although the name Macalī rhymes with Pacalī, its derivation is completely different.[1] The temple has a peculiar interior with the dressed wooden statues of all nine Navadurgā goddesses, their names written below them. The goddess Macalī herself has an altar in the form of a *kalaśa* (pitcher), at which a *nimantraṇa pūjā* is performed. The invitation to this goddess is made because Macalī is the clan goddess (*digudyo*) of the Thakū juju. He has to perform a fire sacrifice in front of the Macalī temple more than four months later at Si Punhi, the full moon of January/February.

The fire-sacrifice

On the subsequent evening of the fourth day of Dasain, two Jyāpu bring the *juju pūjā* from the residence of the Thakū juju to the Citrakār's place. The *juju pūjā* is a brass plate with the usual items of worship, which in this case is accompanied by an earthen pot with rice beer (*thvaṃ*). Together they are a sign that Pacalī is now expected to come to the *lāykū*, the 'palace' of the Thakū juju. After the *juju pūjā* is brought, the Kohiti Citrakār opens the Pacalī jar and start with pouring liquor (*jalpay luyegu*) into it. Just before the jar is taken to the *lāykū*, the Thakū juju's rice beer is also emptied into it. A *dhimay* group of musicians accompanies Pacalī on the trip to the Thakū juju's courtyard, where he is given a ceremonial welcome (*lasakusa*) by the Thakū juju (Photo 13) and his *ācāju*.

The *lasakusa* is a welcoming worship common for divinities but also for e.g. a bride arriving in the groom's family. The essential items are a wooden measuring pot (*siṃphaṃ*) filled with popped rice, coins and flowers, which is turned over to the arriving one, and a key to the house which is symbolically handed over. After the *lasakusa* Pacalī is received in a small room at the groundfloor of the present residence – the old *lāykū* was destroyed by fire about a century ago – local people bring *pūjā* to Pacalī and the *ācāju* performs another *juju pūjā*. Again liquor and *samay baji* is poured into the jar, first by the Thakū juju and then by other people.

While the others are still busy, the Thakū juju and his *ācāju* silently set out for a mission of their own. The jar of Pacalī Bhairava, which has been accompanied by *dhimay* music on the way to and during its reception at the *lāykū*, is also silently moved from the *lāykū*: the music only joins in after some part of the distance has already been covered. The reason given is that Pacalī Bhairava does not like to go from the *lāykū* to his *pīṭha*: he is captured, as it were, by the Jyāpu carrying him off. The Thakū juju plays his part in the mystery by engaging himself in a parallel enterprise at the time of Pacalī's departure.

Every *pigaṃdyo* (deity with a *pīṭha*) of Kathmandu has a yearly festival in which the procession image (*yātrā mūrti*) is brought to the *pīṭha* to stay overnight and receive sacrifice. Pacalī, however, appears reluctant to make that journey and, unlike the other *pigaṃdyo*, he does so only in the dead of night. Moreover, Pacalī's moves are according to a straight up and down plan: he does not have an elaborate procession around town like the other, female *pigaṃdyo*. Pacalī is called a *mvādyo*, a living god (New. *mvāye*: to be alive), and it seems as if his mythical concealment is reflected in his furtive movements. At the same time he is considered one of the most powerful gods of Kathmandu: Pṛthvī Nārāyaṇa Śhāha, it is said, could not have conquered the Valley without being Pacalī himself.

The Thakū juju and his *ācāju* do a *pūjā* in front of the temple of Atkonārāyaṇa which Pacalī will pass one night later on his way to Hanumānḍhokā. The purpose is said to be the invitation of Atkonārāyaṇa to the *yātrā*, and as such the worship there is an extension of the *nimantraṇa pūjā* the night before. Following this is a *pūjā*, which takes place on the other side of the street passing Atkonārāyaṇa and which appears to be the real purpose of the excursion. It is called *bali pūjā* and is

Photo 13.
Thakū juju, the ritual king of the southern half of Kathmandu (Kvane), receiving Pacalī Bhairava at the main entrance of his house.

directed at the *bhūtpret*. Every sacrifice has to take into account the ghosts who are prone to disturb it. Mostly this is done by preparing special ghostfood in a bowl (*baupāḥ*) as part of the sacrificial proceedings. By his very nature as Āju (ancestor) and more particularly *mvādyo*, Pacalī stands closer to the *bhūtpret* than most other gods, as may also be seen from the inclusion of Daitya in his *gaṇa* at the *pīṭha*. Hence it can be understood that the *bhūtpret pūjā* is also more than a simple means of distracting the ghosts from the sacrifice.

The particular form which it takes is mysteriously called *kāṃ jośī bvākegu*, 'making the blind Jośī run'. A Jośī is an astrologer, in ritual practice often the assistant of the Brāhman. While a Jośī also used to assist the *ācāju* of the Thakū juju in the past, he was neither blind nor chased. There is no such precedent in Pacalī's mythology either, so the only way to deal with the mystery is to look at the ritual practice. For the *bali pūjā* a large copper cauldron (*khāsi*) has been carried by two Jyāpu from the *lāykū* to the roadside at Atkonārāyaṇa. The *khāsi* is placed on the road and the *ācāju* surrounds it with six *gvaḥjā* and four small earthen pots according to the instructions given in the *ācāju*'s text – which is secret to the non-initiated. First *kanhāysvāṃ* and *pañcapatā* (small five-coloured flags) are put in the *khāsi*. Then, with accompanying *mantras*, the *gvaḥjā*-like *kavaṃcā* ('little ghosts') are put there in the name of the different evil forces mentioned.

When the *khāsi* is thus filled, the *ācāju* gives a *ṭikā* to the carriers and to a torch-bearer who lights a *tiṃpvāy*, a bundle of thin bamboos. Accompanied by *nāykhiṃ* (the special music of drum and cymbals played by the Butcher's caste) the group rushes off to the Kaṣṭhamaṇḍapa just above Atkonārāyaṇa in the centre of town. From there they rush back and then make three short rounds along the triangle Bhimsensthān (just above the Thakū juju's residence), Kaṣṭhamaṇḍapa and Atkonārāyaṇa. Meanwhile the Thakū juju has gone swiftly to the Pacalī *pīṭha*. On penalty of a fine he has to arrive there before the *khāsi* will be brought and disposed of. The latter will be put hastily on the very hole in the metal sheet below which Pacalī is buried, but from there immediately taken back to the *betāl*, the demon whose copper body lies at the threshold of the *pīṭha*. In the process, some of the contents of the *khāsi* drop on Pacalī, but the greater part ends up on the *betāl*.

By then the Pacalī jar, which was quicker in arriving at the shrine than the *khāsi*, has been placed by the Jyāpu in a *pāṭī* (shelter) facing the *pīṭha*. From about midnight till near dawn, there will be no move in the scenery. The destination of Pacalī's *yātrā mūrti* is the pithole in the *pīṭha*, but, as a rule, it cannot move to or from the *pīṭha* without the music of the Gathu, the Gardeners. The *guthi* of Gardeners also stages the divine dances, in which the *gaṇa* – foremost Pacalī Bhairava – is represented by masked performers. In those dances, which will be treated in the next chapter, the music is also of primary importance: it makes the gods move.

The transition of procession images to their permanent place of power in the *pīṭha*s is always critical, as if two distinct spheres touch each other there: the motionless stone image which expresses the descent of the deity onto earth, and the moving brass or copper statute which represents its dynamic in the human world.

Devotees try to touch the *yātrā mūrtis* exactly at the moment of transition, both before and after they have been placed in their permanent seat of power. The procession images are in all cases highly charged at these critical moments, but there is no other example in which they are so reluctant to join or to leave their stone counterparts as in the case of Pacalī.

The nightly scene at the *pīṭha* comes to life again with the arrival of the Gathu musicians, and a ritual of a high intensity unfolds which culminates in the fire-sacrifice in front of the shrine. Before the jar is brought to the pit the Sthāpit repeats the pouring of liquid from three pitchers which he did the night before in *nimantraṇa pūjā*. The *ācāju* then draws a *maṇḍala* (a sacred diagram) behind the pit and asks to install the Pacalī jar there. At the solemn tunes of the music Pacalī is carried to his ancestral place, the pithole below which are the stone remains of the erstwhile king of Pharping. The *ācāju* continues with an elaborate worship (Photo 14) in which *kotaḥ pūjā*s of both the Thakū juju and the Sthāpit are performed, with different kind of *gvaḥjā* (beside the conical ones a multi-armed Viśvadeva and a Gaṇeśa are brought in), *kavaṃcā*, foods, fruits, incenses, wicks, and flowers for all members of the *pigaṃ*, the divine host in the *pīṭha*. The Thakū juju rings the bells of the shrine, the Sthāpit assists in the *pūjā* and the Gathu music sounds.

Photo 14.
The Karmācārya priest (left) performing a worship to Pacalī Bhairava in the night of the fire sacrifice at Pacalī Bhairava's piṭha. Standing next to him are the Thakū juju of Kvane (right) and his double, Sthāpit (centre) (1992).

Pacalī will now be further filled up with liquor, beer, *samay baji*, and eggs, to the delight of the god. In the subsequent *homa* a special medicine will be burned to relieve Pacalī from his hangover. The first liquor poured into the jar is the Sthāpit's portion, the last is that of the Thakū juju which is poured from a small water jar identified with the goddess, Ajimā. In between other people take their turns, among whom are several *guthi*s. After the Sthāpit empties the Thakū juju's Ajimā *gvaṃpa* the feasting of Pacalī is finished.

Worshippers continue to come, first those who participate in the *navarātri melā*, (taking a bath at nine sacred bathing places (*tīrtha*) at the confluences of the Bāgmatī, Viṣṇumatī and other rivers during the very early mornings of Dasain and visiting Teku Dhoban at dawn on the fifth day of Dasain). Some of them come early enough to contribute to the *jalpay luyegu* (liquor pouring), others are in the crowd which comes with *pūjā* items and sacrificial offerings (mostly cock) in the early morning. Although the Pacalī jar can accept animal sacrifice when it is in the *dyocheṃ*, all blood sacrifices at the Pacalī *pīṭha* are presented to the *betāl* as his intermediary.

The fire sacrifice, which is the most important task of the Thakū juju as *jajmān*, attracts few spectators from the crowd. The Thakū juju's *ācāju* comments on the basis of his text that the *homa* is directed at Agni, the (god of) Fire itself, with Pacalī as a witness sharing in the effect like the human beings do. Others consider the fire sacrifice rather as embedded in the context and mention Pacalī as the main beneficiary. The *homa* at the Pacalī *pīṭha* is again peculiar when compared to fire sacrifices that precede the *yātrā*s of other divinities. Usually a blood sacrifice is made before, commonly the night before the *homa*, and the non-vegetarian part of the oblations in the fire derives from that previous sacrifice: the lungs, the heart or the head of the animal which has been slaughtered at the shrine. In the Pacalī Bhairava *homa* the animal, a he-goat, is slaughtered above the fire – or as close to the fire as is possible in the heat. Agni likes to eat everything, comments the *ācāju*, and indeed, the whole animal will subsequently be committed to the fire.

For the *homa* to start, the party of the Thakū juju, the Sthāpit and the *ācāju* have to await the arrival of the Nāy, the Butchers who kill the victims. The vegetarian part of the *homa*, which consists of offering nine kinds of grain into the fire, may already be started before, but in that case the fire has to be kept burning until the Nāy arrive. The leading elder is dressed in the long white robes and round hat that are considered characteristic of the early Malla or pre-Malla kings. It indicates the Nāy's claimed descent from royalty and nobility of bygone days, before they were degraded to a low caste.

They start with killing the Sthāpit's goat, cutting its throat while the animal is held up to the fire. With the Nāy *nāyaḥ* still holding the animal in the air, his assistant removes the entrails – those are the Nāy's part – and cuts the rest of the animal into twelve pieces which are collected in a basket held by the Sthāpit. The *ācāju* takes the head and keeps it separately in an earthen pot. Reciting *mantra*s from his text, he gives the other pieces one by one to the Sthāpit, who throws them in the fire.

The same procedure is followed for the Thakū juju's goat. In neither of the two cases does the goat have to give the usual consent to be sacrificed by shivering. The *ācāju*'s text does not give a reason for cutting up the bodies into twelve pieces, but according to the Thakū juju each of the pieces is offered in the name of one of the members of the *gaṇa*, the divine host. The two heads, which are offered together at the end of the *homa*, are presented in the name of Pacalī himself. The equivalences of the sacrificed heads with the two *jajmān*s and the main divinity are striking. The idea of self-sacrifice is at the core of any sacrifice but usually immolation and burnt oblation are separated from each other: the animal is first to be immolated at the shrine of the divinity, and the sign of its consent is indicating that divinity has taken possession of it. In case of Pacalī, blood sacrifice and fire sacrifice coincide, while at the same time a curious doubling exists: the *jajmān*, himself a descendant of Pacalī Bhairava, is in need of a double in the form of the Sthāpit.

The divinity is by exception not involved in the immolation: he is a witness to both the animal sacrifice and the *homa*, of which the Fire is the only receiver. In cases where the animal is first offered to the divinity and subsequently (part of it) to the fire, one cannot without justification consider the deity a *jajmān* as well, whose task is consequently carried out by his human counterpart. Both man and god sit at the sacrifice and share the same capacity. Man has brought the animal to slaughter, god has appropriated it by taking possession of the animal, and the subsequent burnt oblation is a matter of both of them.[2] In the case of Pacalī the god does not take possession of the animal and does not partake in the bloodshed. Agni stands in to receive the blood and the Sthāpit is to receive the dismembered animal. As the *betāl* does in ordinary blood sacrifices, the Sthāpit fulfils the role of intermediary in the fire cum blood sacrifice. The duality of man and god in the fire sacrifice is reflected in the Thakū juju and his double, who both act as *jajmān*s and contribute identical shares. Instead of separating the animal sacrifice from the fire sacrifice, they are combined and executed twice.

At the conclusion the *ācāju* instructs the Thakū juju and the Sthāpit to throw paddy into the fire three times each. Then he distributes flowers and blessing marks (*ṭikā*s) to the team and surrounding people, while the Thakū juju distributes pancakes (*catāṃmari*) to the participants. Finally they take the soot of the *homa* as *prasāda* from the *dhagaḥ*, the sacrificialladle. Other people approach the *homakuṇḍa* to take the *ṭikā* of ashes as *prasāda* straight from the smouldering fire.

The yātrā

After the *homa* is completed people flock to the shrine on the fifth day of Dasain to do *pūjā* or to offer sacrifice. The Pacalī yātrā starts only at night after first the Nāy Ajimā and then the Nāy Gaṇeśa are brought to the *pīṭha*. The decorated *pātra* (bowl) representing Nāy Ajimā comes from the same *dyocheṃ* as the procession image of Pacalī. The Nāy Gaṇeśa comes from a Nāy (Butcher) *guthi* which celebrates its own Gaṇeśa yātrā parallel to the Pacalī yātrā. The *guthi* also goes to Pacalī late at night after the *nimantraṇa pūjā* to feast Pacalī in the name of his son Gaṇeśa. In the night of the *yātrā* the Nāy *nāyaḥ* (who slaughtered the goats at sacrifice) brings their statue of the god Gaṇeśa attached to a drum.

The Pacalī jar itself can only be taken out on its round when the whole company is complete: the Ajimā and the Gaṇeśa *mūrti*s as well as the Gathu musicians. Almost every year, however, impatient youngsters carry the heavy jar away before all are present, but then again return it after a rowdy round of the shrine. The brassband of the *rājguru* and a carrier with the Nepalese king's sword are also part of the company. Remarkably absent is the Thakū juju whose presence is not required because, in his own view, Pacalī's *yātrā* and reception at Hanumānḍhokā are a matter of the present kings of Nepal (whose predecessors have taken over the royal status once held by his ancestors).

The Nāy Gaṇeśa and Ajimā are the first to leave the *pīṭha*, carried by a Nāy and a Jyāpu, both of whom are possessed by the respective divinities in their hands and supported by other members of their *guthi*s. The whole company including the musicians circumambulates the shrine thrice before quickly going on their way. Ajimā makes capricious moves up and down the route according to her whims – the possessed carrier is helpless – but never falls back behind Pacalī. The heavy jar of the main god is very roughly carried and sometimes dropped down by a group of inebriated men who assure that Pacalī is enjoying it all because the god himself is filled up with what he likes. Two beer-spouting gods (Hāthudyo) along the way add lustre to the Dionysian company.

A feature of all other *yātrā*s is that the gods are on their way received by humans and especially by *mhyāymasta*, the out-married daughters of the quarter where the deity comes from. Pacalī's *yātrā* in the dead of night has none of those characteristic features: apart from being occasionally dropped down the god moves straight to the palace square, makes a round of the Kāla Bhairava statue there and is announced at Hanumānḍhokā. Before it is Pacalī's turn, his mythical partner the Nāy Ajimā receives a buffalo for sacrifice from a shutter in the main gate. That buffalo is slaughtered on the spot, and the head separated from the body by the Jyāpu retinue of Ajimā. This time the head of the sacrifice will be divided among the elders of the Jyāpu *guthi*.

At the time of Pacalī's reception at Hanumānḍhokā, the royal Kumārī is carried from her abode near by to a courtyard of the palace compound adjoining the main gate (Photo 15). Her action is confined to sitting there as if she has come just to reconfirm the connection between the central power and its distant predecessor.

While Ajimā is already carried away, Pacalī receives a *pūjā* from the palace gate (a *juju pūjā*) without an accompanying sacrifice: instead of the customary *pūjā* items, there is only a coconut to break. After the *pūjā* he is carried straight to his next Jyāpu *dyocheṃ* in the Kvane part of town to stay there for the coming year (Photo 16). At arrival the ladies of the house give a ceremonial welcome (*lasakusa*) to Pacalī, and a feast is given to all those who followed the *yātrā* to its end.

Photo 15.
The goddess Kumārī, represented by a Śākya girl, awaiting Pacalī Bhairava at Hanumānḍhokā on the fifth day of Dasain (1990).

Conclusion

For the *guthi* members the sacred period herewith comes to an end: eight days before the *yātrā yaciṃ laḥ* (pure river water) was distributed among the members. This holy water is to purify them and to indicate the start of a period in which they cannot accept food touched by anybody else including family members and, most important of all, in which they cannot observe death pollution. As a sign of this vow they take a bath, cut their nails and shave their heads.

The *guthi* members come from nine different wards (*tvāḥ*) in Kvane. All these *tvāḥ* also send their boys to Pacalī for the *vaḥlāḥ* (initiation) ceremony organized every twelve years by the Ākāśa Bhairava *guthi*. As discussed in the previous chapter, the *vaḥlāḥ* takes place for three subsequent years in the night before and the night of

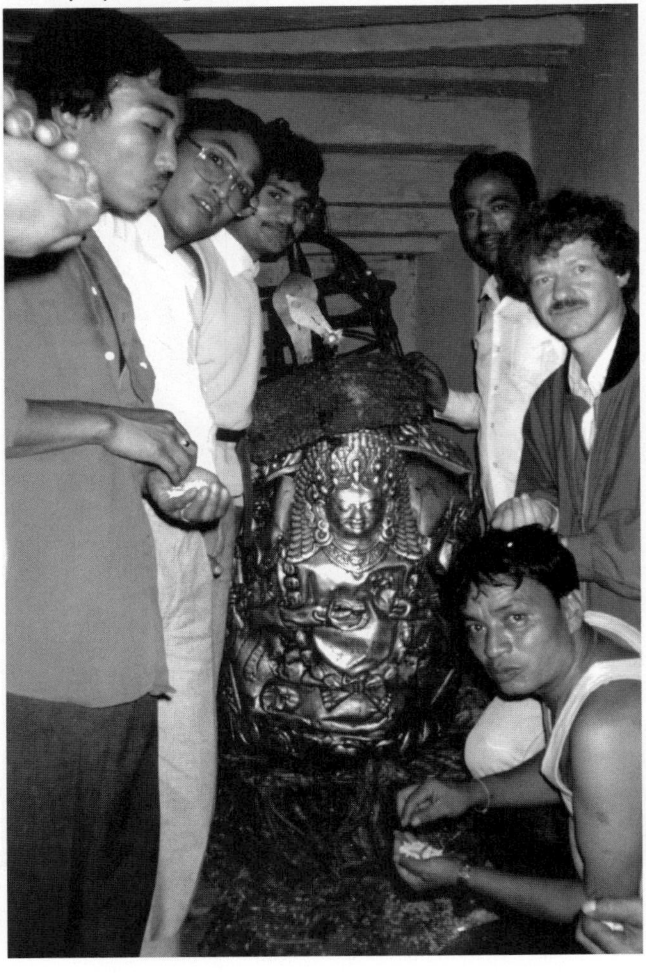

Photo 16.
At the end of his procession, Pacalī Bhairava rests at a Jyāpu guardian's home where he will remain until the start of next year's procession. The author (centre, right) is attending the ceremony (1991).

the *homa*, but the boys use to sleep when the ceremonies for Pacalī are performed. In the final year, however, they have their own (vegetarian) *homa*s conducted by Vajrācārya priests in a fire pit made of bricks. Those small *homa*s are carried out in the *paṭī*s surrounding the Pacalī shrine and tend to be simultaneous with the Thakū juju's *homa* though without any connection.

Although members of different castes partake in the Pacalī yātrā, the Jyāpu of Kvane shoulder most of the overall responsibilities. As Annick Hollé and others (1993) have pointed out, the Farmers form the core of old Kathmandu City, in spite of the fact that they constitute less than a quarter of its population according to a 1971 survey (Greenwold 1974). With regard to the Kvane part of town the authors remark that 'The lower half of Kathmandu still has its own urban fabric, its own temples (Pacalī Bhairav), and its own religious practices differing slightly from those of the upper half. It constitutes a world unto itself. There is good reason to believe that this area was incorporated into the city proper at a later stage.'

It is remarkable indeed that the *yātrā* of Pacalī Bhairava does not pass into the Thane part of town. A parallel can only be found in the *yātrā* of Cakaṃdyo of Thamel (Thabahil), which is confined to the northern part of town (Gutschow 1982: 141), but then, Thamel quarter is located outside the old city's boundaries. The goddess Nilvārāhī, however, who also belongs to Kvane and has her *dyocheṃ* in Kohiti, has her *yātrā* in the spring festival of Pāhāṃ Carhe and, like the other goddesses in that festival, she circumambulates both the Kvane and the Thane parts of town.

Rather than based on a supposedly original status as a separate town (a doubtful supposition, see chapter 1), the restrictions of the Pacalī yātrā both in time (the middle of the night) and in space (the up and down track limited to Kvane) may have to do with the nature of the god himself. In the mythical accounts Pacalī established himself in Kathmandu as a god in hiding. Like Indradyo he started as a furtive visitor and became a captive god once he was caught in the act of his transgression. Moreover Pacalī partakes in both the divine and the human world: he is a *mvādyo*, a living god, and as such the founding father of the ancient Thakū juju dynasty.

It is as a perennial king that Pacalī marches to the centre of the present royal power. Both the god himself – the jar being filled up with liquor – and his attendants and carriers are inebriated when they make their move to Hanumānḍhokā. The Jyāpu *guthi* members have their foreheads painted orange, which adds to the altogether violent appearance of the procession. It is as if, in the dead of night, an assault is being made on the royal palace. The approach is particularly violent, with the retainers of Pacalī and Ajimā hammering the gate with their fists in order to extract the sacrifice from Hanumānḍhokā.

Kingship is variously represented at this moment: it is on the one hand present in the full and agressively moving jar of Pacalī himself. On the other hand, as we shall see in the next chapter, in the royal sword of the ruling monarch the military brassband and the appearance of the royal Kumārī. Ancient conceptions of kingship enter into and are controlled by present-day kingship in this particular night. After that night Pacalī will be put to rest again in his next *dyocheṃ* until he is woken up next year.

He had to be revived as it were, with vitalizing food and a non-vegeterian burnt oblation – in which the fresh blood of goats is sprinkled and all of their meat offered. From the spatial point of view king Pacalī may seem a distant spectator, but at the same time he embodies the fire like the Vedic god Rudra. He is the Fire, which is lighting up and then expiring again, the king who dies but is revived through the fire and the intoxicating liquid poured into him. And, as a human touch, the fire receives a medicine to counter Pacalī's intoxination, which all the more accentuates the identification between Pacalī and Agni.

His origin as a god who was caught and then petrified at the site of his *pīṭha* contains a ghostly aspect – of being in between the two worlds – which also appears in the *pūjā*. Pacalī is the only god who, together with his *gaṇa*, receives both *gvaḥjā* – used to invoke gods – and the rare *kavaṃcā* – explained as *gvaḥjā* for the demons. The mysterious *kāṃ jośī bvākegu* episode cannot be interpreted as an act to chase away the demons. The *khāsi* with the *bhūtpret pūjā* is not dumped somewhere at a place appropriate to the ghosts, but instead brought to and thrown over Pacalī Bhairava himself. Although no participants' explanation exists, it seems here as if the legion of bhūtpret[3] is not expelled or dispersed but collected to serve Pacalī. The god Śiva, of whom the Bhairavas are considered the terrific manifestations, is well-known in Nepal as heading the legion of *bhūtpret*. Pacalī Bhairava appears to share that quality but more than that: as will become more apparent from the next chapter on the Gathu divine dances – in which Pacalī is the main character – the god possesses the attributes of the Lord of Death himself.

Pacalī's hide out amidst cremation *ghāṭ*s, where he was in some versions of the myth wrapped in a *pulu*, a cover for corpses, gives already clear indication of his close association with Death. It must be said, conversely, that all cremation *ghāṭ*s have their nearby *pīṭha* which always includes a form of Bhairava. The fire of Pacalī's *homa*, which consumes whole bodies of goats, has through that capacity an unmistakable affinity with the cremation fire. The connection between Pacalī Bhairava, the cremation fire, and the bodies destined for it, thus comes to the foreground. Pacalī is the hinge of life and death and his movements are covered in darkness. Like all celebrations of death, it is for the participants a rumbustious, albeit somewhat frightening affair. The deliberate unconsciousness or trance of the carriers of Pacalī's companions, the Nāy Ajimā and the Nāy Gaṇeśa, enhances this frightening aspect. The host of attendants with their orange-coloured foreheads, adds further force to the march of the king of Death.

In his *yātrā* Pacalī visits the palace without meeting the king of Nepal. In the twelve-yearly dances of the Gathu, however, Pacalī exchanges his sword with the king – an act which is most often interpreted as empowering the king, especially with regard to the battlefield. In the Pacalī yātrā the connection is made between the Thakū juju – the lord of the sacrificial night – and the present king, whose turn it is to receive Pacalī in the subsequent night. At the same time it seems as if the Jyāpu have appropriated both Pacalī and the Nāy Ajimā by housing them in their *dyocheṃ* and by being guardians of the shrine. After the *lasakusa* in the Thakū juju's residence,

Pacalī is captured in silence, albeit with the equally silent consent of the Thakū juju himself. Both Jyāpu and Thakū juju have the material resources to serve the god: the Thakū juju has lands belonging to Bhimsensthān, another temple in which he is involved, and the Jyāpu *guthi* has lands for the special purpose of the Pacalī yātrā. Several specific items, such as the wood for the *homa*, are supplied by the Guthi Saṃsthān, the government's office for religious endowments.

It is thus not clear to which group of people Pacalī belongs. On the basis of mythology the Nāy can put the greatest claim on him, as it was in their circle that Pacalī ended up. The Thakū juju on the other hand claim to be the descendants of Pacalī Bhairava, but their role in the ritual is confined to the *nimantraṇa pūjā* and the sacrificial night. As lords of the sacrifice their role is equal to that of many *jajmān*s in Kathmandu's fire-sacrifices. The god Pacalī Bhairava, however, transcends the boundaries of specific associations and also those of the Kvane quarter of town. His nightly visit to Hanumānḍhokā in the presence of Kumārī and the royal sword is not witnessed by many people. Impersonated by the Gathu dancers, however, Pacalī Bhairava's fame is spread over the Valley and, together with the goddess Bhadrakālī, he is raised to the level of a national god.

Chapter 7

The Dying Gods

The Divine Dances of the Gathu[1]

Introduction

Divine dances (*dyo pyākhaṃ*) performed by members of the Gāthu (Gardeners) caste are based at four centres in the Kathmandu Valley: Kirtipur, Kathmandu, Theco, and Bhaktapur. The dancing groups all go on tour and the areas of their performances, which together cover a large part of the Valley, in some cases overlap. Yet the dances of the four groups take place independently from each other and follow different cycles. The twelve-yearly cycle of the Kirtipur *dyo pyākhaṃ* coincides with that of the Bhadrakālī *pyākhaṃ* in Kathmandu, and only in this case the two groups may, in principle, assist each other. Whether the Gathu dances are performed in a twelve-yearly cycle, or annually – as in Bhaktapur – they have one feature in common: the divine dancers 'die' at the end of their performance. Surviving them are the *guru*s (teachers), the (six) musicians who accompany and lead the group. The season of actual performance starts at the concluding, tenth, day (Vijayā Daśamī) of the great autumn festival Dasain in September/October and ends at Bhala Bhala Aṣṭamī (eighth of the dark half of Asāra or) around the end of June, depending on the lunar calendar.

Prior to their dances the performers are empowered in several stages, the first of which consists of giving a pledge and 'raising the divinities' (*gama thanegu*), from their permanent seat (*pīṭha*) more than two months before the first performance. A local etymology of the caste-name Gathu is derived from this act, *gaṃ* (Skt. *gaṇa*) + *thaṃ* ('to lift'), the lifting of the *gaṇa* of gods in order to embody them. The names of the gods are somewhat different in each of the four groups but the *gaṇa* (the divine group) always includes a form of the goddess Kālī and her male counterpart Bhairava as the main divinities, as well as the indispensable and crucial god Gaṇeśa and the lion- and tiger-faced female attendants Siṃhinī and Vyāghinī. The rest of the *gaṇa* is made up of the *mātṛkā*s, the mostly eight goddesses whose seats of power (*pīṭha*) surround Newar towns and villages. In the Gathu *pyākhaṃ* of Kathmandu the names of those goddesses are, with some colloquial variations, given as: Mahālakṣmī, Indrāyaṇī, Bhadrakālī, Vārāhī, Vaiṣṇavī, Kumārī, Rudrāyaṇī and Brahmāyaṇī. Most often those eight *mātṛkā*s are, besides being the main divinities of their own *pīṭha*s, also represented together in each of those shrines, as a row or demi-circle of stone images on both sides of the main divinity – and so are Gaṇeśa, Bhairava and the attendants Siṃhinī and Vyāghinī. The *pīṭha* of Bhadrakālī, which is an open-air shrine south-west of Kathmandu's old city, thus includes stone representations of all the divinities which are lifted from there to be embodied by the Gathu dancers.

One month after their first pledge the dancers receive their *ghaṃgalā*, the jingling bracelets worn below the knees, which are distinct for each of the divinities.

From that moment onwards, they are already considered to be divinely empowered or possessed when they practice their dance wearing these *ghaṃgalā*s. While the period of the dance performances stretches over eight and a half months, all ceremonies together, starting from the first pledge on the day of Gathāṃmugaḥ, take nearly eleven months of the lunar calendar. Taking the wearing of the *ghaṃgalā* as a starting point, the period of divine empowerment continues for almost ten months. Six weeks after receiving the *ghaṃgalā* bracelets the dancers will receive their most distinctive feature: the masks which show the faces of the gods and which will be worn during all public perform-ances. The masks also have to be empowered before being joined to the dancers who, at least partly, possess the *śakti*, the power of the divinities, already. The junction is made through a fire-sacrifice on the eve, or in real terms, the morning of the festival's tenth day (*Vijayā Daśamī*), when their first performance as masked dancers is to take place. The *homa* or fire-sacrifice is the *jīva nyāsa*, the inserting of life into masks and dancers together. The masks are again central in the final episode when the *śakti* abandons the dancers, that is, when the gods die. The final disjunction is not brought about by a *homa*, but by a cremation in which the masks are burned in a way similar to dead persons.

With the elaborate fire-sacrifice, the only ceremony which is not performed by the Gathu themselves but by a Buddhist (Vajrācārya) priest, the power is generated which turns thirteen papier-mâché masks into representations of the divinities portrayed, and the wearers of the masks – who are all male – into the embodiment of these gods and goddesses. In the night of their death – whether the term 'death' is fully applicable will be considered further on – a fire will again be lit. This time, however, it is a funeral pyre on the banks of the Bāgmatī river in which all masks are to be cremated. The cremation of the masks should immediately follow the death of the gods on Bhala Bhala Aṣṭamī; in 1992 it happened on the 23rd of June or rather in the early morning of the 24th.

The next Bhadrakālī dances will start only eleven years later, but the same association of Gathu will stage the similar Pacalī Bhairava dances (which also follow a twelve-yearly cycle) after eight years. The twelve-yearly cycles of divine dances (*dyo pyākhaṃ*) in Kathmandu resemble the better documented (Gutschow 1987, Levy 1987) annual Navadurgā dances of Bhaktapur, both with regard to the nature and the course of life of the divinities embodied and with regard to the caste of the performers, the Gathu (also called Mālī or Mālākāra, part of their traditional profession being to make and sell flower garlands for worship). The end of the affair, the cremation of the divine masks, however, is done in secret in Bhaktapur whereas it is a public event in Kathmandu as well as in Kirtipur.[2] As if an epidemic rages through the Valley, all divinities embodied pass away in the night of Bhala Bhala Aṣṭamī, which is always close to *dakṣiṇāyana*, the summer solstice, and to the onset of the monsoon.

The time of the gods' 'death' suggests interesting equations: the Sun's southward turn marks its journey to the realm of Yama, the god of Death. Furthermore, if not the actual commencement of the dances, but the first stage of divine empowerment is taken as a point of departure, their whole enactment lasts over nine months, a gestation period as it were, of which the rains appear to be the fruitful consequence. Let us not, however, start the interpretation before having gathered the facts. Death, so much can be said, is as important in the whole sequence as is the genesis of the dancing gods. While the genesis of these gods is a long and complicated process their death and subsequent cremation take place within the span of one protracted night. In that respect the demise of the dancers sharply contrasts with that of human beings. In the latter case the mortuary rites and their aftermath constitute a process which is more elaborate and complicated than the rituals surrounding birth.

Generally speaking, both the birth and the death of gods contain a mystery. Death is exceptional in the divine realm and birth is more often than not miraculous. The eccentric genesis of Gaṇeśa and the generation of Draupadī as also the birth of the demon killing goddess from the sacrificial fire are popular examples. The Ādityas, the main Vedic gods, are according to the Yajurvedic Maitrāyaṇī Saṃhitā born from the remnants of a sacrificial porridge (*odana*) eaten by the goddess Āditi. When Āditi reversed the sequence and ate the porridge herself before offering it, Mārtāṇḍa ('born from dead egg'), the progenitor of Yama, was born (e.g. M.S.1,6,12; Krick 1982: 270). One might speak in this regard of 'the birth of death', for Yama was the first to die in this world – a fact quite unobtrusively introduced in Maitrāyaṇī Saṃhitā itself. To mitigate the grief of Yamī, Yama's twin sister and lover, the gods created night. By his dying Yama became the ancestor of another race, mankind, without however losing his divinity. Yama is one of the Vedic gods who, like Indra, is still actively worshipped in Nepal. Under his own name, Yama or Yamarāja, he is especially revered during Svanti (Tihār) at the turn of the lunar year. As Mahākāla or Bhairava he enjoys a pre-eminent position in the religion of Nepal. In Bhaktapur's Gāi yātrā, the yearly festival of the dead, a straw effigy of Bhairava is carried along with the effigies for the dead of Taumadhi quarter, to be disposed of at Masān *ghāṭ* along the Hanumante river (see chapter 4).

Yet, even though the mortal aspect of Yama can be tracked down to the most ancient texts, and even if the mortality of Bhairava can be alluded to as the god of Death, death remains an exception in the realm of the gods. Gods and men have many things in common and can not be distinguished from each other in terms of good and evil, superiority and inferiority, not even in terms of power: great sacrificers, ascetics and *tāntrik*s among men have been able to match or even control the gods. The distinctive feature of the gods appears to be exactly their immortality, which makes them revered among men, but which at the same time excludes them from the way to salvation that is open to mortals alone – with the exception of the great Gods Śiva and Viṣṇu who came to embody the universe itself. To sum up this bird's-eye view: the death of a god is contrary to the essence of a divine being, yet it occurs. Likewise, immortality is contrary to the very definition of man as a mortal creature, yet it is constantly aspired to and sometimes achieved. The fence between gods and men is not completely closed and it is on the interface of their respective domains that the mystery play of the divine dancers is situated.

The social setting

To account for the fact that the Gathu performers can, albeit very temporarily, assume a divine nature and like gods (as it is said) acquire exemption from death pollution, one need to go one step beyond the performance of the divine dances themselves. The special power of the Gathu primarily derives from the divine sound they produce by the grace of Nāsaḥdyo, the god of music and dance. The Gathu are the only ones who by their music can set into motion the procession image of the reluctant god Pacalī Bhairava (as we saw, a brass jar heavy with liquor and festive foods) in his nightly *yātrā* from the Pacalī *pīṭha* to the Hanumānḍhokā palace in the centre of town. The Bhadrakālī and Pacalī Bhairava dances, in both of which Pacalī Bhairava is the main god (*mū dyo*) can be considered an extension of the musical performance. All the divine characters of the dances belong to the families of the four principal musicians. Bhairava himself, Gaṇeśa, Rudrāyaṇī and Siṃhinī belong to the family of the nāyaḥ (the eldest of the *guthi*) and his brother who is the *nvakū* (second eldest) of the *guthi.* They play a horned drum (*khiṃ*) and horned cymbals (*chusyā*) respectively. The roles of Bhadrakālī, Kumārī, Indrāyaṇī and Vyāghinī fall to the family of the player of the smaller cymbals (*tāḥ*). Vārāhī, Vaiṣṇavī, Brahmāyaṇī and Mahālakṣmī are assigned to the family of the musician who plays a special kind of cymbals (*babhū*). Those families may invite somebody from another Gathu family to perform in the dances but, conversely, it is impossible for anybody outside their circle to claim a part in the divine drama.

There are two masks, which do not require performers: one is Svet Bhairava, who is considered an aspect of the main Bhairava, and is enacted by the Pacalī Bhairava dancer after an intricate and secret change of masks. The other is Mahālakṣmī who completes the circle of eight goddesses (*aṣṭamātṛkā*), but who has a singular appearance as a very small mask that is carried on a stick ahead of the masked dancers.[3] There are also two more musicians, who play the *pvaṃgā*, a pipe, which is only blown at critical moments and passages. The horn blowers cannot claim roles in the drama, but they are included in the *sī guthi* (funeral association) of the Gathu performers, which consists of the six musicians, the Bhairava and Bhadrakālī dancers and one additional member. The *sī guthi* does not coincide with the group of divine performers but its composition appears to be closely related to the authority over and the formation of the dancing team.

The six *guru*-musicians also constitute the backbone of the *sī guthi*, the funeral association of the Tarhaṃ Gathu *guthi*. Another *sī guthi* of Gathu, called '*Cīrhaṃ*' (small as opposed to big) belongs to the area of Kālimātī, south of Kathmandu proper, and is not involved in the dances. The task of the *sī guthi* in its strictest sense is that of a funeral association which takes care of the cremation of community members. In this context the *khiṃ* player and chusyā player are the *nāyaḥ* (eldest) and the nvakū (second eldest) of the Tarhaṃ Gathu *sī guthi*, which has, like all *sī guthi*s of the different communities in Kathmandu, a yearly sacrifice and feast (*sī kāḥ bhvay*) of its own. Up to 1992 the Tarhaṃ Gathu *guthi* built a temporary shed of wood and straw for this purpose, a custom which was once common among all *sī guthi*s but which is gradually abandoned by most of them. *sī guthi* feasts are not accessible to outsiders, but, as the *nāyaḥ* told me, the musicians play on that occasion the very music which accompanies the divine dancers – also in years that the dances are not per-formed: the power of the musicians does not abandon them until the moment of their physical death. The Bhadrakālī and Bhairava members of the *sī guthi* fulfill, by serving beer from a *pātra* (bowl) and by doing *pūjā* (worship) for the other *guthi*-members respectively, a task which they also have in the context of the masked dances. They do not, however, perform their dance during the *sī guthi* feast.

In years that either the Bhadrakālī or Pacalī Bhairava *pyākhaṃ* is performed, the *khalaḥ* ('family') includes, in addition to the six musicians and eleven dancers, a number of other members, all of whom are, confusingly, also called *nāyaḥ*s, 'elders'. Among those *nāyaḥ*s are three main *nāyaḥ*s, who are the attendants of the three main deities, Bhairava, Bhadrakālī and Vārāhī, and who are called *dhvaṃpvami*, *dātipvami*, and *mipvami nāyaḥ* respectively (this designation of the order of *nāyaḥ*s occurs in the given context only). The remaining *nāyaḥ*s include a variable number of children (*macā nāyaḥ*, in 1992 only two), *taḥdhimha nāyaḥ* (a 'big' *nāyaḥ*, in charge of the *mahāpātra* (drinking bowl) and of the *kṣetrapāla*, the 'lord of the area' (a sacrificial stone in a sacred site which is often identified with Bhairava), as well as a variable number of *cīdhima nāyaḥ* ('small' *nāyaḥ*, in 1992 only one). In 1992 the *khalaḥ* had, with 24 members in total, a minimal composition.

Apart from attending to the divinities, these *nāyaḥ*s must also be capable to replace any one of them in case of need: they are fully sanctified, trained and also exempted from death pollution as the dancers are. Likewise exempted from death pollution are five ladies, who carry the essential items of worship to the places where dances and other ceremonies are performed. They are together called *pañcakumārī* and belong to the families of the *guru*-musicians, but they are not considered to be members of the *khalaḥ*. After the final ceremonies the whole team disbands; it is only the *sī guthi* which remains, thus showing the intrinsic relationship between the dancing 'family' and the funeral association. Here, as in other cases (Van den Hoek & Shrestha 1992: 64, 65) the *sī guthi* proves to be more than a funeral association. In case of the Gathu the double function of the *sī guthi* harbours a contradiction. Because the *khalaḥ* as a whole cannot be touched by death pollution, the *sī guthi*, which consists of the musicians and three central figures within the team, cannot function as a funeral association.

Strictly speaking this prohibition extends to the cremation of the divine masks themselves. The dancers are relieved from divine possession shortly after the gods in them die, but their sanctity remains until *bicāḥ pūjā*, a last worship in the Bhadrakālī temple. Then only they 'return' the *mohanī* (charm in the form of a soot mark on the forehead) which they received at the start of their performance. Therefore, the other (Cīrhaṃ) *sī guthi* should come to build the pyre and watch over the cremation of the masks. In return for this service, the non-dancing Gathu *sī guthi* is to receive one of the dresses of the divine dancers, to be used as a shroud (*devaṃ*) in their funeral as well as festive services. The latter aspect of the relationship has been badly maintained, as the chief *guru* (*khiṃ* player) and *nāyaḥ* of the Tarhaṃ *sī guthi* admitted, and the exchange belongs to the past. Nowadays, in a kind of conflation, the dancers themselves have to build the pyre and to watch over the cremation of their alter egos. The only noticeable exchange between the two *guthi*s was the part of the goddess Rudrāyaṇī, performed by a member of the Cīrhaṃ *guthi* – but he, it was explained, had left the Tarhaṃ *guthi* to which he originally belonged. There is, the chief *guru* noted, also a tinge of democracy in the air, by which the 'small' *guthi* and even a recently split-off segment (degraded because of a low-caste marriage within their ranks) could eventually be reintegrated into the one Gathu *sī guthi* which supposedly existed in Kathmandu in days gone by.

The build-up of divine power

The activities of the Gathu start four days before Gathāṃmugaḥ Carhe, the day before the new moon in Srāvaṇa (July/August) when, in a spectacular way, the inhabitants of the Valley's towns expel the evil spirits which had been given a temporary refuge there during the rice planting season. The Gathu do not see a special link between this festival and the start of their activities, except for the fact that it is an auspicious day to start an enterprise like theirs. Four days before Gathāṃmugaḥ Carhe they send *gvay dāṃ* (consisting of rice, a coin and the *gvay*, betelnut, itself) to the king of Nepal to notify him of the advent of the dances. On Gathāṃmugaḥ Carhe each dancer brings a basket (*kalaḥ*) with items for worship (*pūjā*) to the Bhadrakālī *pīṭha* and offers this *kalaḥ pūjā* to the divinity whom he is to embody in the dances. The most significant item in it is *kisali*, a plate of husked rice, a coin and betelnut, similar in composition to the *gvay dāṃ* and commonly indicating a pledge or a bond. Besides the kisali, each of them offers a raw egg and *samay baji* (a ritual dish of five ingredients: beaten rice mixed with puffed rice, roast meat, black soya beans, raw ginger and liquor) and some other customary *pūjā* items like flowers, lights, incense, uncooked rice, *ṭikā*-powder. The uncommon thing is that all items offered are then taken back again, and put in cotton bags. The bags are carried by each of the dancers to the place of their instruction (*ākhāḥcheṃ*, a house for practicing music and dance) in Vatu quarter, in the northern part of Kathmandu. This particular *ākhāḥcheṃ* is also a godhouse (*dyocheṃ*) of Nāsaḥdyo, the god of music and dance, whose shrines are more often in the open air, also those inside the city itself.

Not only the *kalaḥ pūjā* of the dancers is first offered to the *gaṇa* of gods and then taken away. A sacrificial goat together with a brass plate (*kotaḥ*) of *pūjā* items is also dedicated to Bhadrakālī and then, with the *kotaḥ pūjā* still intact and the goat still alive, carried to the Nāsaḥdyocheṃ in Vatu. The *kotaḥ pūjā* belongs to the whole group of participants, and so does the goat, the sacrifice of which will only be executed in front of Nāsaḥdyo. The first sacrifice thus involves a rare and perhaps unique shift: the sacrificial animal is given a dedication (*saṃkalpa*) in front of

Bhadrakālī, the protagonist of the coming dances, but it is executed in front of the god who is thought to bestow the divine grace of music and dance. The question to whom the goat is sacrificed hence gives rise to some uncertainty. The ritual connection is complex. The placing of the offerings for the respective divinities by the dancers who are to embody them, and the goat sacrifice that is dedicated to Bhadrakālī by and for the whole *gaṇa*, are part of the process of 'raising the gods' (*dyo thanegu*) and 'drawing the gods along' (*dyo sālegu*). The gods, in other words, are supposed to follow the sacrifice, not automatically but by the tantric powers of the ritual. They are represented in the Nāsaḥdyocheṃ, which, on the south- and west-facing walls, has a row of nails from which eventually the divine masks will be hung – but only after the start of the dances.

On Gathāṃmugaḥ Carhe itself, each of the dancers hangs his cotton bag with the assembled *kalaḥ pūjā* items from the nail which corresponds to the divinity in the Bhadrakālī *pīṭha* to whom he has offered the *pūjā*. In this way the gods are transferred to the Nāsaḥdyocheṃ inside town, where they remain in rest for a full month. The dancers will only take their respective bags with *pūjā* remnants from the nails on the day before the next new moon, Pañcadān Carhe. The nails with the bags are, on Gathāṃmugaḥ, all sprinkled with the blood of the goat sacrificed in front of Nāsaḥdyo. The significant part of the sacrificed goat, the head, is divided into eight parts (*sī*) and distributed among the members of the *sī guthi* which includes the performers of Bhairava and Ajimā, but not any of the other dancers. By raising the company of gods (*dyogamaṃ thanegu*) from the pīṭha, and moving them into the Nāsaḥdyocheṃ (*dyo sālegu*), the goat sacrificed in front of Nāsaḥdyo is in essence sacrificed to the divinities to whom it was first consecrated: Bhadrakālī and her *gaṇa*.

In the month to come the dancers will start training in the *ākhāḥcheṃ*, the house of practice, on subsequent Saturdays. The house, which already had a permanent shrine of Nāsaḥdyo, has now also been turned into a kind of repository of the divine powers represented in the Bhadrakālī *pīṭha*. The dancers themselves do not as yet have any divine attributes or ornaments, and practice in their ordinary dress. The musical instruments which accompany them are all duplicates of the ceremonial ones that are to be used during the divine dances. The latter will be brought out, worshipped and put into use only two days before the start of the actual performance, more than two months later. The build-up of divine power in the dancers proceeds more gradually. One month after *dyo sālegu* at a ceremony called *ghaṃgalā* svanegu they receive their *ghaṃgalā* mentioned above. *ghaṃgalā* are a significant attribute of all divine dancers in the Kathmandu Valley: by wearing them the dancers partake in the divinity they embody or who, conversely, possesses them. The *ghaṃgalā* worn by the eleven Gathu dancers in Kathmandu are considered to be distinct from each other, signifying the divinity to whom they belong. On the day before the next moon, Pañcadān Carhe, they are together worshipped in the shrine of Nāsaḥdyo. For this worship, the dedication of their *ghaṃgalā*, the dancers take the bags with the one-month-old *pūjā* remnants from the respective nails on the wall. The eggs included in the *kalaḥ pūjā* offered at the Bhadrakālī *pīṭha* are broken only now as a sacrifice for

Nāsaḥdyo. Together with these remnants of the *dyo sālegu pūjā*, a buffalo is sacrificed. After putting on their *ghaṃgalā*, the five main divinities among the dancers, Gaṇeśa, Kumārī, Vārāhī, Ajimā and Bhairava drink the blood of the buffalo fresh from the carotid artery. Drinking the blood straight from the vein of a sacrificial victim – buffalo, goat, duck, or cock – is a prominent and often recurring feature of the Gathu *pyākhaṃ*. During the performances all dancers partake in it except Rudrāyaṇī, who, remarkably, is a vegetarian. At the time of *ghaṃgalā svanegu* only the five main gods are allowed to wear their bracelets. The others may take the *ghaṃgalā* with them but have to wait till the next Carhe (fourteenth day of a lunar fortnight) before putting them on. Even then, however, they are not sufficiently empowered to drink the blood of a victim. Curiously, the five main dancers appear to be not sufficiently empowered either: on the occasion of *ghaṃgalā svanegu*, as well as on the next occasion that they drink the blood of a buffalo sacrificed, they faint immediately. The main *guru*, the *nāyaḥ* of the *sī guthi*, has to sprinkle them with purified water (*nīlaḥ*) before they can regain consciousness. The *nāyaḥ* himself, after giving it some thought, offered two subsequent but opposite explanations for this phenomenon: firstly, that the dancers faint because the gods are not present in them there and then, secondly, that they are overpowered by the gods taking possession of them. Common to both explanations is that the dancers are not yet fully prepared to take the sacrificial blood in a self-controlled way. They are revived with *nīlaḥ* and a piece of raw buffalo meat in what seems to be a homoeopathic treatment. Evidently, the fresh blood possesses a life-power, which the piece of raw meat does not, or to a very limited extent.

Together with their *ghaṃgalā*, the dancers receive a pair of red trousers, which they are to wear during the subsequent rehearsals and during the dances themselves. Their full dress, the robes in the colours of the respective divinities, is, like the divine masks, to be worn only in the real performance. After *ghaṃgalā svanegu*, the members have fortnightly sessions in one of the *sataḥ* (pilgrim shelter) which surround the Bhadrakālī *pīṭha*. In contrast with their weekly rehearsals in the house of practice, the Nāsaḥdyocheṃ in Vatu quarter, they put on their *ghaṃgalā* during those Carhe sessions. The next ritual landmark comes more than one month after the *ghaṃgalā svanegu* ceremony, on the seventh day of Dasain, Mahāsaptamī.

Nāsaḥdyo, in the form of a *kalaśa* (in this case a small metal water vessel), is generally kept in the *nāyaḥ*'s house but for the time of the dances the *kalaśa* is brought to the Nāsaḥdyocheṃ and placed in a brass-plated wooden frame. On Mahāsaptamī five dancers of the team go to collect water from five different bathing places (*tīrtha*s) to fill the Nāsaḥdyo *kalaśa*. Bhadrakālī goes to fetch water from the *tīrtha*, which includes the *ghāṭ* where, in the end, the masks of the gods will also be cremated: Kālamocana tīrtha. Bhairava goes to Ṭekudobhān *tīrtha* at the confluence of the Bāgmatī and Viṣṇumatī rivers (where the divine masks are cremated in case of the Pacalī Bhairava dances), Vārāhī collects water from Śamkhamūla *tīrtha* at the confluence of the Bāgmatī and Manoharā. Kumārī and Gaṇeśa collect water from the Rāja*tīrtha* on the Bāgmatī, and from the confluence of Bhacā Khusi and the

Viṣṇumatī (Nirmal *tīrtha*) respectively. These *tīrtha*s are the principal confluences surrounding Kathmandu, and the deities fetching water there are the principal ones of the thirteen-member *gaṇa*. All five *gvaṃpa* (small earthen water jars) are emptied into the Nāsaḥdyo *kalaśa*, for which a goat is sacrificed the following day, Mahāṣṭamī, the eighth day of Dasain. Parts of the head of the sacrifice are assigned to the *sī guthi* members in hierarchical order, while the meat is shared as *prasāda* by the whole team.

Mahānavamī is the crucial day in the build-up of power. After keeping a fast for the whole day the dancers and the five main divinities (*pañcakumārī*) set out for the Bhadrakālī *pīṭha* at night. The seven main dancers walk in a row carrying the tools and attributes of the gods in the *gaṇa* whereas the *pañcakumārī* carry the ingredients for the *pūjā* in the Bhadrakālī *pīṭha* that night. This *pūjā* includes the sacrifice of two buffaloes that are slaughtered in front of three pots containing *bau* (food for the departed and the ghosts, which is later strewn around the *pīṭha*). The first buffalo sacrifice is dedicated to the *gaṇa* of gods in the *pīṭha*, the second one to the dancers representing them. The blood of the latter is drunk by the main gods of the group: Bhairava, Bhadrakālī, Vārāhī, Kumārī and Gaṇeśa, who are still without masks, in the process of becoming divine rather than fully being so. Like at *ghaṃgalā svanegu*, the five dancers faint after drinking the buffalo blood and have to be restored to consciousness by the *nāyaḥ*.

Before the masks will finally be collected from the Citrakār's (Painter's) home all dancers go to collect water from Kālamocana, the site which, at the end, this time as well as twelve years ago, is the cremation ground for the masks. Since the ashes of the cremated masks are swept into the river it is tempting to see in this otherwise inexplicable excursion an effort to close the circle, to recover the seed of the last rites (*antyeṣṭi*) for the divinities' present rebirth. The power of the divine host, to be sure, is permanently stored in the stones which represent the *gaṇa* in the Bhadrakālī *pīṭha*. The trick is, as it were, to loosen that power and turn it from a static disposition into the dynamic *śakti*, power, impersonated by the dancing troupe. This may explain why the pots with the water collected at Kālamocana are smashed over the *maṇḍala* stone in front of the entrance to the *pīṭha*.

The masks, on the other hand, which lie ready in a room of the Citrakār's house, do not as yet have any power of their own, They are made from a mixture of papier mâché, jute and starch, which, when it is still kneadable, is put into an earthen mould, from where it is, once hardened, taken out again. Then the whole process of fashioning, painting and decorating the masks follows, in which the maker has to work according to precept, but can nevertheless allow himself some artistic freedom. As the work is done by one man who uses existing earthen moulds, it is, socially and perhaps also symbolically, simpler than the shaping of the Navadurgā masks in Bhaktapur. In the latter case the process followed seems to suggest that all elements together, earth, water, fire and air, are contained in the final products, which thus have an added value of their own and are, in contrast to those in Kathmandu, exhibited and admired by the citizens before their consecration (Gutschow & Basukala 1987: 140-145).

The Kathmandu dance group comes to collect the masks in the dead of night and performs *pūjā* in the Citrakār's house. The *pūjā* for the masks includes secret *mantras*, and not even the Citrakār is allowed to witness it. In the Kathmandu *pyākhaṃ* this is one of the rare examples of a secret ceremony. The two other secret occasions will be treated below. After the secret *pūjā* for the masks they are carried to the Bhadrakālī *pīṭha* and placed before the corresponding stone figures. The masks have by now acquired their divine power but their consecration by no means marks the end of that night's ceremonies. The multi-faceted procedure may be related to the fact that not one but two entities have to be empowered before they can be joined to constitute the single body of the divine dancer or the dancing divinity. Such a build-up is confirmed by the last rites in which those powers have to be disjoined again.

The remaining ceremony in the ongoing sequence takes place in the morning of the concluding day of Dasain, Vijayā Daśamī, when an elaborate *homa* (fire sacrifice) is conducted by a Vajrācārya priest in front of the *pīṭha*. The *homa* has a standard part, which consists of oblations of various grains and ghee into the fire. The concluding part is generally of a more esoteric nature, and in this case included the offering of selected parts of the sacrificed buffaloes into the sacrificial fire: pieces of the lungs, the heart, the intestines and of the meat.[4] During the first part of the *homa*, the fire needs to be surrounded only by the *nāyaḥ* and the five main divine characters who had just before drunk the blood from the second buffalo sacrificed: Bhairava, Bhadrakālī, Vārāhī, Kumārī and Gaṇeśa, in addition, of course, to the Vajrācārya officiant. In the concluding part of the *homa* and at the distribution of *prasāda* by the Vajrācārya, the whole *gaṇa* of dancers is to surround the *homakuṇḍa*, the temporary fire-pit made of bricks. For, as the *nāyaḥ* explained, it is from the sacrificial fire that the *śakti* is born which enables the dancers to wear the divine masks and thereby to embody the deities themselves. During the last episode the dancers are connected with each other and with the masks in the *pīṭha* by a cotton thread which also ties in the *kalaśa* in front of the fire through which the Vajrācārya has evoked and transferred the divinities. As in the case of the brass statues of deities which also have to be empowered by a fire-sacrifice prior to a procession through their realm,[5] the *homa* for the divine dancers can be considered to precede the extended *yātrā* of the deities embodied by them.

To sum up the present section: the power of the divine dancers is built up, respectively, by water (filling the Nāsaḥdyo *kalaśa* and wetting the stone *maṇḍala* in front of the Bhadrakālī *pīṭha*), by joining the masks to their *pīṭha* doubles after a secret *pūjā*, and by a *homa* out of which the *śakti* of the dancing divinities is born, that is: put into motion. The whole sequence is repeated on Pāhāṃ Carhe in March, during the annual festival of Bhadrakālī (and the procession statues of other deities from her *gaṇa*), albeit on a somewhat reduced scale. At that time the Citrakār is asked to repair the cracks which the masks may have incurred, after which the secret *pūjā* for the masks must be repeated as well as the *homa* that generates the *śakti* for the dancers to wear them. On this intermediate occasion all rituals are carried out inside the Nāsaḥdyocheṃ.

After the masks and the dancers have both been empowered they must still be joined to each other. This junction is made in half-secrecy, immediately prior to the first appearance of the dancing gods. Full secrecy is hard to obtain amidst the crowds which by that time surround the open Bhadrakālī *pīṭha*. The point, however, does not seem to be secrecy as such but rather the mystery of man's insurmountable distance from the gods that must still be overcome.

It has meanwhile become Vijayā Daśamī evening. After the rituals of *navamī* (ninth) night and, by extension, the *homa* of *daśamī* (tenth) morning, the dancers could enjoy only little rest before they had to start their first performance.

The manifestation and exchange of power

To obtain a certain degree of secrecy, a curtain is drawn around the dancers assembled in the *pīṭha* and a smoke-screen is formed by burning a particular smoky kind of incense (*guṃgū*). Behind the screen the Gaṇeśa performer applies to the forehead of the dancers a previously prepared soot mark (*mohanī*) which constitutes the final touch before the masks are taken up, handed over, and, with the assistance of the other *khalaḥ* members, put on by the dancers.

A salient feature is that Bhairava, in addition to his mask, receives (with a *namaskāra*, hommage) a metal snake, which was attached to the Nāsaḥdyo *kalaśa* (also present in the *pīṭha*) before. Like Bhairava himself the serpent is also called Āju, grandfather or ancestor. The serpent, which – unless killed – is commonly considered immortal, may hold an important clue.

Since ancient times (e.g. Pañcaviṃsa Brāmaṇa XXV 15,4) serpents are imagined to gain rebirth by creeping out of their old skin without properly dying. The serpent which will adorn Pacalī Bhairava's neck is said to be particularly powerful. A *nāyaḥ* who once tried to replace the old metal snake by a bright new silver one, was subsequently haunted by nightmares. Kathmandu Valley, once a serpent kingdom, is full of serpent symbolism of course; yet the particular identification of the serpent Āju with the god who, so to speak, dies without dying, or is reborn like he was before, is a telling detail in the context of the transient but recurrent manifestation of the divine dancers.

Another striking detail is that, at the moment when all masked dancers set out from the *pīṭha*, Bhadrakālī herself remains seated for a while with her stone double, as if the one is reluctant to go or the other is reluctant to release the *śakti* required. A parallel will again be found during the funeral episode of the divine dancers treated below, in which, reversely, the Bhairava dancer cannot relinquish his *śakti*. It is generally understood that in the twelve-yearly cycle of the Pacalī Bhairava dances, Pacalī is the most important deity, while in the similar cycle of Bhadrakālī dances the goddess Bhadrakālī is pre-eminent. This shift in pre-eminence can be contested on numerous grounds, but it is confirmed by the first grand act of the deities embodied by the dancers: their meeting with the king of Nepal. In the Pacalī cycle it is the god, commonly called Aju, who exchanges swords with the king, while in the

Photo 17.
The late King Birendra exchanging swords with the Bhadrakālī dancer (see also Photo 18) during the twelve-yearly Bhadrakālī dances (1991).

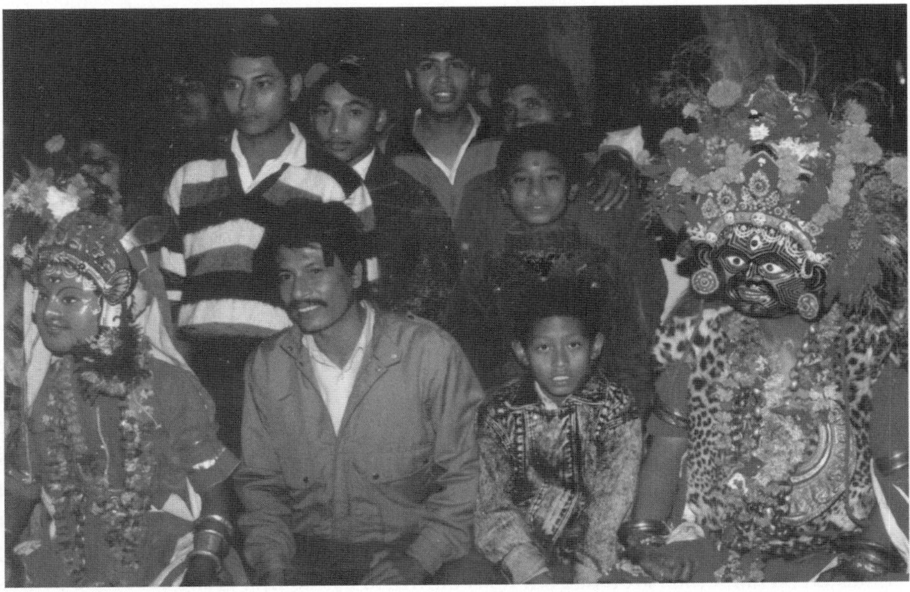

Photo 18.
Bhadrakālī dancer (right), the principle character of the Gathu dancers, with the maker of the masks Prem Man Chitrakār (centre), sitting next to the Indrāyaṇī dancer (left) (1991).

Bhadrakālī cycle it is the goddess, commonly called Ajimā, who has the honour to exchange swords with the king (Photo 17). (Pacalī) Āju and (Lumari) Ajimā are the two main *pīṭha*s of Kathmandu Kvane, the lower (southern) part of the city, and it is sometimes said that the two gods are husband and wife. The difference between the Pacalī and the Bhadrakālī dances seems to concern a shift in locality – from Bhadrakālī *pīṭha* to Pacalī *pīṭha*, from an *ākhāḥ* (rehearsal place) in the northern part of town to one in the southern part, and from Kālamocana Ghāṭ to Teku Ghāṭ – rather than a change in the dance performance itself.

The Gathu *nāyaḥ*'s records mention Ratna Malla of Bhaktapur, who vanquished the Thakuri kings of Kathmandu in 605 NS (1484 AD), as the king who established the sword exchange. On the one hand, that date may be too early to account for the present situation, on the other hand it may be too late to account for the sword exchange as such.[6] It might be that the first Malla kings of Kathmandu wished to sustain relations with the different parts of the city that was internally divided before becoming a kingdom in itself. The shifting pre-eminence of Bhadrakālī and Pacalī Bhairava is accompanied by a shift in the colour of the Bhadrakālī's mask: in the Pacalī dances she is red (the usual colour of Kālī), in the Bhadrakālī dances she is blue, as if she has assumed the colour of her counterpart Bhairava (Photo 18).

A current explanation has it that blue is the colour of Bhadrakālī in her Vatu *dyocheṃ* in the northern part of Kathmandu (the name Vatu is even thought to derive from the colour of the goddess: *vacu*, blue). For Bhadrakālī is the only *mātṛkā* goddess having two *dyocheṃ*s, the other one being in Tebāhāl in the southern part of the city. The colour contrast would thus reflect the recurrent distinction between the Upper (Thane) and the Lower (Kvane) part of town. This explanation is in accordance with the fact that the death of the gods occurs in the Northern part of the city in case of the Bhadrakālī dances and in the Southern part in case of the Pacalī Bhairava dances. Likewise, the first real dance performance of the Bhadrakālī *pyākhaṃ* takes place in the Upper part and the first dance of the Pacalī *pyākhaṃ* in the Lower part of town (Photo 19). As will be seen below, several dress items which remain as *prasāda* of the dances, are given to the Vatu *dyocheṃ* after the Bhadrakālī *pyākhaṃ* and to the Tebāhāl *dyocheṃ* – equally related to the Bhadrakālī *pīṭha* south-east of the city – in case of the Pacalī Bhairava dances. Pacalī Bhairava himself has no permanent *dyocheṃ*: the residence of his procession image is as we have seen (see chapter 6, section 2) shifting among twelve Jyāpu (Farmer) families.

The sword exchange between Bhadrakālī and the king, as it happens today, need not be elaborated upon here (see also below, chapter 8). As a major event it is recorded in books on culture, tourist guides (although it is nowadays very hard to approach the scene), newspaper articles and, more recently, also in Nepal Television broadcasts. Led by Bhadrakālī carrying her sword the masked dancers follow a more or less straight route from Bhadrakālī *pīṭha* to Makhan Tol, passing Martyrs Gate, New Road Gate, Pyukhā, Vatu, and Indrachowk. The king's sword was brought to Makhan from the other direction, Hanumānḍhokā, by a sword-carrying party (*pāyāḥ*) which goes out on itself every year in the night of Vijayā Daśamī.[7] The king himself arrived and left without any sword. The sword, which is ritually exchanged belongs to his predecessors, the Malla kings. Bhadrakālī and the king exchange their swords three times back and forth. It is no exchange in the real sense of the word: in the end each party keeps its own sword. Yet the result of the transaction is, according to the Gathu, that the king is provided with *śakti*, divine power. The king is, to put it in human terms, empowered through his Gardeners in what constitutes a major event in the ritual calendar. After the event is over, the sword party continues its own way while the Gathu go to the *Nāsaḥdyocheṃ* to remove their divine garments.

One feature, which is most characteristic of the dancers in the whole period to follow is strikingly absent in their first encounter. The Gathu dancers, in their own words, go only there where sacrifice awaits them. Yet, when received by the king of Nepal, the divine dancers had to go without sacrifice, such in contrast to their reception, a few weeks later, by the Thakū juju, the ritual 'king' and patron of the Pacalī Bhairava festival in South Kathmandu. What makes the difference? The Thakū juju is entitled to participate in the sword party, but not to carry the king's sword (which is, quite prosaically, carried by a ranking officer) nor to exchange his own or any other sword with Bhadrakālī. A tentative interpretation of the role of the king of Nepal will be given in the concluding section of the next chapter.[8]

The full exploits of the divine host can not be followed here. Twice more they will visit the area of Hanumānḍhokā, but on those occasions they perform in Nāsalcok, inside the palace compound (Photo 20). In addition, they have thirty more

Photo 19.
The divine dancers (Gathu pyākhaṃ) performing during the night, at Thakū juju's courtyard in Kvane (1991).

destinations, in the Upper (Thane) and the Lower town (Kvane) of Kathmandu, but also in other parts of the Valley. However, they will only go there where they are provided for (i.e. with sacrifice), a condition, which led to the dropping of ten out of the 31 projected destinations.

The relationship with the dancing teams of Kirtipur and Bhaktapur is peculiar. If need be, the Gathu dancers of Kirtipur and Kathmandu can assist each other and even exchange dancers. There is no such relationship with Bhaktapur. The Kathmandu dancers do, however, visit the court of Bhaktapur, as well as that of Pāṭan. The Kirtipur dancers visit Hanumānḍhokā, but their visit is not returned by the dancers of Kathmandu. The contours of a hierarchy emerge, in which Bhaktapur is self-contained and in which Kirtipur is subordinate to Kathmandu.

The day after their sword exchange with the king of Nepal, on Ekādaśī (eleventh), the dancers make a round of Kathmandu city. They follow the same route as Kumārī does in the celebrated festival of Indra yātrā, but unlike Kumārī, they do not split their tour into a southern (Kvane) and a northern (Thane) part.

Photo 20.
Pacalī Bhairava dancer in a worshipping gesture during the Gathu dance performance at Hanumānaḍhokā palace (1991).

The 'last waltz'

The Gathu dancers dedicate three of their performances to their divine patron, Nāsaḥdyo alone, in front of his *dyocheṃ*. The first of these, on the thirteenth day (*trayodaśī*) of Dasain, is also the first of their performances during the coming period.[9] The last dance before their demise is similar to this first one and for our present purposes, a short-cut will be made to that last performance before the final dance of death.

Instead of going into the details of the whole repertoire attention will be focussed on the sacrificial aspect of the last dance. Only one dramatic episode will be recounted as an example that compares well with the Bhaktapur Navadurgā and with the Kirtipur *pyākhaṃ*, suggesting an original scenario common to all. The repertoire, it should be noted, is to a large extent standardized and the sequence of the solo performances and the dramatic exchanges of the masked dancers do not, in this last dance, differ from the shows which have been given before at other places. Most other performances, however, have a patron who invites the troupe to perform, such as the Kvane Thakū juju in the courtyard of his *lāykū* (residence). Like the first dance on the thirteenth day of Dasain, the last performance is not sponsored by a patron, but totally dedicated to Nāsaḥdyocheṃ and the god Nāsaḥdyo himself. For the major evening performance not only the god's *kalaśa* but also its decorated wooden frame will be brought out from the *dyocheṃ* and placed at the Vatu thorough-fare, facing south-west, just as it did when standing inside the *dyocheṃ*. The immobile Nāsaḥdyo, a niche without statue in the wall of the *dyocheṃ*, faces south however. The masks themselves are, when they are not worn by the dancers, hung from the two walls of the *dyocheṃ* which face south and west. There is no prohibition on entering the *dyocheṃ*, not even when the dancers change their human dresses for the divine ones. Only just before the climax performance a curtain is drawn around them, like it was done at the start in the Bhadrakālī *pīṭha*, to allow for a short spell of secrecy in which Gaṇeśa gives the *mohanī* mark to himself and to the *gaṇa* as a whole.

During the performance the musicians take place in a *pāṭī* opposite the *dyocheṃ*, facing north. The dances are enacted between this *pāṭī* and the *dyocheṃ* in full view of the Nāsaḥdyo *kalaśa*. Towards evening the Pacalī Bhairava dancer worships Nāsaḥdyo and goes on to perform *pūjā* for the musicians and the other dancers and members of the team. Apart from giving the customary *pūjā* and *ṭikā*, Pacalī offers, left-handedly, an egg to Nāsaḥdyo and to all dancers but the vegetarian Rudrāyaṇī, who is given some milky paste on the mouth of her mask. The other dancers have to lift their masks a bit to suck their raw eggs. Pacalī himself is served by the *dhvaṃpvami nāyaḥ*, his special attendant.

In a sequence which is standard for other performances as well, a he-goat is subsequently dedicated (*saṃkalpa*) to Nāsaḥdyo and killed with a knife by Pacalī, who passes the corpse on to the other dancers (except the vegetarian Rudrāyaṇī) who suck the blood from its neck, with Pacalī himself taking the last turn. Pacalī appears to be the host or *jajmān* of the divine troupe. The head of the goat is then severed and put in front of the Nāsaḥdyo *kalaśa*, while the corpse is carried away inside the *dyocheṃ*. In a grand feast the next day hundreds of invitees will get a tiny piece of the goat's meat as *prasāda*. In addition to the *sī guthi*, this time three other members of the dancing team partake of the (sub-) divided shares of the head of the sacrifice.

Two more acts of distribution conclude the sacrificial session. Vārāhī throws, again left-handedly, *samay baji* (a standard mixture of *prasāda* food) to the bystanders and Bhadrakālī serves rice beer (*thvaṃ*) to the dancers. A duck which is unobtrusively brought and placed in the *pāṭī* near the musicians will play a crucial role later that night. After that the general public is given the opportunity to worship the Bhadrakālī *gaṇa*, which they do with offerings of light, incense, *ṭikā*-powder, paddy, foods like *samay baji*, sweat bread, bananas and other fruits, as well as with gifts of cloth and money. The programme will later resume in a much lighter form with Siṃhinī and Vyāghinī (Simbā and Dhuṃbā) performing humorous sketches and chasing the children – who enjoy everything except being caught. The musician who plays the *babhū* cymbals recites by heart the accompany-ing stories.

Meanwhile Bhadrakālī was invited for a private reception in a house nearby. Standing motionless like a statue the dancer first received the welcoming ceremony (*lasakusa*) at the gate. Pacalī Bhairava was also privately received in another house. When the night programme was about to start the first great thunderstorm of the monsoon broke out and everybody took refuge in the Nāsaḥdyocheṃ which thereby got the ambiance of an overcrowded bar. Amidst the bustle the small mask of Svet Bhairava, which is covered with a white cloth while attached to the wall, was inconspicuously lifted and carried away. Some time later the duck mentioned above was brought in decapitated, and thrown in Nāsaḥdyo's cavity. What had happened in-between was the transformation of Pacalī or Kāla (Black) Bhairava into the peaceful vegetarian form of Svet (White) Bhairava, a procedure so secret that not even the other dancers may attend it. The musicians, primarily the *nāyaḥ*, conduct the secret ceremony, which does not take place in Nāsaḥ *dyocheṃ* but in the almost adjoining Bhadrakālī *dyocheṃ*. Nothing could be heard, however, because on this occasion no music but only *mantra*s are uttered. As the *nāyaḥ* later told me, Bhairava in his fierce form as Pacalī bites the neck of the duck in the sanctum of Bhadrakālī, the fenced space in which five brass procession statues of Bhadrakālī are kept.

After he has sucked the duck's blood the transformation of Bhairava starts. He takes off his fierce mask but is not allowed to see for himself the other part of his identity, which is Svet Bhairava, considered to be Mahādeva or more specifically, Paśupatināth. The Svet Bhairava mask is put on his face while still being covered with cloth, accompanied by *mantra*s, which effect the transformation. No explanation could be obtained as to the reasons why Pacalī Bhairava may not see his double or, to cast it into a single image, why Svet Bhairava can not behold his own self. Here, finally, emerges a secret in the true sense of the word because the mystery cannot be solved. One may, however, turn it the other way around: the fact that Śiva can have such contrasting aspects as Paśupatināth and Pacalī Bhairava is taken for granted mostly, without acknowledging the conflict present in that double identity. In the

Bhadrakālī *pyākhaṃ* then, we come across one of the rare cases, archaic or original, in which the problem appears to have been given shape by hiding the one part of Śiva's identity from the other while still enacting their junction. Still, one would expect the dramatic expression of it to be just reverse. As Rudrāyaṇī turns off her eyes when a victim is slaughtered, being unable to stand the sight, so one would expect Svet Bhairava to be unable to face his terrible alter ego. As it is enacted, however, the bloodthirsty Pacalī is withheld the vision of his own peaceful, transcendental form. That the two masks of the god do indeed share the same identity, and not only the same dancer, will become clear from the dying scene.

Perhaps the vision of his peaceful self would dissolve the very powers that sustain Pacalī and his insatiable thirst for blood. Svet Bhairava, his other self, is also exactly his opposite, which is made very clear by the standard act, which he performs. Coming out of Bhadrakālī *dyocheṃ* Svet Bhairava's mask is still veiled with a white cloth, which is torn away by Gaṇeśa and Kumārī. Here and further on in the drama, the superior form of Bhairava is teased and challenged by the other members of the divine host. After a series of acts with all other members of the *gaṇa*, he is given beer to drink, something Svet Bhairava is not used to, so he gets sick. Indrāyaṇī, the very one who served him the beer, then offers to cure him – she is the doctor of the *gaṇa*. But this time she does not succeed and Svet Bhairava has to vomit, dirtying his clothes, which he then goes to wash in the river. Washing his clothes he catches a fish – thanks to the thunderstorm the fish could be hidden in one of the pools of water in the street and appeared as a real surprise, suddenly floundering in the hands of Svet Bhairava who, surprisingly, starts to cook it. Not for himself, however, but for his teasing companions Simbā and Dhumbā, who came on the stage while Indrāyaṇī retreated. Suddenly he stops, calling: 'Why should I cook something for you which I do not eat myself?!' (the accompanying words are spoken by the reciter among the musicians).

The scene enacted by the Svet Bhairava of the Navadurgā in Bhaktapur and described by Levy (1987: 127) likewise involves the catching of a fish, but gives no indications of the *brahmacārī* (renunciating) character of the god or of the mystery of his double identity. The fish caught by Svet Bhairava also appears in the Kirtipur repertoire, thus pointing to a common source of the three dances – perhaps a textual one. A text on the Bhadrakālī *pyākhaṃ* kept by the Gathu is not accessible to outsiders, and it is not clear whether it contains a detailed screenplay. The scene just described appears to be humorous, yet the *nāyaḥ*, when asked about it, strongly denied that it is a comedy. The serious portent is more important than the fun, the mystery more important than the entertainment.

Svet Bhairava dances only a few times: three times in front of Nāsaḥdyocheṃ, one time in Nāsalcok of Hanumānḍhokā in the presence of the king of Nepal, and one time at Indrachowk at the request of the locality. During the Hanumānḍhokā performance the Bhairava dancer was ill and was therefore replaced by the *nvakū* (second eldest) of the *sī guthi*, who had himself performed the Bhairava role in the Pacalī dances four years earlier. More interesting and noteworthy is that the transformation of Bhairava and the appearance of Svet Bhairava in the last dance was also performed by the *nvakū*, who is also the *chusyā* musician and who, evidently, has a permanent capacity to fulfill this principal role. The reason why he replaced the present Bhairava dancer is also striking: while only a few spectators (and most of them belonging to the *khalaḥ* itself) were present in the dead of night, the *nvakū* took up this crucial role at the request of the public! It was certainly a wonderful performance.

The Bhadrakālī and the Navadurgā *pyākhaṃ* have been called 'fertility cults' and the deities 'protective divinities' on the basis of very little evidence pointing in that direction. When not propitiated with sacrifice, the divine host poses a threat rather than offering shelter. The borderline between demonic and divine forces is particularly hard to draw in Nepal, where even the ghosts expelled from the towns at Gathāṃmugaḥ are addressed as '*bhūdyo*', ghost-god. Yet one may discern in the Bhadrakālī *gaṇa* one definitely benevolent character and one definitely malevolent character. The benevolent Svet Bhairava, who mysteriously springs from the ambivalent Bhairava, can also be consulted with regard to progeny. In principle, every god can be asked for good fortune and progeny, but Svet Bhairava's role is more specific than that. One may privately request Svet Bhairava to come to one's own house or quarter, which he will do only after midnight and going about veiled. On these occasions, four of which occurred during the last Bhadrakālī *pyākhaṃ*, Svet Bhairava is accompanied by Gaṇeśa and Kumārī, one of whom will, at their destination, draw the veil from Svet Bhairava's mask like in the drama. If it is Gaṇeśa who pulls it off, the family will be blessed with the birth of a son, if it is Kumārī a daughter is more likely to be born. Although this act is related to progeny, it rather seems an archaic way of predicting the sex of an unborn child than a fertility cult.

The features of the malevolent character that will be staged next, ironically (but quite incidentally, it was said) resemble those of Svet Bhairava, especially its curled moustache. The bad character is Daitya, the demon whose sole function it is to be beaten by Bhadrakālī. Daitya is not a mask like the others but a wooden shield with on one side his icon and on the other side a handle by which Bhadrakālī can grip it. Daitya is placed in front of Nāsaḥdyo. Before Bhadrakālī's turn comes there is a sudden appearance of Pacalī Bhairava, shortly after Svet Bhairava left the stage. Apparently the reverse transformation does not involve the mystery and does not require the sacrifice and secret ceremony necessary for changing Pacalī into Svet Bhairava. The mask of the latter is again covered with the white veil and hung from the wall of Nāsaḥdyocheṃ where it will remain until it is taken for cremation.

Pacalī performs a wild sword dance as if to assert his fierce side again and then sits down to receive *dakṣiṇā* (i.c. money) and to distribute a five-coloured thread (*pasūkā*) as *prasāda*. While Pacalī brandished his sword into the void, Bhadrakālī subsequently pitches into her Daitya enemy quite literally, wildly hewing the wooden image with her sword. Daitya can not hit back and is, after being beaten, carelessly thrown before Nāsaḥdyo again. Pacalī and Bhadrakālī together make a grand finale, whirling around each other, and then, with Bhadrakālī giving a *namaskāra* towards Nāsaḥdyo, retreating into the *dyocheṃ*. The whole *gaṇa* once more comes out and walks a little westward to announce their departure to the gods by making obeisance to the gods (*dyo lhāyegu*), and thereby the performance is finished. It was about three in the night.

The next day about six hundred people enjoyed a feast at Vatu square in which pieces of the goat sacrificed the previous night were included. In addition to the goat a buffalo ought to be sacrificed on the same occasion. The buffalo was indeed sacrificed and its blood sucked by the dancers, but only next day in order to have the meat served fresh at the feast. On the one hand the dancers tell that blood, liquor and food eaten by them in their divine form leaves them as soon as they put off their masks. On the other hand this particular buffalo was, like the two buffaloes at the *homa*, sacrificed and its blood sucked by the dancers without masks. Hence, divine power can be attributed to both the masks and the consecrated persons wearing them, and the two components of divinity can apparently be separated. Likewise, the mask of Bhairava was in the last dance worn by somebody else then the one thereto designated.

As will be seen in the next section, the complexity of the divine dancer's or the dancing divinity's identity are further revealed at death and in the funeral rites. The intricacy notwithstanding, a clear hierarchy can be observed between the two components of divinity in the lifetime of the dancers. The masks, hung from the walls of the Nāsaḥ *dyochem̩*, can be worshipped without their human embodiment. The consecrated dancers, by contrast, can not be worshipped without their masks. In the composition of divinity, the masks are the encompassing aspect. The only ones who can be worshipped as they are, without masks, are the musicians – who, as was related above, constitute the very source and origin of the Gathus' power to embody the divinities and to put them in motion.

The death of the gods

The gods are to die at a place tellingly called Jamabāhāl: the Cloister of Death. The same *bāhāl* is held to be the original site of the god Seto Macchendranath (Manandhar 1986: 72) as well as a resting place of the goddess Bhadrakālī at the time of her advent to Kathmandu. The courtyard of Jamabāhāl is presently surrounded by office buildings of Tribhuvan University in the quarter which is as a whole called Jamal. The public that turned out to witness the death of the divine dancers was massive, especially when compared to the few spectators at their last dance – but, I was told, yet nothing compared to the crowd in Kirtipur where the whole population bade farewell to their divine dancers. Before the dancers set out for Jamal, the public could still worship them in front of Nāsaḥ *dyochem̩*, and again, at Indrachowk, where the dancers whirled around in their obeisance (*dyo lhāyegu*) to Ākāśa Bhairava and then remained seated for a while opposite that temple. From there the dancers went straight to Jamal via Asan and Kamalāchī.

It turned out that a sequence of dances was yet to be performed before the moment of dying came. A small retreat in Jamabāhāl, where just as in Nāsaḥdyochem̩, the masks could be attached to the walls, proved to be invaluable in another respect. For, when the performance was about to start, the second great shower of the monsoon broke out, delaying everything but making the nature symbolism in the dancers' demise altogether convincing. The setting of the stage with regard to the cardinal directions was equal to that in Vatu: the musicians facing north and Nāsaḥdyo facing west, with the small mask of Mahālakṣmī on a stick to the left of the musicians. The divine dancers all made their last appearance, to start with Gaṇeśa. After solo performances of Brahmāyaṇī, Rudrāyaṇī and Kumārī the complete *gaṇa* made a last whirling dance together. At its conclusion Pacalī worshipped Nāsaḥdyo and the musicians, and performed *pūjā* of the dancers (with the sacrifice of eggs) such as described above. Then, suddenly, a duck was released from the second floor of the house of the eldest of Kathmandu's Vajrācāryas. As usual with cocks and ducks, it was caught by Kumārī who bit its throat, but did not pass it on to the other divinities. Instead, the standard procedure concludes with Vārāhī throwing *samay baji* towards the public in all directions, and Bhadrakālī serving beer to the *gaṇa* of dancers.

Then, from the house of the leading Vajrācārya elder, the parting meal is brought, *sī jā* in Newar, which literally means the food of death.[10] It consists of flattened rice mixed with yoghurt (*dhau baji*) and granulated sugar added to it. It is said that the same kind of death meal is served to those under the sentence of death just before their execution. Bhairava, Bhadrakālī and Vārāhī sit together around the tripod on which the ceremonial plate (New. *thāybhu*) with death-food is placed. The other dancers sit on small banks at a few yards distance. Bhairava, apparently, is the master of death, initiating with the uttering of a mantra the eating of the *sī jā*. Bhairava, Bhadrakālī and Vārāhī, sharing the *sī jā*, throw some of it behind their backs in the directions of the other dancers. Thereupon, all at once, the dancers drop dead and are immediately lifted by the team of assistants. The surprise effect is tremendous: after their rigorous parting dance the death of the divine host occurs in a split second, without any agony. By comparison, the dancers of Kirtipur stumble along for a while after the eating of their *sī jā* and drop dead one by one.

The stiffened bodies of the Bhadrakālī *gaṇa* are at once carried out of the compound of Jamabāhāl. The procession of the dead bodies follows the same route as the one by which the living gods came. Nāy (Butcher) musicians precede the procession but do not yet play their characteristic funeral music. One of the most fascinating aspects is that Pacalī comes back to life thrice. His first resurrection occurs at Asan where Pacalī is supposed to drink from a red-painted tap which is turned upside down (*akhaḥ hiti*) and which, at least at present, contains no water. Pacalī comes into motion very slowly to the accompaniment of the Gathu musicians, but then, in a crescendo, accelerates his pace to end up in a few moments of ecstatic dance from which he drops stone-dead again. The dance of the dead god which takes hardly more than a minute, is repeated in front of Ākāśa Bhairava at Indrachowk and in front of the Nāsaḥdyochem̩ at Vatu. His dramatic resurrections are, it was explained, the result of the fact that Pacalī as the main god of the *gaṇa* is so powerful that his *tyāga*, his abandonment of *śakti*, can not be effected at once.

Pacalī's double, Svet Bhairava, was left behind at Vatu and thus did not share the *sī jā*. Yet he is supposed to have died at the time of Pacalī's death, exactly because the two of them share the same identity. After Pacalī's last resurrection, the mask of Svet Bhairava was taken from Nāsaḥ *dyocheṃ* and put underneath Pacalī's mask, something which must have been done so furtively that I could not witness it. Likewise the wooden shield representing Daitya is put underneath the mask of, tellingly, his slayer Bhadrakālī. He will also be cremated together with Bhadrakālī and the other gods, something which once again indicates the fusion of good and evil, or more specifically, the fundamental affinity between the goddess and the demon slain by her.

From Vatu the procession proceeds along the same road by which, at their first appearance, the dancers went for their meeting with the king of Nepal. The Bhadrakālī *pīṭha* is this time the terminal point for the dancers in their divine composition. At the gate of the *pīṭha* the masks are separated from the dancers' bodies and placed again in front of their respective stone representations, now stripped of flowers and other decorations. This is the moment of disjoining: After the removal of their masks the faces of the dancers are covered with the white cloth which they first wore as a turban (*phetā*) to support their masks. As dead bodies they are carried around the *pīṭha* and then taken to the second floor of the building adjoining the *pīṭha*. In the room from which they once started their long enterprise the dancers are laid down in a row, their faces covered by the white cloth as a shroud. For a moment it seems as if not the divinities, but the dancers embodying them have died. Shortly after, though, the dancers are brought to life by the *nāyaḥ* with holy water (*nīlaḥ*) and accompanying *mantra*s. Those restored to life, however, are not the same any more as those who died. As divine dancers they died indeed and were hence covered with shrouds. At their revival they take off their decorations and most significantly, the *ghaṃgalā*, which marked the divinity of their human bodies. Under the guidance of the *nāyaḥ*, they subsequently worship their former divine identity, the masks in the *pīṭha*. A *pūjā* and goat sacrifice are performed. The blood of the goat sacrifice, which is part of the final *pūjā* for the masks is sprinkled over both the masks and the stone representations of the gods. Svet Bhairava and Daitya, however, remain invisible behind the masks of Pacalī and Bhadrakālī, as if both of them share in the identity of the protagonists of the divine host. The masks now definitely resign the power that had so long been stored in them leaving it to the immobile stones of the *pīṭha*. The decorations are removed from the masks as they were from the dancers, but in contrast to the dancers they are not restored to life. It is for the masks that the last rites are performed.

The play with life and death is intricate: the dancers immediately resurrect but in another identity, while the masks cannot be reborn until the cycle of twelve years has passed. But then, unlike the dancers, they will be recreated and revived in the same identity, which they, time and time again, relinquish at their death.

The cremation and its aftermath

After a break during which the dancers in their room receive a *ṭikā* and *prasāda* from the *nāyaḥ*, they come out to lift the masks, covering them with the pieces of white cloth that in the preceding episode covered the faces of their own dead bodies – a sublime dramatic reversal. Death, which at first touched the divine dancers in their totality, and which was subsequently split, as it were, between the masks and the bodies of the dancers, is now concentrated in the masks alone, the divine and encompassing component of the entity which passed away. From this moment onwards, the Nāy musicians start their true funeral music. Preceded by the Nāsaḥdyo *kalaśa* and the mask of Mahālakṣmī, now also covered, the dancers carry their shrouded masks to Kālamocana *ghāṭ*, still walking in their usual order with Gaṇeśa at the tail end. In that order the masks will also be deposited on the funeral pyre.[11]

At Kālamocana *ghāṭ* just beyond the *pīṭha* of Pacalī, discussion arose about where to burn the masks. The ashes of the cremated masks are considered to be particularly powerful and should not fall into the hands of witches. The cremation platform was considered too accessible and therefore too risky a place to burn the masks. It was finally decided to perform the cremation off the Bāgmatī banks, on a tiny island at the confluence with the Tukuca rivulet, just big enough to accommodate the dancers and their retinue. The pyre was built up of seven layers of wood on which the masks were put over each other, with Gaṇeśa last. The Nāsaḥdyo *kalaśa* could not be burned of course, but its contents, the waters collected from five *tīrtha*s, were released into the Bāgmatī river, as were the flowers and the greenery adorning it. The *kalaśa*, which was later casually taken along when the group departed, was hardly recognizable any more: it seemed just an ordinary metal water vessel, be it small and dented. The cremation itself could not be as solemn as perhaps it should be, because of the splashing and hubbub that accompanied wading through the muddy Bāgmatī and climbing up and down its slippery banks. But it was performed according to rule, that is, apart from the already mentioned fact that the other Gathu *sī guthi*, which was to build the pyre and to complete the burning after it had been set to fire, did not turn up.

The Bhairava dancer, one of the nine members of the dancers' *sī guthi*, made, with the burning straw torch in his hand, three rounds of the pyre, which, among the other divine masks, contained two of his former selves. Just as the chief mourner in human cremations often is, he was supported in his circumambulation, in this case by his special attendant (*dhvaṃpvami nāyaḥ*). After the pyre was lit by him, the dancers sat around it until all masks were reduced to ashes, which took a long time. The divine masks proper burned quickly, but not the solid wooden shield of Daitya. At dawn the dancers were still squatting around the fire, waiting for Daitya to burn to ashes. At last, in full daylight, the ashes of the gods, including the resistant Daitya, could ultimately be swept into the Bāgmatī. After that the group left the tiny island, splashing through the muddy waters, and, being freed from divinity, chattering and laughing like other mortals.

Still four days later, a bicāḥ *pūjā* was performed at the Bhadrakālī *pīṭha* to bid a final farewell to the deities of the *gaṇa* there. As the *bicāḥ pūjā* is a customary feature at the conclusion of every *yātrā* and since the Gathu at that occasion were no longer different from ordinary human beings, its description will be left out here. One interesting detail, though, is that by preparing and giving a *mohanī* (soot) *ṭikā* at the conclusion of *bicāḥ pūjā*, the dancers and members of the group, in their own words, return the *mohanī ṭikā* which they received after the *homa* and the *pūjā* initiating the Bhadrakālī *pyākhaṃ*. A few other details of the aftermath of the divine dances are worth mentioning. The cremation as such left no *prasāda*, but *prasāda* of the dances had already been given (*ṭikā*, flowers and a red thread) by the *nāyaḥ* in Nāsaḥdyocheṃ at the great feast the day after *belākhāḥ*, the last dance. Yet one special *prasāda* could only be given after the completion of the last rites: threads from the garments of the divine dancers were distributed among the public to be used in amulets to avert evil, especially for children. Not all the garments of the gods were torn to pieces. One of them, it was already mentioned, is traditionally given to the Gathu *sī guthi* who used to complete the cremation of the masks. The most valuable dresses are kept by the dancers' own *sī guthi* to be used as a *devaṃ*, a shroud with which the deceased is covered just before cremation, but which is not usually burnt with him. When the *nāyaḥ* of the Gathu *sī guthi* dies, however, the *devaṃ* is to be burnt with him.

The dresses of the gods are the single most expensive item in the Bhadrakālī *pyākhaṃ*. Of the total amount of Rs. 380,000 which His Majesty's Government provided for all ingredients, attributes, sacrifices and feasts which the Gathu have to finance (for which there is no other patron) Rs. 100,000 was spent on garments, which can not be used for the purpose again. The panther skins worn by Bhairava and Bhadrakālī are directly supplied by the palace. Bhairava's panther-skin dress will go to the *nāyaḥ* of the dancers, while a panther skin which is used as a seat for the dancers will go to the Bhadrakālī *pāyāḥ* of Vatu *dyocheṃ*; in the case of the alternate Pacalī Bhairava *pyākhaṃ* it goes to Bhadrakālī's southern *dyocheṃ* in Tebāhāl. Finally, it may be mentioned that Simbā and Dhumbā are entitled to keep their tails of yak hair themselves. The yak tail from Bhadrakālī's headdress goes to the *dhimay* players,[12] who on several occasions head the procession of the Bhadrakālī dancers – the Gathu musicians themselves are always in the rear.

Thus, the material remains of the divine host are dispersed. The dissolution of the divine dancers themselves, to summarize the essence of it, consisted of two parts. The dancers die together with their masks, but are revived in a different quality, as the human beings which they were before they began their divine life and death. The masks, on the other hand, are not revived and will be reborn only twelve years later. The death, cremation and rebirth of the gods show a fundamental difference with that of men. The cremation itself is similar but the further mortuary rites and the subsequent *śrāddha*s are absent. Most important of all, the gods are reborn in the same identity which they left at their death, something which hardly if ever occurs to men. The gods of the Bhadrakālī *pyākhaṃ*, it must be concluded, do indeed die in their earthly manifestation, but their death resembles that of Yama himself, whose secret seems to be that, in dying, he remains essentially the same he was before. In a distant way it resembles the serpents who vanquished death through their (self)-sacrifice,[13] while, on further consideration, the serpent Āju worn around Bhairava's (Āju's) neck might point to that same feat.

Conclusion: The Gathu pyākhaṃ in the ritual structure of Kathmandu

So far little has been said about the separate characters of the divine host, whence they come, who they are and what they pursue. Within the broader network of Kathmandu's divine world, the gods of the *gaṇa* manifest themselves at least on three different levels, one of which has already elaborately been accounted for by Gutschow & Bajracharya (1977) and by Gutschow (1982: 120-122). The eight goddesses of the *gaṇa* can be conceived of as the *aṣṭamātṛkā* which, at least ideally, surround the city, the Valley and the kingdom of Nepal according to the points of the compass. This is the static point of view, which, in the shape of a *maṇḍala*, is complete in itself and does not require any action of the sort that is manifested in the Bhadrakālī *pyākhaṃ*. The protagonists of the divine drama, Pacalī Bhairava and Bhadrakālī, have their *pīṭha*s, their seats of power, on the outskirts of old Kathmandu, but their origin lies elsewhere.

At the level of the Bhadrakālī *pyākhaṃ*, the imaginary circle surrounding Kathmandu is not closed or static at all. Pacalī Bhairava once was a king of Pharping in the south of the Valley, who fell in love with a Nāy girl in Kathmandu and who, when found out, was forced to go into hiding at the site of his present *pīṭha* at Teku. Bhadrakālī was discovered as a small child by a farmer in Tupiyā, a village north of Kathmandu in the neighbourhood of Budhanilakantha. The childless farmer wished to adopt the child found by him, and laid it to rest in the shade while he finished his work. When he returned to the site the baby girl had disappeared, however, and instead he saw a bright light (*jyoti*) shining from the bushes. There and then he had the true vision (*darśana*) of the goddess Bhadrakālī who changed into a child again after expressing her wish to be installed in Kathmandu. On the way to Kathmandu the farmer and the goddess took rest in Jamal, the place where, in the twelve-yearly cycle of the Bhadrakālī *pyākhaṃ*, the gods die.

The divine dancers are also obliged to visit Bhadrakālī's place of origin, and proceed from there in a long march to Gokarna and Sankhu. If they fail to do so (as they did in 1992), they should, following their death and the *bicāḥ pūjā* in Kathmandu, visit Tupiyā and perform a *kṣamā* (apology) *pūjā* at the modest Bhadrakālī temple which is adjoining the paddy field where the farmer once found the godly child. This year they did their *kṣamā pūjā*, accompanied by a goat sacrifice and followed by a feast, on the fourth of July 1992, barely a month from the next Gathāṃmugaḥ Carhe, which marked the beginning of their enterprise the year before. It is the very last ritual of the protracted farewell ceremonies, the climax of which, their collective death and funeral rites, is striking by its shortness.

The external origins attributed to the two main deities of Kathmandu's Gathu *pyākhaṃ* already give an indication of the event's supralocal significance, for which, however, more conclusive evidence can be adduced. Let us first look at the second level on which the *gaṇa* of divinities manifests itself. In contrast to the static representation of *mātṛkā*s in a *maṇḍala* in which each of them is designated a fixed position, each and every *pīṭha* around Kathmandu in fact harbours the whole *gaṇa*. The *pīṭha* of Pacalī Bhairava, by exception dedicated to a male divinity, nevertheless contains the demi-circle of stones representing the *aṣṭamātṛkā* such as they are also represented in the other *pīṭha*s of Kathmandu. From the dynamic, social point of view, the *pīṭha*s surrounding Kathmandu are not of equal importance. Among them, Pacalī Bhairava has an important *yātrā* during Dasain, but his move through the city remains, apart form his leap to the centre, confined to his own, Southern domain of the town (see Gutschow's map, 1982: 134). The goddesses of the most prominent *pīṭha*s of the city, however, cover the greatest area of the city in their respective *yātrā*s – which are left unrecorded in Gutschow's survey of procession routes. They are Bhadrakālī, more popularly called Lumari Ajimā, and Indrāyaṇī, more popularly called Luti Ajimā. Bhadrakālī, as we have seen, has her *pīṭha* south-east of the city proper, while Indrāyaṇī has her seat north-west of it, on the banks of the Viṣṇumatī. The crossing diagonal from south-west to north-east approxi-mately coincides with the ritual division of the city in an Upper (Thane) and a Lower (Kvane) part. Both goddesses, who are considered elder (Bhadrakālī) and younger (Indrāyaṇī) sisters, but who are at the same time conceived of as antagonists, ostentatiously cross the dividing line into each others' territories. As will be clear from the rowdy processions described above as well as, more generally, from the warrior characters of the divinities involved, Kathmandu can be viewed as a ritualized battlefield (see above chapter 1).

The exploits of the Gathu dancers, which cover a vaster domain and transcend the Thane-Kvane division of the city itself,[14] suggest the image of a ritualized war path. The exchange of swords with the king prepares both sides for the sacrifices to come: the king for the real war path which he may choose to follow and in which he may be either victor or victim, the dancers, on the other hand, for their sacrificial march which, as it were, runs parallel to that of the king. Both of them start their move at the time that the harvest is being collected or still ripening in the fields – the appropriate time for war and sacrifice – and both have to be back at the onset of the rains. Although the Gathu are said to take to sacrificial violence at random (and this threat extends to human beings) if they are not properly provided for, their battlefield is a symbolic one and their exploits are likewise ritualized. Every sacrifice, however, including that of war itself, delivers its spoils or fruits, and from that point of view the Gathu do indeed have a generative power. The nature of that power, which is born from sacrifice – like the divinities themselves – would, however, be misjudged by labelling the divine dancers 'protective' or 'fertility' gods. Casting this stereotype on a most intriguing performance deprives it of its depth and unmistakable suspense.

The passage of the divine dancers through life and death, culminating in what might be termed the sacrifice of their own selves, opens up the fence between gods and men. The intricate play with life and death alludes to the secret of the Lord of Death himself who died but yet remained, both in his own divinity and in all mortals alike – for Death is the divinity in Man.

Chapter 8

The Conclusion of Dasain

Sacrifice and Sword Processions

The state level: the royal goddess Taleju

On the seventh day of Dasain the images of the royal goddess Taleju Bhavānī are taken down from their lofty position in the Taleju temple which is overlooking the ancient palace compound of Hanumāndhokā. Taleju is brought to a room of worship at the back of Mūlcok, a courtyard, which is distantly facing the stairs leading up to the temple. On the way down to this special room of worship, Taleju's Pūjā kothā, the four images or emblems representing the goddess are covered with shiny cloth (*tās*). The doors of the Pūjā kothā are closed behind the small procession of priests carrying the covered images, and Taleju will be just as secluded from the public eye as she was in her high temple abode.

Only the initiated Karmācārya and Jośī (non-Brahmin castes of Hindu ritual specialists) who by hereditary right perform Taleju's worship are granted a *darśana*, a sight of the goddess who since Malla times is the main *śakti* (power) of the realm. The Malla kings used to be the main initiates in the worship of Taleju, receiving a secret *mantra* of dedication to the goddess. Nowadays the royal participation is confined to the official fanfare of Mahāsaptamī, the great seventh day of Dasain. That day the king of Nepal visits Mūlcok to view the *phūlpātī*, a canopy of flowers which is brought from the garden of Jīvanpur in Dhāding, an adjoining district of Gorkhā. The *phūlpātī* is received first in Jamal quarter by a delegation from Hanumāndhokā and an assembly of dignitaries from military and government circles.

Dignitaries follow the *phūlpātī* when it is brought from Jamal at the eastern edge of town to Hanumāndhokā, where the king will join the high-ranking company (Photo 21). At that time the bunch of flowers hanging from a bamboo stick is uncovered, and a pumpkin and a goat are sacrificed for it. Subsequently the *phūlpātī* is brought to its own room, known as Dasain Ghar, in the courtyard adjoining Mūlcok (Nāg Pokharī). The worship of the *phūlpātī* is all in the hand of non-Newar (*parvatīyā*) Brahmins who have no access to the main goddess Taleju Bhavānī, but who perform the Gorkhālī part in the ceremonies in the ancient palace. The king also receives *prasāda* (blessed items, i.c. flowers) from Taleju through the main priest (*mū ācāju*) without, however, having a *darśana* himself.

The duality of Newar and non-Newar officiants also pertains to the sacrifices in the night of the eighth day (Mahāṣṭamī) and the morning of the ninth day (Mahānavamī). The sacrifices of the present state are massive, carried out by army personnel with Parvatīyā Brahmins to consecrate the sacrificial goats and buffaloes. The animals are decapitated, in contrast to the Newar way of sacrificing in which the throat of the victim is cut. The Newar officiants have their first sacrifice in the afternoon of the great eight day, when twelve goats are sacrificed by the *ācāju* himself for the *naḥlāsvāṃ*, the grain sprouts sacred to Dasain (see above chapter 6, section 2). The *naḥlāsvāṃ* together with the royal swords have their own *koṭhā*, which is adjoining the Taleju Pūjā *koṭhā* in Mūlcok.

Photo 21.
Ceremonial reception of the Phūlpātī in the presence of the ruling king and dignitaries in the courtyard of Nāsalcok at Hanumānaḍhokā palace (1997).

Both the Newar and the Parvatīyā perform sacrifice during Kālarātri, the 'black night' between the eighth and the ninth of Dasain. First the regiments sacrifice buffaloes and goats in Kamphukoṭ, the military barracks adjacent to Hanumānḍhokā palace. Subsequently the army decapitates 54 goats and 54 buffaloes the one after the other in Mūlcok under the guidance of a *parvatīyā* Brahmin. The priests of Taleju have no function at all in the army sacrifices. Instead the *ācāju*s officiate high up in the temple of Taleju, which is open to public only on the ninth day of Dasain. For the occasion, the procession images of Guhyeśvarī and Bhairava – two *kalaśa*s – are shown to the public at the southern gate of the temple. Many people worship those as being Taleju, but, the *mū ācāju* assured when questioned about it, the real images of Taleju are safely locked up in the Pūjā *koṭhā*, invisible for both the army and the general public.

After the army's massive sacrifice the scene is taken over by the Newar again, who sacrifice eighteen goats, nine for the Pūjā *koṭhā* and nine for the *naḥlāsvāṃ* kothā with the swords which are to be used in procession in the concluding night of Dasain (see below). The meat of the goats is divided among the Shrestha castes who in Malla times held court functions: Karmācārya, Jośī, Rājbhandāri, and

Rājvaṃśī. Subsequently eight buffaloes are slaughtered and their blood sprayed into the two sacred rooms from a distance. This slaughter is carried out by the Nāy (Butchers) among whom also the meat is divided. The ceremony ends in the very late hours of the night, yet at six or seven the sacrificial team has to be ready for another smaller sacrifice.[1]

This latter sacrifice, of a buffalo, a goat, and a duck, is also carried out by the Nāy, below the stairs, which lead to the Taleju temple. No blood is wilfully sprayed in the direction of the stairs, but only on a stone *triśula*, a trident sign at the right side of the steps. In the Taleju temple itself no sacrifice ever takes place. The Kālarātri sacrifice by the priests of Taleju and their Nāy slaughterers is the only one straightly directed at Taleju in her Pūjā *koṭhā*, but the doors remain closed during the massive slaughterings by the army in the morning of Mahānavamī.

Dasain is thought to be a re-enactment of the mythical battle between the goddess and her demon opponents such as described in the Devī Mahātmya. The final days are decisive and hence the goddess is saturated with blood to give her strength. At the same time the animals sacrificed to Taleju, and also to the *mātṛkā* goddesses surrounding the city, are thought to represent her demon enemies. The buffalo in particular embodies her main enemy, Mahiṣāsura, the slaying of whom gave the goddess the epithet of Mahiṣāsuramardinī, killer of the buffalo demon (one of the forms which the demon assumed in the course of the final battle).

Mahānavamī, the great nineth day, is also the day for large-scale private sacrifices especially at the *pīṭha*s surrounding Kathmandu and for all *āyudha*: weapons, implements, and engines. Families who can afford it sacrifice a goat or a sheep, the head of which is divided among the family members in a *sī kāḥ bhvay* that night. At the end or in the course of the *sī kāḥ bhvay*, the male members eat, in order of seniority, the eight parts of the head of the sacrifice (*sī*) : right eye, left eye, right upper jaw, left upper jaw, right and left lower jaws, nose and tongue. Depending on the composition of the family, and perhaps on caste and locality, the sī distribution may follow a different pattern and include females (cf. Toffin 1993b: 97).

While Kālarātri and the morning of Mahānavamī constitute the main period of sacrifice, the festival culminates in Vijayā Daśamī, the 'tenth day of victory'. Both at the family level and at the levels of the quarter, the city and the state it is the day of the victorious sword processions, called *khaḍga yātrā* in Nepali and *pāyāḥ* in Newar. At the family level the swords are kept next to the bed of *naḥlāsvāṃ* in the family shrine. The eldest male member first gives a soot mark to the other male members of the family. After the name of this soot mark, which is taken from a small earthen tray on top of an oil lamp, the festival is in Newar called *mohanī*, lit. 'spell'. The *mohanī ṭikā* is generally given in the course of sacrifices to strengthen the participants.

The *pāyāḥ* or sword procession is in essence a sacrifice executed by the family or group members, albeit one without an animal victim. In most cases the victim is a *bhuyuphasi*, a pumpkin, which represents one of the forms in which Mahiṣāsura hid himself according to the common story. In order of seniority the male family members in turn cleave the pumpkin with the sword. Finally the seniormost member – the father or the eldest brother blesses all family members – with a red (mixed vermillion, curd and rice) ṭikā. The *naḥlavāṃ* is distributed as *prasāda* to put in the hair or above the ear. In the coming days the sprouts will also be given to visiting relatives.

The *naḥlāsvāṃ* can be compared with the gardens of Adonis in ancient Athens (Détienne 1972) and with the *mulappari* of South India (Zanen 1979: 145-151). The unfruitful grain sprouts contrast with, rather than reflect, the process of rice harvesting. According to Pradhan (1986: 294) the seedlings themselves are said to be the swords of the goddess. The sword procession does not mark the harvest but the warpath in which the enemy from without is beaten. The male members march out in a gesture, which is by now entirely a symbolic act and mostly understood as a victory of good over evil. There are no texts read on the occasion, and, besides themes from the Devīmahātmya, the occasion is also said to celebrate the victory of Rāma over Rāvaṇa. As Toffin points out, with references to Kane (1955) and Biardeau (1989), Vijayā Daśamī was the appropriate day of going to war all over ancient India. According to one tradition it is also the day on which the five Pāṇḍavas took up again their arms after their exile in the forest to fight the Kauravas (Toffin 1993b: 97; Underhill 1921: 56).

Daitya and Kumār

Strangely enough the goddess Taleju moves back to her high temple abode in the morning of Vijayā Daśamī, before the sword procession from the palace takes off in the evening of that day. It seems as if the divine battle is over at the moment that the human warpath starts. However, the swords, which were worshipped with sacrifice the night before, are still kept in the *naḥlāsvāṃ koṭhā* adjoining by the then empty room of Taleju. Together with the king's sword, they will represent the *śakti* of the realm in the evenings's sword procession. There is a particular feature of continuity between the movements of Taleju and the procession of the swords: the appearance of two unmasked but decorated dancers embodying the divinities Daitya and Kumār.

Daitya and Kumār make their first appearance on Mahāsaptamī morning when the images of Taleju are brought down from the temple, and their second in Vijayā Daśamī morning when Taleju is brought up again. Both dancers are boys who, at the time of their selection for a five-year period, must be between eight and fifteen years old. Daitya has to belong to the Śākya (Goldsmith) community of Kvane (the lower town), Kumār to the Tulādhar (Merchant) community of Thane. If the timing is accurate, the two deified boys for a short while share a single stage inside the ancient palace on the Mahāsaptamī (seventh) and Vijayā Daśamī mornings of Dasain. They do not form an ensemble, however. When embodying the divinities the two boys are kept strictly separate, and, incidentally, the two of them never met in ordinary life either.

Remarkably Daitya and Kumār are the protectors (*rakṣak*) of the royal goddess at the critical moments of transition. The Kumār dancer of Thane has to protect Taleju from dangers originating in heaven, and he is thereto equipped with a bow and arrow. The Daitya dancer of Kvane has to protect the goddess against dangers from the earth and the netherworld and is thereto equipped with a dagger. The incongruity of the central *śakti* of the realm having to be protected by guardians, one of whom is from the demonical realm himself, has been elaborately treated in an article on Daitya and Kumār (Van den Hoek & Shrestha 1992b). The main point to retain here is that the two divine dancers make their final appearance in Dasain during the sword procession of the palace, after Taleju has safely returned to her temple abode (Photo 22).

The training of the boys is not directed at the goddess Taleju, but totally devoted to Nāsaḥdyo, the Newar god of music and dance (Kasā 1965: gha). The short performances of Daitya and Kumār during Dasain do not clarify their opposed identities of god and demon, nor their function as protectors of the royal goddess. The accompanying music and songs are of a Buddhist devotional type and do not provide a clue to their specific functions either. Yet Daitya and Kumār do, apart from their very first and last dances, only perform their act at three occasions in Dasain. The assignment of the two dancers can, it seems, only become clear from the setting in which they operate just as, conversely, their performances may shed light on the particular contexts.

What we see are two divinized boys who, provided with their proper weapons and accompanied by *pañcatala* music, dashingly approach Hanumānḍhokā from the north and the south to attend Taleju's descent and ascent.

When the two of them meet in the ancient palace, at the very centre of town, their serpentine and threatening movements are not directed at each other, nor are they in co-ordination either. Evidently the ritual divide between Thane and Kvane has to be maintained in the very domain of the central goddess. To protect the goddess, it appears, the two chosen guardians should not form one party, but two separate ones. This opposition seems to be in keeping with their identities as Daitya – from the demonic realm – and Kumār - from the divine realm.

In the night of Vijayā Daśamī Daitya and Kumār join the sword procession when it comes out of the Taleju gate. The *pāyāḥ* from the palace is, at least nowadays, much more sober than various other sword processions which in daytime go out from *dyocheṃ*s in different quarters of town, and to which I will turn below. In the years that the Gathu dancers appear and either Pacalī Bhairava or Bhadrakālī exchanges swords with the king of Nepal at the very time of the sword procession, the occasion is marked by grandeur. In ordinary years the king, who is said to have participated in the *pāyāḥ* during the Malla period (Pradhan 1986: 311), does not appear, and the *pāyāḥ* company is then confined to the priests of Taleju and the carrier of the royal sword. Various other people of traditional rank like, according to his own saying, the Thakū juju of Kvane, may in principle partake in the *pāyāḥ*.

Several Jyāpu fulfill key roles in it and are obliged to come. A wooden image of Hanumān on a stick is given to the Jyāpu who will go ahead of the *pāyāḥ* to announce its coming. According to the Karmācāryas the Jyāpu carrying Hanumān is really possessed because a *mantra* is cast on him by the *mū ācāju* in Mūlcok at the time that the latter wraps a turban around the carrier's head. All sword carriers also have to make shaking movements as if possessed, and Daitya and Kumār, who preceed them, manifest the same symptoms. According to his (Vajrācārya) teacher Daitya, who goes in front, actually participates in the *khaḍga yātrā* brandishing his dagger. Rather than just protecting the goddess, Daitya and Kumār are here seen as leading the *śakti* of the realm in a way that befits their martial character.

Photo 22.
The Kumār dancer returning from the Taleju temple, after participating in the sword procession (pāyāḥ) (1992).

The royal sword is flanked by two Jyāpu who are holding *chali kathi*, silver-ornamented sticks. Significantly again, one of the mace-bearers represents Thane and the other one Kvane. Two other Jyāpu carry *baupāḥ*, bowls with ghostfood, which are disposed of at the northern gate of the Taleju temple in front of two lion guardians who respectively belong to Thane and Kvane. The opposition between the two city halves appears to be part and parcel of the *pāyāḥ*, as if the central *śakti* exists by the grace of parties that are opposed to each other. The procession first makes a move southward to the crossroads just below Kāṣṭhamaṇḍapa, then goes northward through the army quarter of Kamphukoṭ to Makhan and the crossroads at Vaṃgaḥ (Indrachowk), the northernmost point. The south-west to north-east diagonal which the *pāyāḥ* draws through the centre of town touches both the Kvane and the Thane parts.

Once they come back in the palace grounds through the western gate of the Taleju temple the group ascends the stairs and circumambulates the temple. The swords and the Hanumān image are then put at the base of the stairs and receive a *lasakusa* from the *mū ācāju* in the common way: by turning a *siṃphaṃ* over them and symbolically handing over a key. The key is not belonging to the room where they were worshipped over the past days but to another room in the palace where the swords are, according to the *ācāju*, put at rest for the coming year. The royal sword, however, is taken back to its own room in the palace: as a palladium of the realm it has to come out at different occasions.

Daitya and Kumār do not enter the palace this time but each goes his own way. As set forth in the article referred to (Van den Hoek & Shrestha 1992b), the essence of the couple seems to be that they represent opposite sides, suggesting as it were that the warlike expedition incorporates its own adversary. Not only Daitya and Kumār, but also the mace-bearers flanking the royal sword, represent this duality – in their case the opposition between Thane and Kvane. This configuration has the characteristics of a ritualized battlefield, a sacrificial arena (cf. chapter 1). To all appearances, the *śakti* of the realm marches out to meet an outside enemy, but Daitya, the enemy from within, leads the procession. It thus appears that Taleju, the protective goddess, derives her very power from the contest which ever exists, inside and outside.

During the centuries of political division, each of the Malla kings kept Taleju as this protective goddess. Instead of diminishing in importance by being shared, the cult of Taleju flourished and was adopted by small principalities in and outside the Valley: Sankhu (Zanen 1986, Shrestha 2002: 261-3), Panauti (Toffin 1984), and even the once small principality of Gorkhā. Inside the very town of Kathmandu, the ancient Thakū jujus of Kvane established Taleju in their residence, according their own saying copying the example of the Malla kings. Between, and even within the kingdoms, divisions were not transcended at either the political or the religious level. The kings of Pāṭan, Bhaktapur and Kathmandu neverthe-less continued to depend on one and the same protective goddess to bestow the power of victory on each of them.

Of old, the sacrificial nature of warfare was pre-eminent – in spite of all mundane interests involved. War, sacrifice, and capital punishment constituted the closely related sacred tasks of a king since Vedic times. Heesterman touches upon the role of the woman in it all – not the goddess, but the wife of the sacrificer-king. The woman, who passes out of her own family, has to remain an element of insecurity between two lineages, which, through her, establish or maintain a connubial (marital) alliance. In a sacrificial contest – Heesterman's attention centers upon a Vedic midsummer festival – the sacrificer's wife plays a central part because she also represents her own relatives whose connubial link with the sacrificer's party she embodies (Heesterman 1985: 134-136). A similar argument pertains to the battlefield: in a configuration of enemies who are at the same time related to each other – such as existed in case of the Malla kingdoms – women may find themselves embodying both sides in a conflict.

The position of protective goddesses parallels that of a woman who is related to different parties. As argued elsewhere (Van den Hoek & Shrestha 1992a: 73), the power of the protective goddess seems to derive from the very fact that she maintains relations with opposed parties. As the main priest of Taleju explained, Daitya is the demon adversary, but he nevertheless belongs to the *gaṇa*, the retinue of the goddess who slays him: the goddess incorporates her enemy. The sword processions which come out from different Taleju temples at Vijayā Daśamī are not and were not opposed to each other in terms of good and evil – nor were, for that matter, parties in actual war opposed in those terms. Instead, the *pāyāḥ* of the palace with its twofold mace representing Thane and Kvane, and with Daitya and Kumār at the head of it, already displays the two sides of the battlefield or sacrificial arena internally.

Daitya and Kumār, going at the head of the party, can be seen as the protagonists. They have to die young, perhaps because the scriptures prescribe them to be forever youthful, but also because they are heading a sacrificial party which cannot remain without victims at set times. Like the dancers of the Gathu *pyākhaṃ* Daitya and Kumār have to die, not every year, but at the end of their five-year term. The coming into being and the demise of Daitya and Kumār constitute the ritually most elaborate aspect of their divine enactment (Van den Hoek & Shrestha 1992b: 197-207, 214-216). On the occasion of their last dance, which is not part of Dasain, they literally fall off the stage, Kumār in public and Daitya in secret. Both of them fall unconscious, and are covered with a white shroud. It is considered inauspicious to enact this passage of death, and it is therefore – apart from the numerous rules to be followed – hard to find willing candidates. As in the case of Gathu dances (see previous chapter), both the boys and the divinities are reborn, but the *personae* who incorporated the divinities effectively die in that capacity.

The *śakti* of the goddess has to be nourished in many ways, rather than protected in the strict sense of the word. Plenty of sacrifice has therefore been made to her on the eighth and ninth days of Dasain. Yet the ultimate sacrifice is that of war, as expressed by the goddess' slaying of her demon enemy on the tenth day of victory. Although he has to die, Daitya himself is part of the sword procession, which celebrates this feat. In the bipolar composition of the *pāyāḥ*, war seems to be primarily a matter of sacrifice, as it happened to be in days bygone. Daitya and Kumār have to protect the goddess from dangers arising in the netherworld or coming from heaven, but at another level they represent those regions in themselves. In the sacrifice of war the victory of the goddess lies with the victims, who, it should be added, will themselves enjoy the fruits of sacrifice as well. The kingdom will be reborn through sacrifice, whether it is in victory or defeat.

Yet the celebration of death in Dasain is generally directed at victory, and the *pāyāḥ* at the household level does not express the same ambivalences as the sword procession at the royal level. In between one area remains undiscovered, and that is the level of the quarter or ward: several public *pāyāḥ* (the household level being secret) take off mostly from the *dyocheṃ*s of *mātṛkā*s.

The ward level: sword processions and other yātrās

In all great celebrations of death up to Dasain, the ward level is subordinate to a larger entity, that of the city and the state. The festivals are celebrated in the domestic circle as well, but without giving prominence to a particular locality. Dasain seems to fit a pattern of celebrations, which take place at both the supralocal and the domestic level, but not at any intermediate level. The Pacalī Bhairava yātrā at first sight contradicts this pattern because it is only celebrated in the southern part of Kathmandu city. Yet in the end it appears to conform to the supralocal level, if only by the visit of Pacalī to the central palace in the presence of the royal Kumārī. The Pacalī Bhairava dances leave no doubt about the supralocal and royal significance of the god.

It is only at Vijayā Daśamī that the local level of the ward (*tvāḥ*) asserts itself. The ward structure is essential for an understanding of Kathmandu city, but its features remain hidden during the festivals of the fall. On the day of Vijayā Daśamī, however, a prelude is given to the marches of the goddesses, which dominate the ritual calendar after the turn of the year – two weeks after Dasain. During Vijayā Daśamī all goddesses who participate in the spring festival of Pāhāṃ Carhe (approximately in March) have their *pāyāḥ*. In the sword processions, the images of the deities are not brought out, but instead, the human members of the *guthi*s concerned embody themselves the members of the divine *gaṇa*: the *aṣṭamātṛkā*, Gaṇeśa and Bhairava.

The *guthi*s are all Jyāpu (Farmer caste), and in all but one of the cases the members dress in robes, which have the colours of the divine host. Dressed in the robes of the *gaṇa* the participants resemble divine dancers but they wear no masks. They come out of the different *dyocheṃ*s in a possessed state shaking their swords. Central to the performance, as we saw already at the level of the family is the sacrificial act of slaying a pumpkin (Photo 23), which is sometimes executed in public and sometimes before the *gaṇa* comes out. In all cases a *baupāḥ* is put outside to placate the wandering ghosts.

The movements of the different sword processions are short and cover only a limited distance in the vicinity of the *dyocheṃ*s. They follow upon each other so that it is possible to get a glimpse of all of them by crisscrossing the city. The *dyocheṃ* of Bhadrakālī – which is closed to the public at the time of the *pāyāḥ* – in the large courtyard of Tebāhāl is usually the first place of action. The *baupāḥ* carrier is walking in front of the procession, followed by Bhairava and the other members of the *gaṇa*, who are not all identifiable for the onlookers or even for their attendants. Bhadrakālī herself, known by the generic name Ajimā (the Grandmother), is closing the row. Orchestras of *dhimay* and *bāsuri* (flute music) go ahead of the procession, which makes a round of the courtyard and a short excursion eastward to a crossroads with a

Gaṇeśa temple. There the remnants of the *bhuyuphasi*, the pumpkin which was in this case slain before the *pāyāḥ* took off, are dropped. The carrier of the pumpkin pieces has thereafter to be taken on the back of another person, evidently overwhelmed by fulfilling his role.

From other instances, like the Bhadrakālī *dyocheṃ* in Vatu, it becomes clear that all participants in the sword procession tend to fall unconscious after their act, and lay down for a while till they are given some pure water (*nīlaḥ*) to drink. In Vatu too, the party comes out after already having cut the pumpkin. They go round the Vatu square to the south and make short strikes east and west. *Dāphā* music plays in the *pāṭī* in front of the *dyocheṃ* and a *guṃgūmakaḥ* (a vessel with incense) is burned from which the sword carriers inhale the smoke before they go up in the *dyocheṃ* and faint away.

Other processions follow the same pattern, but in two cases, that of Nilvārāhī and of Kaṃkeśvarī, the pumpkin is sacrificed outside the *dyocheṃ* at a crossroads. The members of the *gaṇa* take turns in hewing the *bhuyuphasi* with their swords. On the pumpkin of the Kaṃkeśvarī *pāyāḥ*, sacrificed in front of a local Kumārī shrine, the face of Mahiṣāsura is painted. The cleaving of the pumpkin, whether it is done in secret or in public, thus appears to be the central act of the *pāyāḥ*, as it is at the domestic level.

Not every quarter has its Ajimā and not every *dyocheṃ* has its *pāyāḥ*. The goddesses who have a *pāyāḥ* in Dasain all appear together in the great *yātrā* of Pāhāṃ

Photo 23.
The cleaving of a pumpkin representing the demon king Mahiṣāsur, as part of the procession of the swords (pāyāḥ) on the tenth day of victory (Vijayā Daśamī) in Kathmandu at the Yatkhā quarter (1993).

Carhe more than five months later. At that time the brass procession statues of the divinities are carried around town, meeting each other on the way or, on the contrary, avoiding to meet each other. In Vijayā Daśamī no boundaries are crossed: the *pāyāḥ* groups remain in their own quarter, and have no chance of meeting each other. However similar the sword pro-cessions at the *tvāḥ* level are, they all have their own domain in which the enemy from outside, Mahiṣāsura, has to be beaten.

There are no processions resembling *pāyāḥ* during the spring festival of Pāhāṃ Carhe, except perhaps in one case, which is already an exception in Dasain. The Pāhāṃ Carhe *yātrā* of the goddess Naradevī is overshadowed by a performance of masked dances by the Naradevī *guthi* (consisting of Jyāpu and Tulādhar) which precedes the procession of the metal statues. The masked dancers embody the divine company of Naradevī or Svetakālī and thereby resemble the sword processions which other goddesses have in Dasain. During Dasain, however, the Naradevī dancers have their *pāyāḥ* behind the closed doors of their *dyocheṃ*. They are then not dressed in the robes of the divinities but perform their sword procession in white *jama*s, secluded from the public eye.

The Naradevī dancers (*pyākhaṃ*) are a subject in itself, which properly belong to the context of Pāhāṃ Carhe. Here it is important to note that the Dasain performances are related to a festival that takes place much later. Dasain is open-ended, whether it concerns the ward *pāyāḥ*, the city *pāyāḥ* or the divine dances of the Gathu.

Vijayā Daśamī is the conclusion of the all-embracing festival of Dasain, but at the same time the local level asserts itself, not only in the sword processions but also in three separate *yātrā*s of which the preliminaries already start before the concluding "tenth day of victory". On that day the fire sacrifices take place which mark the start of the elaborate processions of two of the most frequented deities in the heart of town: the goddess Annapūrṇā of Asan and the god Maru Gaṇeśa, named after his quarter Maru.

Most people consider the goddess Annapūrṇā as belonging to *dathu*, the central part of town. A more sophisticated view is that an enshrined stone fish (*nyā lvaha*) in Asan square just north of the Annapūrṇā temple indicates the dividing line between Thane and Kvane. According to the Jyāpu *guthi* which supervises the festival, however, Annapūrṇā belongs to Thane. Shifting perspectives are characteristic of the view on the ritual division of Kathmandu. Apart from the ancient royal palace only Maru quarter, west of the palace, is generally reckoned to belong to Dhatu, the central area of town. Regardless of the classification one is adopting, both Annapūrṇā and Maru Gaṇeśa are within close range of the palace. Both deities have their *dyocheṃ* as well as their temple along the main trade route that crosses Kathmandu from south-west to north-east.

It is significant that the first local *yātrā*s of town belong to temples of the inner city, and not to the *pīṭha*s that surround it. The *pigaṃdyo* (divinities with a *pīṭha*) will get their *yātrā*s only after the turn of the ritual year. As was shown above, the *pāyāḥ* or sword processions are a manifestation of *śakti*, which is different from the actual *yātrā* of the *pigaṃdyo*. Annapūrṇā is not a *pigaṃdyo* and she has no *pāyāḥ* in Vijayā Daśamī, but the *yātrā* of the procession statues is nearly simultaneous with the sword processions. In the late night of Vijayā Daśamī the two procession statues of the goddess are brought down and placed in the temple. Then a fire sacrifice is performed by a Karmācārya officiant, in which thirty-two grains are offered as well as pieces of meat, blood, and lungs of a buffalo sacrificed the previous night.

The preparations for the *yātrā* correspond to a large extent with those common to all *yātrā*s including the Pacalī Bhairava yātrā described above. The *pāḥlā* of the six-member *guthi*, the one whose turn it is to take care of the temple and the *dyocheṃ*, distributes *yaciṃ laḥ* to the other *guthi* members on the first day of Dasain. As in the case of Pacalī Bhairava, this pure river water indicates that the members have from then on to abstain from eating touched food and also from mourning the dead.

In the late night of *phūlpātī* (the seventh day of Dasain) the *guthi* goes out from the *dyocheṃ* to invite other divinities in a ceremony which is similar in outline to the *nimantrāṇā pūjā* of Pacalī Bhairava. The specific offerings, however, consist of *bvaṃcā*, small earthen pots which are filled with special rice beer and covered on top with straw and food items: *samay baji*, fish and *catāṃmari* (thin pancakes). The *bvaṃcā* are offered to Kamalāchī Mahādeva, Akhaḥhiti Bhairava, Hikvādyo, Gaṇeśa, the Nyā lvaha (Fish Stone) and to Annapūrṇā herself. The *bvaṃcā* are collected at the respective places by representatives of the divinities, the one offered to Annapūrṇā itself by a Tulādhar *guthi*. Moreover, in a resthouse thirty-two *bvaṃcā* are put and subsequently taken by the *guthi* members themselves to be consumed afterwards. On that day special food, *maraḥjā*, is given to eleven children who represent Bhairava, Gaṇeśa and the *gaṇa* of goddesses. The *maraḥjā* consists of rice and sixteen other dishes, the children are selected from the families of the *guthi* members. *Maraḥjā* feedings to children, which are sometimes large and open to everybody, are a recurrent feature of Kathmandu's festivals.

In the evening of Ekādaśī (one day after Vijayā Daśamī) the palanquin of Annapūrṇā makes, under great public interest, a small tour of upper Kathmandu which takes more than five hours to complete due to all *pūjā* offered to the goddess on the way. The next day Annapūrṇā makes a big round of the whole city which ends only at three o'clock in the night with a *lasakusa* at the *dyocheṃ*. The goddess makes many stops on the way to give the devotees the occasion to offer their *pūjā* to her. A singular feature of this *yātrā* is that the goddess makes a very small round of her own quarter (Asan/Bhotāhiṭī) two nights later, which is followed by another *lasakusa* at the *dyocheṃ* and a duck- and goat sacrifice inside.

There is no ritual connection between Taleju and Annapūrṇā, but the *yātrā* takes place in the span of time between Vijayā Daśamī and the full moon as the end of the month (Katiṃ Punhi), in which human beings have to visit their relatives to receive a Dasain blessing consisting of a *ṭikā* and *naḥlāsvāṃ*. Annapūrṇā herself especially visits the *mhyāymasta*, the daughters who have been married out from Bhotāhiṭī quarter. Jyāpu are the main participants in many of Kathmandu's *yātrā*s and, since they practice *tvāḥ*-exogamy, there are numerous *mhyāymasta* with their kin to be visited during *yātrās*. The same holds true for the Maru Gaṇeśa yātrā which is almost simultaneous with that of Annapūrṇā, and which will presently be touched upon very briefly.

The *yātrā* statue of Maru Gaṇeśa is already brought out on the eighth evening (Mahāṣṭamī), and on the ninth (Mahānavamī) evening makes a short round of his own domain: Maru and adjacent quarters. On Vijayā Daśamī a *homa* is performed in front of the temple by a Vajrācārya priest. At the same time the Maru Gaṇeśa *guthi* (the same as that of Indradyo) sacrifices a goat in the temple, but nothing from it is offered into the fire: only grains are used in this *homa*. In the evening of that day Gaṇeśa is carried to those places from where he has received ornaments. The next day, on the eleventh (Ekādaśī), Maru Gaṇeśa makes a big round of town. Both the Maru Gaṇeśa and the Annapūrṇā yātrā are part of the Dasain period but unlike Pacalī Bhairava they have no royal features.

One day before the full moon that concludes the Dasain holidays (*Katiṃ Punhi*) a Buddhist divinity, Sighahdyo, is brought out by a Śākya (Goldsmith) *guthi* of Asan, again in the central part of town. The deity is carried in silence from the house of the *guthi* eldest to the Sighah *caitya* (*stupa*) a few hundred yards away. Sighahbāhāl is built as a copy of the great *stupa* of Svayambhū on a hillock west of town. Like Svayambhū, Sighah houses Jyāpu boys who are to be initiated there (*vaḥlāḥ*) in the two nights preceding Katiṃ Punhi. Sighahdyo as a Buddhist deity does not receive blood sacrifice, but a fire sacrifice is carried out in front of him on the full moon day, before the *yātrā* starts. The procession, now accompanied by several orchestras, does not cross the city, but moves almost straight back to the house where the deity came from the day before, without even passing by the palace area of Hanumānḍhokā.

After Vijayā Daśamī, then, the unity of the festival gives way to a number of local processions, in which the palace is no longer the focal point. The dismissal of the divinities (*visarjana*) in the *naḥlāsvāṃ* room of the old royal palace takes place on the day before the full moon, when the sacred bed of seedlings is, after a *pūjā*, finally removed and disposed of at the main Taleju gate. Within two weeks another national festival, Tihār, will be celebrated, but then the proceedings are all at the level of the household, without accompanying royal ceremonies.

Conclusion

The above observations on Dasain were mostly made from the Newar point of view. The bringing of the *phūlpātī* from Gorkhā, the military display at the parade ground on the same day, the massive army sacrifices, all are additions which took shape in the course of Gorkhā rule since 1768. While the Pacalī Bhairava yātrā, the rituals surrounding Taleju, the divine dances and the sword processions remain a Newar affair, the Gorkhālī additions are of little concern to the Newars. Unlike in Indra yātrā, in which the ceremonies of the state are embedded in Newar ritual, the new dynasty asserts itself in Dasain. Although the king can in principle obtain the *dīkṣā* which would give him acess to the worship of Taleju, he does not engage in it, but instead draws all attention towards the reception of the *phūlpātī*, and towards the big military display which that day, the seventh (*saptamī*), takes place in the parade ground Tundikhel, in the presence of the king.

In Indra yātrā the role of the king is submissive in a number of respects, in particular with regard to the living goddess Kumārī who by her blessing confirms his reign. All imagery points to the fact that the king is a victim in the sacrificial sense of the word. Dasain can be seen as an extension of Indra yātrā, in which the king still plays his sacrificial role, but in which the threat to his authority no longer comes from within. The enemy within is not killed or subdued like Daitya is in the dances of Indra yātrā, but is incorporated in the forces that march out during the *khaḍga yātrā* of the palace. Daitya *is* the sacrifice, heading the *khaḍga yātrā* to meet his equal, and, in the end, to meet with his own death. Like the king himself, he is the consecrated warrior, who leaves the bonds of settled life to set out for the wilderness. In that respect he can be compared to the seemingly anomalous *vrātyas* of Vedic times (Heesterman 1993: 178-179, 183).

The theme gets all the more force by the various duplicates of the royal war party, among which are the tours of the *pāyāḥ*s inside town and more particularly the appearance of the divine dancers. The sword exchange between the divine dancers and the king highlights the king's role as the prime warrior of the country. At the same time the parallellism between the moves of the divine dancers and those of the king indicates that the battlefield is no longer confined to the inner arena of the realm, but that it reaches out to the world beyond. The same thought is expressed by the nature of the enemy, Mahiṣāsura, as a conqueror of the three worlds. Mahiṣāsura is the chosen enemy who is also equivalent to the king: his sacrifice is a king's sacrifice. The goddess who effects victory and defeat is standing in between the combatants as the very image of sacrificial death.

The theme does not change in value when other stories are taken into account for the great war and victory. Whether Vijayā Daśamī is told to be the defeat of Mahiṣāsura by the hands of Durgā, or the defeat of Rāvana by Rāma with Sītā in between (an explanation also common in Nepal), or the defeat of the Kauravas by the Pāṇḍavas with Draupadī in between (Biardeau 1981: 217, 222), the purport of the message does not change. It is a sacrifice of war in which the goddess holds the key. Even the comparatively modern elaborations of this royal ritual in Nepal do not basically alter this scheme, but they do bring it somewhat closer to realities on the ground.[2]

Oldfield, who wrote in the 1850s, during the reign of Prime Minister Jang Bāhadur Rāṇā, is the first who makes elaborate mention of the army sacrifices: 'Every regimental officer, from the rank of jemadar upwards, is expected to present a buffalo (the higher officers giving two or three) as an offering to the colours of his own corps. On the ninth day of the festival these offerings are presented at the head-quarters of the respective regiments. The colours are erected in a prominent position and decorated with garlands of flowers, streamers etc., and amid a continuous firing of guns and muskets, the animals, with their horns and heads painted and with wreaths of flowers round their necks are brought up and secured in the proper position.' Oldfield contrasts at length the clean way of decapitating practised by the Gorkhās with the, to him, disgusting way of searching and slitting the throat veins of the animal as practised by the Newars (Oldfield 1880 II: 344-349).

Landon, in his eulogy of the reign of Prime Minister (Mahārāja) Chandra Shamsher half a century later, remarks in passing that 'the peasant of Nepal is no longer compelled to furnish the beasts required for the annual sacrifices of the Durgā Pūjā festival at low or even nominal rates. Nothing perhaps has brought so directly to the knowledge of the people the new spirit which actuates the Nepal Government than this relief' (Landon 1928 II: 160). The remark is very characteristic of the centralized way in which Dasain was organized in the time of Rāṇā rule. The king and principal *sardars*, Oldfield (1880 II: 345) reports, were usually present at the Koṭ to witness the scene. The sacrifices occur at the headquarters of every regiment of the country, yet they are tied up, in Kathmandu and other places, with the older worship of Taleju – preceding and following as they do the secret Kālarātri sacrifices to the images of Taleju in her Pūjā *koṭhā*.

Among the efforts to make Dasain a state affair, Oldfield (1880 II: 343) also mentions that 'the 'Panjanni' or annual period for the renewal of all public service, is always brought to a close by the first day of the Dassera'. On the other hand he notes (II: 351) that 'the grand cutting of the rice-crops is always postponed till the Dassera is over and commences all over the valley the very day afterwards.' As the harvest depends on the condition of the crops, the latter observation can hardly be true to life, but it indicates again the effort to make Dasain a turning point, after which the government and the landowners can claim their respective shares in the harvest. Legitimate claims thus parallel the possible spoils of the army if it marches out into other territory, reminding us of the Vedic notion that (in whatever way) the king is the 'eater' of his people (Heesterman 1985: 109).

In contrast with Indra yātrā, the king in Dasain does not have to bow in order to receive a blessing mark, but he himself places the *ṭikā* on the forehead of his ministers, officials and subjects alike. The custom was already en vogue at the time of Jang Bāhadur in the 1850s, with the difference that at that time also the Prime Minister held his 'Darbār': "On the tenth or last day of the festival, it is usual for the king to hold a public Darbār, at which the Ministers and all Sardars and officers above the rank of Jemadar attend, make their salaam, present a small offering, from one rupee upwards, to His Majesty, and have their caste and position confirmed by his touching their foreheads, and so investing them with the 'tikka' or caste-mark. During the day all officers and public officials at the capital pay a visit of respect to the Minister and his brothers, and make to him and them a small pecuniary payment, verging from a rupee upwards" (Oldfield 1880 II: 351). Not only the king, but also his ministers and generals thus received a *dakṣiṇā* in return for their priestly function of blessing and reaffirming people in their established positions. Evidently the priestly role of the king is the model for this kind of ritualistic exchange, and nowadays only the king still has his open Darbār in the new palace of Nārāyaṇahiti on Vijayā Daśamī.

The role of the Brahmin in Dasain is very limited, both for the Gorkhā or Parvatīyā people and for the Newars. For the latter the Brahmin does not even appear on the sacrificial stage, yet there is one task for a Rājopādhāya Brahmin: Taleju has a Brahmin cook, who every morning comes to a room in Mūlcok to cook rice for the goddess. On the seventh day of Dasain the Brahmin also comes to prepare the two *baupāḥ*s, the bowls with ghost-food, which are carried by the Jyāpu in the *pāyāḥ* of Vijayā Daśamī. The three days in between the Rājopādhyāya comes to offer pūjā to the *baupāḥ*s in the *naḥlāsvāṃ koṭhā*. Taleju's own Pūjā *koṭhā*, however, remains closed to him.

In contrast with Indra yātrā – which includes several processions for the deceased ones, Dasain manifests death in its sacrificial aspect only. The two weeks between the full moon of Indra yātrā, until the first day of Dasain (*Ghaṭasthāpanā*), however, are called sohra *śrāddha*, the sixteen days of ancestor worship. They close with *pitṛ visarjana*, the dismissal of the ancestors, on the day before Ghaṭasthāpanā. The *sohra śrāddha* is not comparable to the processions in which the dead souls are banned from this world. It is celebrated at the household level only, and there the celebration can be termed an auspicious *śrāddha*. While the regular monthly or yearly *śrāddha*s are meant to keep the ancestors at bay, the auspicious *śrāddha*s such as those preceding a marriage are intended to invite the ancestors to a place of honour – not downstairs but upstairs.

In the *sohra śrāddha* both the ancestors of the male side (up to seven generations) and the ancestors of the female side (up to three generations) are invited to give their blessings to the family.[3] It is a preliminary to the festival of victory – Dasain. Yet it is not the end of the invocations of death. In a dramatic reversal the Lord of Death – the ever-living – is invited to bless the household during Yama pañcak, the five days of Yama. These include the three days of Tihār, the turn of the ritual year, which is celebrated fourteen days after Dasain, with the dark moon being in the center of the festival week. We shall now turn to this festival.

Chapter 9

Tihār

The Turn of the Ritual Year

Introduction

Tihār, or *Svanti* in Newar, is one of the greatest festivals of the year, yet it is entirely celebrated in the domestic sphere. Unlike domestic rites proper, such as *the rites de passage*, Svanti takes place in each and every household in the same period of five days, which is also called Yamapañcak, the five days of the Lord of Death. The five days are dedicated to Yama and his messengers, with the exception, it appears, of the third day which is dedicated to Lakṣmī, the Goddess of Wealth. Lakṣmī pūjā usually falls on the new moon night of the month of Kārtik; the following day, the first of the bright half of Kārtik, is celebrated as New Year according to the lunar calendar.

On New Year's day Death is worshipped as the divinity in man. In Newar the worship is called Mha pūjā, the worship of the Self or the Body, Sanskritized as Ātmā pūjā. Mha pūjā, and Svanti as a whole, contrast with all those celebrations in which death and the deceased are kept at bay. Svanti is an invitation to Death as a living god. Unlike Pacalī Bhairava the general manifestation of Yamarāj has no *yātrā*, but is invoked in every household by molding his form out of rice flour like a *gvaḥjā*, or by representing him as a *maṇḍala*, a cosmic diagram.

The Newar ritual cycle knows one other day when Yama is honoured as the general Lord of Death under his own name. That is the day when Yama opens the gate of his kingdom to let in the deceased of the past year. It is the festival of Gāi yātrā (Sāpāru), which was treated above in chapter 4. The reception of the dead by Yama is directly opposed to the reception of Yama by the living. As will be understood from the accompanying stories, the invitation to Yama is not to take the living away, but to be among them.

In the two days of Yama pañcak, which precede the Tihār festival, crows and dogs are honoured as the messengers from the realm of death. Like serpents, crows are considered immortal in Nepal unless they are violently killed. Serpent sacrifies occur in Nepal (Van den Hoek & Shrestha 1992a) but crow sacrifices are not known. The crows are the ever-living messengers of death and more particularly of the ancestors abiding in Yama's realm. Dogs are the carriers (*vāhana*) of Lord Bhairava and the gatekeepers of Yamaloka. It appears that crows and dogs are announcing the coming of their master. Both species are propitiated with food and *pūjā*.

On the first day of the sequence of five, crows receive their due. In the lively words of Anderson (1975: 166): 'People set out small dishes made of green leaves sewn together, containing food, coins, burning incense and oil wicks to propitiate this black, predatory bird whose rancous scolding often foretells a death or impending disaster.' As a matter of fact the crows are, together with the ancestors, provided with a portion of cooked rice every day, which is placed for them on the roofside.

The day after Ko pūjā, the crow's worship, it is the turn of the dogs in Khicā pūjā. All dogs receive a *ṭikā*, a red mark on their foreheads, and a garland of flowers. They are fed with delicious food for one day. The strange thing is that after this reception of the messengers of Death, it is not Yamarāj who will come into the houses next day, but the goddess of Wealth, Lakṣmī. Death makes his appearance only the day after that.

Lakṣmī pūjā

In the morning of the day called Lakṣmī pūjā, cows are worshipped with a blessing mark on their forehead, and with garlands and painted decorations.[1] The reason is different from the cow decorations in Gāi yātrā, in which cows are paraded because they have direct access to Yamaloka (the world of Yama). In Lakṣmī pūjā they embody the Goddess of Wealth. But yet, something peculiar is there in the worship of cows and of Wealth during those days that bear the impression of Yama, Lord of Death. One is reminded of Naciketas in the *Katha Upanisad*, who is allowed to ask Yama three boons, the last of which is the following question to Yama:

> 'This doubt there is about a man departed,
> Some say 'He is', some 'He does not exist'
> This would I know, instructed by thee
> of the three gifts, this gift is the third'
>
> *Katha Upanisad* 1, 20 (translation J.N. Rawson 1934)

Instead of answering the question Yama begs Naciketas to choose another boon, and offers him all riches of the world, in cattle, in women and in wealth, which Naciketas all refuses because they are as perishable as life is. Yama as the supplier of transient wealth here equals the quality of Lakṣmī. One may well wonder whether during Lakṣmī pūjā the goddess of wealth does not represent Yama in his capacity as a supplier of transient wealth, his counterpart as it were. The explanation may seem far-fetched, but then, as will appear from the two other days of Tihār, its celebrations may be the most profound of any of Nepal's festivals.

In the night of the dark moon, Lakṣmī is invited by a show of oil lamps as well as electric bulbs to lead her on the way. Households are vying with each other to attract the attention of the goddess by a show of light on all houses and in the alleys leading to them. Strips of cowdung are also laid out from the roadside through the houses up to the *dhukū*, the treasure store upstairs. There, or in the sacred room of the house, an image of Lakṣmī painted on paper is receiving *pūjā* from the family members in secret – this being in striking contrast with openness to outsiders of the ceremonies of the subsequent days, which, to all appearances, harbour greater secrets of their own.

Lakṣmī pūjā is an ordinary *pūjā* with flowers, incense, *ṭikā* powder and other customary items. Additional is the inclusion of at least one new silver coin and one new household utensil. Those will only be taken away the day after Tihār, and then too the *ṭikā* of Lakṣmī will be distributed. In a way Lakṣmī is thus present in her secluded space during the three last days of Tihār, but will not come to prominence again before the festival is over.

The night of Lakṣmī pūjā is marked by institutionalized (and government-allowed) gambling. Lakṣmī cannot or does not bestow the same wealth on everybody, as already is clear from the households' vying for her favour. Or is the gambling and general license already a sign of the advent of Yama who will preside over the following days? It seems anyway a divine play (*līlā*) enacted by humans who, once in the gambling mood, may forget themselves and the whole context of the game. Heavy losses may thus occur in this black night of Lakṣmī pūjā which is considered nevertheless an auspicious occasion in Nepal and India (Divālī) alike.

Only next morning the New Year will be celebrated with some fanfare, occasional firecrackers (as a modern introduction) and, as a customary feature, the wearing of new clothes by everybody. But above all New Year's Day contains one of the most serious *pūjās* of the year: the worship of the self.

Mha pūjā

Ritual manuals such as the *Nepāl varṣa kriyā* prescribe that Mha or Ātma pūjā should take place in the morning, but, nowadays at least, it starts after sunset on the previous day. It is not identical for all castes and families but it has the same significant features in all cases. Central is the drawing of *maṇḍalas* (New. *mandaḥ*) for gods and humans alike. These cosmic diagrams are drawn on the top floor of the house where the kitchen is located and the meals are taken (Photo 24).

First, water is sprinkled in the form of the particular diagram, then the actual *mandaḥ* is drawn with *potāy*, the flour of parched rice. The *mandaḥs* vary from family to family but are always complex diagrams within a circle. They may be drawn by hand by any member of the family or put more mechanically by making use of a paper stencil for the appropriate lines and dots. They are laid out in a row according to the line in which the family members will sit during the *pūjā*.

At the head of the row a few small *mandaḥs* are drawn to represent the 330 million gods. Together with this collectivity of gods there are three distinct images of riceflour which represent Gaṇeśa, and, in the case described, Yamadūta and Śivadūta as messengers of death and gatekeepers of the *pātāla*, the underworld. Sometimes Yamadūta is said to be the gatekeeper of the underworld and Śivadūta that of the splendid Mount Kailasa. In other cases not the messengers of death but Yamarāj and his scribe Citragupta themselves are imagined to be present. Against the wall (at the head of the row) a winnowing fan, a brush and a waterpot are placed to receive worship as well. Finally a *sukundā*, an auspicious lamp used during rituals[2] is put

Photo 24.
The author (centre, left) participating in a Mha pūjā, a worship of the self, with a Shrestha family in Sankhu (1991).

amidst the gods. The worship will start with lighting the *sukundā*, but first the *mandaḥs* have to be completed.

Mandaḥs are made for all family members including infants, guests, and those who are absent. The diagrams of the white *potāy* powder first receive a small circle of oil in their centre with a read mark inside. Subsequently popped rice, husked rice and black soyabeans are scattered over the *mandaḥs*. All added elements also belong to the structure of the *mandaḥs*: they represent the five gross elements (ether, air, fire, water, and earth), *mahābhūtas*, which correspond with the five subtle elements of the human body, *pañcatattva*. The participants' view on philosophical matters is not clearcut. What matters is that the *mandaḥs* represent their own human bodies. However, in the view of some people they are also an expression of Yama himself.

This ambiguity may reflect a profound and ancient thought. In the concluding paragraph of the chapter on the dying gods we already saw that the mystery play of the divine dancers alluded to the secret of life and death and finally led to the conclusion that Death is the divinity in man. Heesterman reaches a similar conclusion on quite different (textual) grounds where he analyses the victory of the Lord of Life, Prajāpati over Mṛtyu, Death. Prajāpati's victory, however, does not eliminate Death, who is on the one hand assimilated by his conquerer as part of himself but on the other hand remains a separate entity who through a compact with the lord of Life is entitled to the body of the deceased as his share (Heesterman 1993: 54). Most revealing is a passage from the Śatapatha Brāhmaṇa quoted by Heesterman, in which the sacred ambivalence is stated more generally and explicitly: 'Death becomes the self of him who knows thus; when he departs from this world, he passes into that self and becomes immortal, for Death is his own self' (Heesterman 1993: 57, 221 f.). Death is the divinity in man and, in a seemingly paradoxical way, the source of his immortality.

No classical (or any other) texts are recited during Mha or Ātmā pūjā, but the interpretation of the *mandaḥ* points to the same thought: it is a microcosmic as well as macrocosmic representation of the Self and, at the same time, of Death. The underlying thought is expressed in other ways too in the course of the ritual, especially in its individualistic set-up and the absence of exchange.

There is no clear division of labour in drawing the *mandaḥs* and supplying them with their ingredients. Any family member can do it and, although in the subsequent rituals women do most of the work, it would be a misconception to view this ceremony as a service of women to men. After all, women are to participate in Mha pūjā in a way equal to men. The *mandaḥs* will be worshipped on their own, and hierarchy exists only in the order of seating: the eldest male at the head followed by all other male family members including infants. The eldest female, other female family members and in-married women follow. The ladies, who offer ritual services to the group, have at the end to do it for each other also since nobody is excluded from participation. If someone is away from the parental home, his *mandaḥ* at home will still be worshipped by others during Mha pūjā.

First a number of other items is placed in and around the *mandaḥs*, among which are various fruits. One of those fruits has a special significance and will be worshipped subsequently. It is a big wild citrus fruit called *taḥsi*, which is not normally eaten.[3] Its speciality is that, unlike all other items used in worship, it does not become *cipa* (Nep. *jutho*, polluted) after being used. In the next ceremony it is as ritually fresh as it was before and indeed it will be used again in the ceremony of the following day, Kijā pūjā, the worship of brothers. The same can never be done with for example a banana which has once been used in worship.

A walnut placed in the centre of the *mandaḥ* has as its speciality that it does not rot. The *pūjā* items for the *mandaḥs* also include several kinds of flowers among which the dark purple *gvaysvāṃ* is essential. Its special quality is that it does not wither, but dries up instead, retaining its colour. In front of the *mandaḥ*, next to the *taḥsi*, a standing lamp (*tvāḥdevā*) is put for every person. With those essential items the worship of the *mandaḥ* and the person sitting behind it can start.

First of all the eldest male at the head of the row worships the *sukundā* (which also has its own *mandaḥ*), lights it and pays hommage to Gaṇeśa, Yamadūta, Śivadūta and the other gods. Incense is burned for the gods and put into each of the *tvāḥ deva* in front of the other *mandaḥs*. This is the start of the worship of the mystical diagrams. An in-married woman or a daughter will give a *ṭikā* to all those present and finally put one on her own forehead. The whole group will then throw rice as *pūjā* to the gods, to the roof (*pūjā* for the house) and on each of their *mandaḥs*. The *mandaḥ* is further worshipped with an offering of light in the form of a burning wick (*itāḥ*). The *taḥsi* fruits, which are displayed on the *mandaḥ* together with other fruits; a garland of flowers and a thread of cloth are handed over together with a *ṭikā* on the foreheads of the participants.

The head of the household then kindles (with the flame of the *sukundā*) a very long wick (*kheluitāḥ*), which consists of twenty-one oil-soaked threads. Similar *kheluitāḥ* are then passed on along the row of people, with each person lighting his own *kheluitāḥ* from the flame of the one of the person before him. After circling the long and brightly burning wick three times above his *mandaḥ*, each person places it on the diagram, which will be covered by the long flaming string. At the moment that the *kheluitāḥ* is laid on the *mandaḥ* the essential connection is made between the mystical diagram and the person sitting behind it. The *kheluitāḥ*, which makes the connection represents the lifeline of the individual concerned. Jocular remarks are made about well-burning *kheluitāḥs* and soft-burning ones; extinguishing (at start) *kheluitāḥs* are immediately rekindled.

One of the ladies of the house then carries out a ceremony called *siṃphaṃ luyegu* or the pouring things out from a measuring pot. She uses a *kule*, a measuring pot like a *siṃpha*, filled with rice, popped rice, peanuts, acorns, steamed rice flakes as well as a few coins. With the *kule* she touches first the right knee and the right shoulder of each person and then pours the contents over the bowed head of the recipient and his *mandaḥ*. The action is repeated with the left knee and the left shoulder and once more with the left and the right shoulder. Variations exist: in some cases the body will first be touched cross-wise (left shoulder, right knee etc.) but the essence remains the same. The body is honoured and both head and *mandaḥ* receive the shower of the ingredients from the kule. At the end of the row, logically, two women have to bestow the honour upon each other.

Finally the head of the household cuts small pieces from the skin of one *taḥsi* and passes them on as *prasāda*. Mha pūjā is completed with the handing over by one or two women of the fruits assembled next to the *mandaḥ* plus a cotton string ending in a multicoloured cotton pieces. There is no counterprestation to the women who present all these items, something, which will be quite different in the ceremony of the next day.

After the presentation of these ritual presents the whole row is cleared away, first with a mixture of cowdung, red earth and straw to secure the purity of the act, then only with a brush. Following the removal of the sacred diagrams, in some cases with the *kheluitāḥ* still burning on them, *sagaṃ* is eaten. *Sagaṃ* is taken at the completion of numerous family ceremonies in Nepal, and consists of a piece of bread with an egg, a piece of roast meat and a dried fish, to be consumed with an earthen plate or bowl with alcohol in the other hand. After that an eleborate feast is eaten.

The Mha pūjā as described above is the ceremony such as celebrated by a Shrestha family in the small town of Sankhu (see also Shrestha 2002). Place, caste, and family variations exist and it might be worthwhile to conduct a comparative study on Tihār. I mention only one of the most frequent variations: in most cases Śivadūta and Yamadūta, or Yamarāj and Citragupta, are positioned each on either side of the row of people. They need not be represented by riceflour images but may just be present by their own , which will be worshipped like the others. In the Shrestha family taken as an example, Yamadūta and Śivadūta are, in the ceremony of the next day, shifted from the head to the tail of the row. But then, their treatment will also be different.

Kijā pūjā

Kijā pūjā is, as far as the ingredients are concerned, almost similar to Mha pūjā, but it is very different in its purport and social composition. The name Kijā pūjā (Nep. *Bhāi ṭikā*) would literally amount to the worship (by their sisters) of younger brothers, but among the Newars generally sisters worship all their brothers (Photo 25). If possible, all married women return to their parental house on this day to worship their brothers.

For Kijā pūjā a row of *mandaḥs* is drawn, which are exactly the same as the day before. The difference is in the position of Yamadūta and Śivadūta, which are shifted to the tail end and are not, at start, worshipped with *pūjā* (red powder, flowers, rice, etc.) but with a thread of cloth only. Furthermore the *mandaḥs* are this time drawn for the male members of the family only – the women just have a serving role.

The worship starts like the day before with lighting the sukundā and offering pūjā to the gods by the eldest male at the head of the row, and continues in much the same way with the worship of the *mandaḥs* and the *taḥsi* fruits. The different social set-up manifests itself in the handing over of the *kheluitāḥ* by the sisters, who are this time not taking them themselves. The men receive the burning *kheluitāḥ* by first throwing pūjā of vākijāki (a mixture of paddy and rice) and then put them, like the day before, crosswise over the *mandaḥ* (with the walnut as a hold).

The sisters worship the bodies of the brothers and pour the contents of the kule over their heads and *mandaḥs* three times. Then the sisters give all fruits to the brothers together with strings of *gvaysvāṃ*, a gift, which is again greeted with a *pūjā* of *vākijāki*. The garland of *gvaysvāṃ* is the most significant because it will be durable. Sweetmeats are added to it, and then *sagaṃ*, and finally pieces of *taḥsi* skin in yoghurt are served. At the tail end, Yamadūta and Śivadūta receive none of all this, but only crushed rice with yoghurt and ginger, items which are more generally used to ward off evil forces. It appears that on this occasion the messengers of Death are not treated as honoured guests but as intruders to be kept at bay – their usual position. Still they are not neglected or left out, but a telling story makes clear how they are this time not seen as part of the inner self but as takers of bodies.

Once Yamarāj came to take a man's body on the day of Kijā pūjā and at the moment that his sister was worshipping him. The sister pleaded with Yamarāj to let her complete the worship, which included the *pūjā* for Yamarāj himself. The latter,

Photo 25.
Kijā pūjā, the ceremony of sisters worshipping brothers (1991).

pleased by this worship of himself, offered her a boon. The sister then asked him not to take away her brother before the *mandaḥ* of oil had dried up, the walnut was rotten and the *gvaysvāṃ* had withered. According to some versions Yama waited a long time before giving up. In other accounts of the story he immediately rewarded the sister for her cleverness and dedication and extended her brother's life.

In the story the imperishable items of the worship, which are also used in Mha pūjā, are suddenly provided with a meaningful context. At the same time it is clear that Yama does not forsake his claims, not even on the days that he is himself received by the living – although he has a certain pliancy. The ambivalence is well expressed by the different positions, which Yamadūta and Śivadūta occupy in the two subsequent ceremonies: as guests of honour at the head of the row and as guests in the rear to be kept at bay.

Again it must be stressed that Kijā pūjā is not performed in every house in the same way. It also happens that during Mha pūjā Yamadūta has the form of a *mandaḥ* at the head of the row while Śivadūta has his *mandaḥ* at the tail. During Kijā pūjā they retain their positions and receive on their *mandaḥs* the same items of worship as the human participants get. The need for a comparative study is obvious, but made difficult because it concerns a household ceremony for which one has to be invited.

After the pieces of *taḥsi* in yoghurt have been served, all *mandaḥs* are cleared including those of Yamadūta and Śivadūta if they are represented in that way. In case of the riceflour images they are likewise done away with, like *gvaḥjās*, which are also treated as garbage once the gods invoked in them are dismissed. The clearing is first done as before, in a pure way, with a mixture of cowdung, earth and a straw bunch – or simply with a banana skin. After that a brush is used to do the true cleaning.

At this point again Kijā pūjā deviates from Mha pūjā with regard to the exchange expected. In return for their worship of the brothers the sisters expect and receive a *dakṣiṇā* which must preferably consist of money together with a *sārī* or a piece of cloth. The interaction is completely different from Mha pūjā, in which each person in principle performs his *pūjā* on his own behalf. The ending of Kijā pūjā is the same again as in Mha pūjā: a feast is enjoyed by everybody, men first.

Conclusion

Comparison of the three consecutive days of Lakṣmī pūjā, Mha pūjā and Kijā pūjā shows the elementary social relationships in an almost crystallized way. The conjugal relation-ships within the extended family occupy a central position in Lakṣmī pūjā, directed as it is at the prosperity and productivity of the family. Kijā pūjā, on the contrary, shows the enduring importance of the brother-sister relationship in a society, which is usually characterized as completely patrilineal, and in which indeed married daughters do no longer have access to the family shrine in their parental home. The two ceremonies are sharply opposed to each other in social terms: during Lakṣmī pūjā the out-married sisters are not allowed to attend, while during Kijā pūjā they are obliged to come.

In between those two days stands Mha pūjā, on the day of the turn of the year. Its emphasis on individual participation and the total absence of exchange appears to transcend the ceremonies of the preceding and the following day. Mha pūjā is a society-transcending occasion, in which each participant is essentially connected with the mystical diagram of his own self. The *mandaḥ* might be called the external soul of the person, and is intimately connected with death. Ideas of transmigration do not appear to play any role, but the divinity of the external soul is apparent from the worship, which the *mandaḥ* receives.

The *mandaḥs*, which are drawn on the day of Kijā pūjā are identical with those of the previous days and cannot have an entirely different meaning: again they represent the external soul with death as its divine aspect. In this case, however, the sisters explicitly ask the divinity to give their brothers a long life. A split is brought about between the two aspects of the diagram: the representation of the Self and the representation of Death. When they hand over the burning *kheluitāḥ* to be put on the *mandaḥ* the sisters ask Death to extend the life of their brothers. Death as a divinity is set apart and faced with a request for life. Such a notion of Death is not absent from Mha pūjā either: the presence of Yamadūta and Śivadūta or Yamarāj and Citragupta as guests indicate their identities as gods outside man. In the , however, death and the self are fused, and no exchange takes place in which death as a divinity is requested to extend individual lives. The jocular remarks about the burning of the *kheluitāḥ* indicate, however, that the idea of lengthening life is also present there, albeit subdued.

The two aspects of Death, as a god claiming bodies and as a part of the self, do not differ from the dualistic view on death in the Brāhmaṇas. As pointed out above, Prajāpati, by conquering Mṛtyu, also assimilated him as part of his own self. At the same time, however, Death remains a separate entity.

In this connection it is interesting that in the view of the late Vedic prose texts (Brāhmaṇas) Prajāpati is equated with the Year, that is with (finite) Time, and so with Death. The conception of Death as the Year, in which Death is assimilated to Prajāpati, on the one hand, and of Death as the independent claimer of bodies on the other hand, fits in well with the ceremonies of the Turn of the Year in Nepal. During Mha pūjā, on the actual New Year's Day, the assimilated aspect of death receives the emphasis: Death as immanent in the Self. During Kijā pūjā the next day Death is foremost seen as the god (Yama) who claims lives. An exchange is established in which the sisters serve as priests for their brothers and receive a *dakṣiṇā*. It is, of course, also seen as an act of devotion of sisters for brothers, but it must be kept in mind that the common model of female-male devotion is the relation between husband and wife, and not the bond between brother and sister.

The conjugal relationships receive their emphasis during Lakṣmī pūjā as a family ceremony, but the latter event is an ordinary *pūjā* in which no *mandaḥs* are drawn for the participants. Death although announced by crows and dogs as messengers, gives no direct sign of his presence in Lakṣmī pūjā. Wealth and procreation, the transient prosperity of life, can, however, be seen as the panoply of Death. Similarly the licentious behaviour, which manifests itself in gambling, can be seen as bearing the imprint of Yama. The passage in the Jaiminīya Brāhmaṇa about the contest between Prajāpati and Mṛtyu is, it should be mentioned, also meant to explain the Mahāvrata festival, which is stylized in its classical form, but containing 'the remnants of a rowdy and orgiastic New Year festival' (Heesterman 1985: 55).

Tihār is a particular celebration of death, in which neither mourning nor sacrifice occur. It is the god of death himself who is worshipped both as a guest to this world and as immanent in everybody living. Yet there is a connection between the Dasain sacrifice, made in every family on the ninth day and the feast in the night of Lakṣmī pūjā. The meal must contain small pieces of dried meat (*sukūlā*) of chicken, goat, and buffalo. At least one of the dried meats, usually that of the goat, derives from the sacrifice during Dasain. In that way the feast in Lakṣmī pūjā contains an element which turns it into a sacrificial meal and which establishes a straight connection between the slaughter of Dasain and the peaceful transition of the year.

All five days together, called Yama pañcak, are sometimes also termed *pañcarātri*, in contradistinction, but also in line with the designation *navarātri* for Dasain. Neither Lakṣmī nor Yama receive a sacrifice during *pañcarātri*, but a tiny piece of *prasād* of *navarātri* establishes the link between the sacrificial outburst of Dasain and the feast of Lakṣmī pūjā in the new moon night of Tihār. At the same time Tihār is a conclusion and a new beginning. It is the conclusion of the period of the great celebrations of death. Sacrifices will continue to precede or accompany every local *yātrā*, but the period in which sacrifice stood on its own and occupied a central position is over. Likewise *śrāddhas* for the deceased will continue on different occasions, but the massive explosions of grief and joy are over.

Tihār concludes the cycle of festivals in which the memorial as well as the agonistic celebration of death dominated the ritual scene. The break should not be exaggerated, but there is a clear shift from ceremonies of death to those of life. One might see the start of this shift in Kijā pūjā itself already, in which Death is in fact asked to leave – formulated as a request by the sisters on behalf of their brothers. After Tihār the marriage season starts, although, at least nowadays, the practice is to wait with marriages till the end of the month of Kārtik. In Tihār the first rice of the new harvest can be consumed. Talks about the shares in the harvest and the rent to be paid by tenants will have started before, but during Tihār such talks should not be conducted. Gambling is allowed, but talk about debts must be postponed.

Life takes a new turn after Tihār, also on the ritual level. The massive celebrations of death are over and give way to various local festivals in which those of the goddesses prevail. The coming period may therefore be termed 'Marches of the Goddesses' – a brief survey of which will be found as an appendix at the end of this book. Ritual life becomes localized and moves away from the palace as the centre and the general populace as the celebrants. Remarkably the first march of a (*mātṛkā*) goddess, which crosses Kathmandu starts during Tihār itself. It is the *yātrā* of the goddess Maitidevī whose *pīṭha* is located east of Kathmandu. Because her *yātrā* coincides with Tihār, the *guthi* members celebrate Mha pūjā with their goddess, but do so after the *yātrā* is completed, a few days after the turn of the year. Thus we see that Tihār constitutes a break in the ritual cycle and a definite shift of emphasis to the local family level, but not an interruption in the string of Kathmandu's festivals.

Concluding Remarks

J.C. Heesterman and Sj.M. Zanen

One may be inclined to assume that the festivals of the 'four months' period (*caturmāsa, caumāsa*) from the middle of the rainy season till the end of the year reflect the course of the agricultural activity of this part of the year, working up to the climax, the harvest. However, as we have come to see, the festive calendar of the 'four months' is not directly related to agriculture. We did not even find clear traces of a harvest festival. Nor does the – admittedly rather hackneyed – notion of fertility rites have much explanatory capacity. The purport of the festivals studied in the preceding chapters lies elsewhere.

Although there is no sharp divide between these festivals and those of the other part of the year, the former differ in their overriding concern with death – a concern they have, each in its own way, in common and thereby stand apart from other festive occasions of the year. The *caturmāsa* festivals are different in that they are collective affairs, tending to be supralocal, crossing the border between the upper and the lower part of the town, and so involving the town as a whole. The festivals preceding or following the 'four months', on the other hand, put greater emphasis on the local and familial aspect.

The concern with death that characterizes the *Caturmāsa* festivals does not mean that they are imbued with a gloomy *memento mori* atmosphere. Nor do the care for the departed or the cult of the ancestors dominate the festive proceedings. There is, to be sure, room for mourning the deceased and the thought of their afterlife. Nor are episodes of solemnity missing. But the overall impression is one of overwhelming exuberance. The autumn festivals are celebrations – hence the title of the present study, 'Celebrations of Death'.

The point is these festivals are basically *sacrificial* feasts. Apart from formal sacrifices forming part of the successive festivals the underlying notion appears in various ways to be that of sacrifice, more specifically of sacrificial death. Generally speaking, sacrifice is the way to deal with – as different from solving – the riddle of life and death. Significantly, in the Vedic ritual texts cremation is viewed as man's ultimate sacrifice (*antyeṣṭi*). If the dominant feature of the festivals is the procession (*yātrā*), it should be recalled that sacrifice is not the static event, not passing beyond the narrowly circumscribed sacrificial area we know from the late Vedic *srauta* ritual; it is essentially a process involving ample spatial movement of which the otherwise static Vedic sacrifice still shows telling traces.

The sacrificial space is defined – though not restricted – by the central part of the city with the royal palace at Hanumānḍhokā on the one hand and on the other by the open air sanctuaries (*pīṭha*) of the eight *mātṛkā* goddesses which surrounded the city. This area is further marked by a SW–NE running dividing line (part of an old trade route) between northern upper and the southern lower town (Thane and Kvane) suggesting an agonistic tension. In fact, many *yātrās* – not only the sword processions – have a distinct agonistic aspect, as also the dancers' performances. Put differenlty, the sacrificial area formed by Kathmandu is not just a "sacred space" but a sacrificial arena.

Related to the notion of sacrifice underlying the celebrations of the *caturmāsa* is the theme of kingship, which comes to the fore in the last and most impressive part, in the Indra yātrā and in Dasain. Here the king appears as the exemplar of sacrifice, being both sacrificer and victim. As such he presides over the sacrifice meant to control, assuage and channel 'the agonistic tenstions.' The two main themes, then, of the series of 'celebrations of death' are sacrifice and kingship. A brief review of the *Caturmāsa* festivals should illustrate how the two themes are ritually enacted so as to elucidate the enigmatic process of life and death.

Gathāṃmugaḥ at the start of the festival cycle, on the new moon day of the month Srāvaṇa (July-August), is itself a fire sacrifice. It centres on the cremation of a reed effigy of the ghost-god that gave his name to the festival. A man of the Poḍe (Sweeper, Fisherman) caste sets fire to the effigy and then must take place on a heap of straw put before the effigy. Together with the burning mass he is quickly dragged to the cremation ground on the riverside and immersed in the water. Not surprisingly it is not easy to find a Poḍe willing to play the game. What we see here is a crude but clear reflection of the funerary cremation – man's ultimate sacrifice – and the expulsion of the as yet unpacified ghost. It even seems to suggest an original background of human sacrifice (or self-sacrifice) – a suggestion that is supported by the legend of the man-eating ogre Gathāṃmugaḥ.

Is Gathāṃmugaḥ a representation of death, cremation and expulsion, Gāi yātrā, the 'Procession of the Cows', following two or three days later, is concerned with the way to heaven of the departed who died during the past year. Each family in which a death occurred sends out a procession featuring cows represented by boys with cow masks as well as, in the case of wealthy families, live cows. The individual procession groups join in a long string following the procession path round the town. Recalling the Vedic notion that the cows given as a gift (*dakṣiṇā*) to the Brahmin officiants make the sacrificer reach heaven after his death, the 'Procession of the Cows' represents the way to heaven of the recently departed. Although sacrifice is lacking in the Gāi yātrā as such, the notion of the *dakṣiṇā* suggests a sacrificial aspect. Indeed the live cows that were taken along in the procession are afterwards given to Brahmins. Thus Gāi yātrā is, as it were, the conclusion of the sacrifice of Gathāṃmugaḥ.

The festival season rises to an ever increasing degree of intensity with the eight days of Indra yātrā – starting three days before the full moon in the middle of the month Bhādra (roughly September) followed at the beginning of the next month by its exuberant climax during the ten days of Dasain. Mourning is continued on the first day with another circumambulation of the town. But the distinguishing feature of Indra yātrā is that here the theme of sacrifice is intimately connected with kingship. This theme is already signalled in the morning of the first day by raising a pole, some 25 m. high, in honour of Indra, divine warrior and king of the gods, on the central square opposite the royal palace. Here, however, Indra is not the victorious king whose victory is celebrated by the raising of the pole – as one might expect – but, on the contrary, he is a captive, guilty of transgression.

The motif of the captive king is reinforced by the severed head of Bhairava, the transgressive violent form of Śiva. Bhairava, whose head is on display at various places in the town, some of them at set times spouting rice beer through a tube placed in its mouth, takes up an even more important place in the festival than Indra. He is however, not the recipient of sacrifice but the victim whose severed head holds the life-giving beverage. The captive warrior king and the beer spouting head fit in well with the sacrificial background. To this background they add a further dimension, the violent sacrificial contest. Bhairava having been – according to local legend – a king killed by Kṛṣṇa who severed his head in an epic battle, that is in the 'sacrifice of battle' (*raṇayajña*) as it is called in the Mahābhārata. The notion of such sacrificial fights also finds expression in the dances performed during the festival's processions as well as by less ritualized street fights.

In more general terms, what it comes down to is the precarious ambiguity of kingship. The king must be strengthened by the blessing of the divine patron of the realm, the goddess Taleju. Impersonated by a prepuberal girl – the living goddess referred to as Kumārī, Princess –, Taleju makes her appearance during various processions accompanied by dancers and musicians. It is on the last day of the festival, when she has made a round of the displayed images of the captive Indra and Bhairava's severed head that Kumārī confirms the king in his reign by putting the *ṭikā* marking her blessing on the king's forehead.

Even though the king is confirmed by Kumārī's blessing, this does not change the fundamental ambiguity of his kingship. His role is still that of the exemplar of sacrifice. So Indra yātrā cannot and does not guarantee the stability of the social and cosmic order that depends on the king. These remain subject to the uncertainty of the sacrificial context. Indra yātrā, then, prepares the way for the upheaval of Dasain.

The interrelated motifs of sacrifice – kingship and the 'battle of sacrifice' – are again deployed in Dasain, albeit with greater, even riotous intensity. The first five days are devoted to another form of Bhairava, the mythic king Pacalī, killed for sexual transgression. His open-air shrine (*pīṭha*), south of the town – several gods have such shrines outside the town –, is the place where Pacalī was killed, or where he hid when pursued, appositely near a burning *ghāṭ*. Represented by a big jar – his head –, which after elaborate rites of enlivening and being filled with rice beer, he is taken in a rowdy procession during the night of the fifth day to the central square where the Bhairava yātrā ends in a mock assault on the royal palace.

An important feature of Dasain is the cult of Taleju we already met in the Indra yātrā. Her image is brought down on the seventh day from her temple overlooking the royal palace compound in the town centre to a special room in the palace facing her temple. In the 'dark' night of the eighth day a massive sacrifice of buffaloes and goats is performed, first in the barracks by army personnel assisted by non-Newar officiants and then again in the courtyard between her room in the palace and the temple another such sacrifice, which is entirely a Newar affair.

In contradistinction to Indra yātrā, where the aspect of kingship is completely integrated in Newar ritual, we see here a split between the sacrifice as a state solemnity of the royal house of the Gorkhā dynasty on the one hand and on the other the Newar sacrifice harking back to the ancient Newar kings. Apart from the nightly double sacrifice in honour of state and kingship private sacrifices are performed on the next, the ninth, day at the *pīṭhas* surrounding Kathmandu.

The climax of the festival, however, is the last, the 'Tenth Day of Victory' (Vijayā Daśamī). It is marked by local sword processions (*pāyāḥ*) that set out from local shrines (*dyocheṃs*) for a short circuit in the locality. Later, at night a *pāyāḥ* sets out also from the royal palace, which is, however, hardly more impressive than the local daytime processions. This is entirely different, though, when the royal *pāyāḥ* involves the rite known as *khaḍga siddhi*, the exchange of swords between a 'divine' dancer from a special dancing troupe, representing either Pacalī or the goddess Bhadrakālī and the king. This occurs once in twelve years in the case of Pacalī and once in another twelve year cycle when it is Bhadrakālī's turn (that is, four years after Pacalī the king's counterpart is Bhadrakālī and so eight years after that it is again Pacalī's turn).

Mythologically speaking, the 'victory' evoked by the dancers of the 'triumphant tenth' day is the victory of the goddess over the buffalo demon, Mahiṣāsura, who on being slain turns into her devotee. A similar paradoxical relationship is enacted in the case of Kumārī and Daitya as evoked by the dancers of Indra yātrā. What these and numerous other performances during the festival express is not just the triumphant strengthening of the always precarious position of the king. It is above all the predicament of man faced with the mystery of life and death that the dancers leading the processions make all but tangible throughout the autumnal cycle of festivals. When the king comes to the fore – as he does in the two last festivals –, he does so as the exemplar of man's predicament.

Finally, it is to man in his earthly domestic circumstances – be they ever so homely – that the next feast, Tihār, showing in the new year, veers round again. During this feast a shift occurs from attention to death to the generation of life and prosperity, highlighted by the worship of Lakṣmī, the goddess of Wealth, on the third day of the feast. During Yama pañcak, the five days of Yama, when neither mourning nor sacrifice occur, death is celebrated as a visitor among the living and as part of their own selves. The first two days are dedicated to crows as the immortal messengers from the realm of Death, and to dogs as the carriers and gatekeepers of Yama. The third day cows are worshipped, pointing either to their role as intermediaries between this and yonder world, as in Gāi yātrā, or as the worship of wealth embodied, preceding the visit of Lakṣmī herself.

New Year's day of the Nepal era follows upon the new moon night of Lakṣmī pūjā and is celebrated by the worship of the Self during Mha pūjā, and, the following day, by Kijā pūjā, the worship of brothers by their sisters. During both worships *mandaḥs* (*maṇḍalas*), drawn in front of all members of the family, represent the Self of every person but also Death as the divinity in man. It seems that these rituals signify that, on the one hand, Death is part of every mortal being, on the other hand Death remains a deity outside man, the claimer of bodies. The same duality can be traced in the Brāhmaṇas in which Death is conquered by and assimilated to Prajāpati, and yet remains present as a separate deity.

The conception of Death as the Year, as in the Vedas Prajāpati is equated with the Year, fits in well with the rituals of the turn of the year in Nepal. Whereas during Mha pūjā, New Year's Eve, the assimilated aspect of death receives the emphasis, during Kijā pūjā, New Year's Day, on the contrary, Death is seen as the external god (Yama, Mṛtyu) who claims lives.

Tihār thus implies a conclusion and a new beginning. It is the conclusion of the period of the great celebrations of death and sacrifice, and a beginning of festivals of life, which concern marital exchange and fertility. The latter festivals are more localized, away from the palace and from the general public, and usually involve goddesses. The transition is clearly marked during *Kijā pūjā*, when Death is in fact asked to leave the living in peace.

APPENDIX I:
Festivals observed during the period of Caturmāsa

Newar months are reckoned from new moon to new moon, the full moon marking the middle of the month. The two halves of the month are marked by waxing and waning, resp. the 'bright' and 'dark' halves of the month.

Name of Festival	**Nepali dates (beginning/end)**	**Western calendar** (approximately)
Hariśayanī Ekādaśī, Lord Viṣṇu's sleep, the beginning of Caturmāsa	11th day of the bright half of Dillā (Āṣādha)	June/July
Tulasī piye, the plantation of *tulasī* plant in the following day (Chapter 2)	12th day of the bright half of Dillā (Āṣādha)	June/July
Gathāṃmugaḥ, purification of houses and the expulsion of the "ghost god" from every quarter of town (Chapter 3)	14th day of the dark half of Dillā (Śrāvan)	July/August
Janai pūrṇimā and Gāi jātrā (Sāpāru), the procession of cows (Chapter 4)	full-moon day to 7th day of the dark half of Guṃlā (Śrāvan/Bhādra)	August
Kāyāṣṭamī, the day of pilgrimage to the shrine of Kāgeśvar Mahādev and the performances of the annual Devī dances (Chapter 5)	8th day of the bright half of Yaṃlā (Bhādra)	September
Indra yātrā: the erection of Indra pole (*yaḥsiṃ thane*), the procession of Kumāri, etc. (Chapter 5)	12th day of the bright half of Yaṃlā to 4th day of the dark half of Yaṃlā (Bhādra/Āśvin)	September
Sorha śrāddha, the sixteen days dedicated to *śrāddha* rituals for the deceased (Chapter 5)	1st to 15th day of the dark half of Yaṃlā (Āśvin)	September
Dasain (Mohanī) -Pacalī bhairav yātrā (Chapter 6) -Twelve-yearly divine dances of the Gathu (Chapter 7) -Sacrifice & sword processions (Chapter 8)	1st to 10th day of the bright half of Kaulā (Āśvin)	Sept./October
Katiṃ punhi (Chapter 8)	full-moon day of Kaulā (Āsvin)	October
Tihār, the turn of the ritual year, Yamapañcaka (Chapter 8)	13th day of the dark half of Kaulā to 2nd day of the bright half of Kachalā (Kārtik)	Oct./November
Haribodhinī Ekādaśī: the awakening of Viṣṇu	11th day of the bright half of Kachalā (Kārtik)	Oct./November
The end of Caturmāsa	full-moon day of Kachalā	November

APPENDIX II:
Marches of the Goddesses

The second part of A.W. van den Hoek's projected study of *The Ritual Structure of Kathmandu City* was called 'Marches of the Goddesses.' Part one is the present book. Part two was planned to contain the following chapters:

Transition: The Turn of the Ritual Year

The Goddess Maiti Devī celebrates Tihār – in secret.
- Sacrifice and homa on the eve of Lakṣmī pūjā.
- *Yātrā* during Tihār.
- Celebration of Tihār at the conclusion of the *yātrā*.
- The transition: Ajimā yātrās and human marriages.

Guhyeśvarī yātrā: From the centre to the jungle.
- From Taleju Bhavānī to the Guhyeśvarī *pīṭha* in Mṛgasthalī.
- The overnight stay of the Guhyeśvarī and Bhairava images (*yantras*) at the pīṭha; sacrifice.
- The return journey via Paśupatināth.
- The absence of fire-sacrifice.
- Conclusion: general and specific aspects.

Indrāyaṇī yātrā: The festival of the Northern part of town.
- Preparatory acts and invitation (*nimantraṇa*)
- Participating gods and *guthis*; the Thakū juju ('ceremonial king') as yajamāna.
- Three buffalo sacrifices and their fruits, esp. the heads of the sacrifice.
- The *sarpahoma* – sacrifice of serpents and other wild animals into the fire. Comparison with *sarpahoma* in Sankhu, Theco and Pālung
- The Kirtipur connection.
- The *yātrā* route and its deviations (by invitation) to pious devotees and *mhyāy masta*, i.e. out-married daughters.
- The *lasakusa* – welcoming ceremony.
- The *Bicāḥ* (<Skt. Visarjana?) *Pūjā*.
- Story of Indrāyaṇī (Luti Ajimā) and her sisters; connections with the Bhadrakālī (Lumari Ajimā) *yātrā*.

Hāritī Ajimā: The short twelve-yearly journey of the goddess of smallpox.
- Context: Misā Samyek, the gathering of women on the day after the great Samyek (12 yearly) of the high Buddhist casts celebrated according to the solar calendar on Māgh Saṃkrānti (14th of January) and graced by the king.

- The journey of Hāritī downhill from Svayambhū and up again.
- The story of the goddess: from ogress to protectress of children.
- Hāritī Ajimā and faith – healing.
- Conclusion: Pecularities of the shortest *yātrā*.

Milā Punhi: The end of Pauṣa, the darkest month.
- Cāṃgu Nārāyaṇa's journey (as *kalaśa*) from his hilltop sanctuary to the Hanumānḍhokā palace in Kathmandu.
- Start of the Svasthānī - reading, and of the Svasthāni - *vrata* in Sankhu. Journeys of the *vratins* in Kathmandu Valley.
- Completion of Svasthānī *vrata* at the next full moon (Si Punhi); *aśvamedha* in Sankhu.

Holi Punhi and the feeding of the ogre Gurumāpā.
- Holi in Nepal, stories and significance. The official celebration.
- The feeding of Gurumāpā at Tundikhel; the Kilāgal *guthi*.
- The aftermath of Holi: Cakaṃdyo yātrā in north Kathmandu.
- Conclusion: interconnections; the Pradhāns of Kathmandu.

Pāhāṃ Cahre: The host of goddess marches.
- Duru *cyaṃ cyaṃ*: Lord Paśupatināth announces Pāhāṃ Cahre.
- The twofold *yātrā* of Bhadrakālī; (Lumari Ajimā) the two *Dyocheṃs* (god-houses) and the *pīṭha* (seat of the goddess). The *homa* at the *pīṭha*.
- Kaṃkesvarī (Kaṃga Ajimā) yātrā. The *homa* at he *pīṭha*.
- Naradevī yātrā. The secret *homa* in the temple. The yearly Sveta Kālī dances and their twelve-yearly cycle.
- The Naradevī *guthis*.
- Luṃcubhulu Ajimā yātrā.
- Takhti Ajimā (Nilvārāhī) yātrā.
- Nhāykaṃtalā Ajimā yātrā.
- Gaṇeśa yātrās and Narasiṃha yātrā.
- The worship of Luku Mahādyo, the hidden Śiva.
- Conclusion: Spatial distribution, coherence (get-together of three goddesses at Tundikhel and Asan); avoidence and challenges. Comparison with the Khaḍga yātrā of Dasain, and with Bālā Carhe (Indrāyaṇī yātrā).

Lhuti Punhi: Completing the round of Kathmandu's goddesses.
- Preceding the full moon: Caitra Dasain and Seto-Matsyendranāth yātrā.
- Mhaypi Ajimā yātrā: from Nāy Tvāḥ to the *pīṭha* on a forested hill north of Kathmandu; secret *homa* in Caturdaśī night. Buddhist Shrestha *yajamānas*, Jyapu and Prajāpati *guthis* and a Vajrācārya officiant.
- In Punhi night the statues depart for a round of the northern quarters of the city – outside the city boundaries proper. Rest at Talāchi near the *dyocheṃ*.

Visits to *mhyay masta*.
- On Pāru (Pratipadā) the *khat* (palanquin) with Mhaypi is carried around the city and at night received with *lasakusa* in the *dyocheṃ*.
- Connection with the Indrāyaṇī yātrā of Manamaiju, of which the Thamel Pradhān are the patrons.
- Pāsikva Ajimā yātrā: is reduced to a day of exhibition of the procession statues in the *pīṭha*.
- Kamalādī Gaṇeśa yātrā.
- Towards the periphery: the journey of Kanelacok Bhagavatī to Nuwākoṭ to witness the *homa* there. Bālāju Melā with Gaṇeśa yātrā from Purāno Guhyeśvarī.
- The eastward line: Hadigaon Ajimā yātrās and the start of Sankhu Vajrayoginī yātrā and Bhaktapur Bisket yātrā: the official New Year according to the solar calendar on April 14. Thimi and Bode yātrās.

Transition: Feeding the Ghosts and the Spirits (From Akṣaya Tṛtīyā to Sithi Nakhaḥ)
- *bau holegu*: feasting the *bhūtpret* along the city's procession route, luring them into the city.
- Feasting the Digudyo at the ancestral shrines.
- Cleaning the wells on Sithi Nakhaḥ day, the last day of Digudyo (*kuldevatā*) worship.
- Kumār yātrā, the last festival before the rice-planting season.
- The sequel up to next Gathāṃugaḥ: Bhala Bhala Aṣṭamī and the mystery of divine death; Nāga Pañcamī: the household worship of the immortal serpents who sustain the world.
- Conclusion: the intangible forces propitiated; family and lineage solidarity resuscitated or broken up.

Conclusion: The Ritual Structure of Kathmandu

Notes

Notes to Preface

1. See: Bal Gopal Shrestha and Han F. Vermeulen (2001), 'In Memoriam Bert van den Hoek (1951-2001).' *European Bulletin of Himalayan Research* 20-21: 151-163. This obituary includes a bibliography of A.W. van den Hoek. An updated version of this list is included after the bibliography at the end of this book.
2. The film *Sacrifice of Serpents* was first shown at the opening of the festival of South Asian documentaries 'Film South Asia 1997' at Kathmandu, October 25-28, 1997. It was selected for the Septième Bilan du Film Ethnographique in Paris, March 23-28, 1998; the Ethnographic Filmfestival 'Beeld voor Beeld 1998' in Amsterdam, June 4-7, 1998; the Interntional Convention of Asia Scholars (ICAS-1) at Noordwijkerhout, June 25-28 1998; and the Filmfestival of the Society for Visual Anthropology during the Annual Meeting of the American Anthropological Association in Philadelphia, December 2-4, 1998. At the latter festival the film received an Award of Commendation from the Society for Visual Anthropology for making "a thorough documentation of a multi-day festival which is slow paced with spare narration and 'time to see.' A depth of Vedic scholarship and many years of fieldwork by the anthropologist are combined with Nepalese team assistants who were community members to make an informed film record of the event."
3. In July 2001, Bert had successfully applied for a research affiliation at the Centre for Nepal and Asian Studies (CNAS), Tribhuvan University, Kathmandu, to complement *Caturmāsa*. The study of the other festivals of the annual cycle would have completed his research on '*The Ritual Structure of Kathmandu*' (See Appendix II).

Notes to Chapter 1

1. Revised version of a paper presented at the CNWS Symposium 'Urban Images' in Leiden, January 6-9, 1992, and published in Peter J.M. Nas (ed.) *Urban Symbolism*, Leiden/New York/Köln: E.J. Brill, 1993, pp. 360-377.
2. The latter juju also worships the goddess Taleju in his lāykū (New. palace) but according to his own saying, the worship of this royal goddess was probably copied from the Malla example in later times.
3. For the festival of Pacalī Bhairava and and the story connected with him, see chapter 6.
4. On Bhadrakālī, see further below, chapter 7.

Notes to Chapter 2

1. During this period, with the exception of two auspicious days in Dasain, no favourable moments for marriage occur.

Notes to Chapter 3

1. Āsakaji Vajrācārya traces the expulsion of Ghaṇṭākarṇa in the Rudrāyamala Tantra, where it could, however, not to be found by me.
2. Dhooswan Sayami (1985: 5) writes that farmers keep a piece of land uncultivated to honour Gathāṃmugaḥ as protector of the fields. To be sure, many farmers maintain such a piece of land (called *dumbo*) as a refuge for the inhabitants of the earth, serpents in particular, and sometimes in memory of a dead ancestor. The worship of Gathāṃmugaḥ in that context has not been encountered by the present author.

Notes to Chapter 4

1. In Sankhu, however, the Poḍe caste does participate in the procession (Shrestha 2002: 139, 247). (eds.)
2. The part of the cow in the Gāi yātrā is reminiscent of the cow sacrificed at a funeral (as the anustaraṇī cow) or given as *dakṣiṇā* to a Brahmin. This cow should help the deceased to pass the Vaitaraṇī river or, conversely bring the mourners, holding on to its tail, safely back to their home after the cremation (see Caland 1896: 8; Śatapatha Brāḥmaṇa 13.8.4.6 and Eggeling 1900: 438n.). Interestingly, if a cow is taken in the Gāi yātrā procession it is to be given as a *dakṣiṇā* to a Brahmin. It would seem that the *dakṣiṇā* gift, as often, has come to replace the sacrificial immolation (cf. Heesterman 1993: 209). The Gāi yātrā cow, then, still bears the mark of the sacrificial origin.
3. The story goes that a Malla king whose wife was grief-stricken by the death of her son, started Gāi yātrā and included the comics to make his wife smile again (Sayami 1980: 7; Varya 1987: 233). Since then Gāi yātrā served as a yearly census of death for the kingdom. This story can hardly account for the omnipresence of the festival throughout the Valley in all its different manifestations.

Notes to Chapter 5

1. As Oldfield (1880 II: 319-320) observes, the 'only part the Gorkhās take in the Indrajatra is in the erection of a triumphal flagstaff in front of the Darbar The flagstaff is raised at night-time, and the salute fired the same time, to record the exact hour when the city fell into the power of the Gorkhas.' The raising of the Indra pole, then, though decidedly of ancient local origin, has been appropriated by the conquering Shah dynasty.
2. Other names of Indra, such as Yeṃnyādyo or Yemā, may have originated rom a connection of Indra via Yendyāta (ancient Newarī for Indra yātrā, Manandhar 1986: 216). Or they suggest an association, if not a conflaction, with Yama, the god ruling the realm of the dead.
3. Indeed in Pāṭan and Bhaktapur high crosses are erected during Indra yātrā with the mask of the god in the middle.
4. According to Surendra Man Shrestha and Baldev Juju the five ingredients represent the five elements (alcohol: *tejas*, meat: *pṛthivī*, soyabeans: *vāyu*, beaten

rice: *ākāśa*, ginger: *jala*) and are together representative of the sacrifice *par excellence*: the human one.

5. They belong to the so-called 700 (nhaysaḥ) Sāymi of Kathmandu, who are divided over nine *tvāḥ* (quarters). The Bākādeśa Mānandhar are descendants of one common ancestor and (like most of the Jyāpu *guthis*) the *guthi* members cannot marry among each other.
6. Furthermore, in Hasrat's chronicle both the dice game with Taleju and the dream which led to the worship of Kumārī are ascribed to Trailokya Malla who ruled more than one and a half century before Jayaprakāśa.
7. In 1993 the Nepālbhāṣā Academy staged a modern ballet based on the Naradevī *pyākhaṃ* with the shifting relationship between Kumārī and Daitya as the central theme.
8. The custom was revived after more than forty years in 1993, but now in a stadium and sponsored by a Kilāgal youth-club.
9. Amidst heavy security measures the king casts a perfunctory glance at the stage of the Daśāvatāra, a show with epic scenes which has been performed every evening of Indra yātrā at the high temple next to the Kumārīcheṃ.
10. In the Śatapatha Brāhmaṇa (XIV, 1, 1; Eggeling 1900: 441-443) it is Viṣṇu who is beheaded in a particular way releasing vital sap from his decapitated body (Van den Hoek 1990b: 153).
11. The innovative additions by the last Newar king, Jayaprakāśa Malla, and the conquering Shāhī dynasty, about the middle of and later in the eighteenth century – resp. Kumārī's procession (with a special three-tiered pagoda-like procession chariot) and the elaborate raising of the Indra pole at Hanumānḍhokā – clearly signalize centralization of royal authority, while making Kathmandu its exclusive seat.

Notes to Chapter 6

1. According to the *ācāju* it comes from Maccheśvarī, according to Slusser (1982 I: 324) from Martyeśvarī.
   One is reminded here of the late Vedic Prajāpati, the Lord of Creatures, who is sacrificer, victim and godhead rolled into one. This pattern equally appears to apply to Pacalī, the beheaded king and god.
2. One of the occasions in which Śiva comes together with his legion of *bhūtpret*, is his marriage with Pārvatī (Iltis 1985: 291-295).

Notes to Chapter 7

1. An earlier version of this chapter was published as an article under the title 'The Death of the Divine Dancers: The Conclusion of the Bhadrakālī *pyākhaṃ* in Kathmandu' in: Michael Allen (ed.) *Anthropology of Nepal: Peoples, Problems and Processes*. Kathmandu: Mandala Bookpoint, 1994, pp. 374-404.
2. In its highlights, the Gathu *pyākhaṃ* of Kirtipur exactly with Kathmandu's Bhadrakālī *pyākhaṃ*. Surprisingly death and cremation do not feature in the yearly

Theco dances, nor in their twelve-yearly special performance which is preceded by a serpent sacrifice (*sarpahoma*).

3. Cf. the special form of Mahālakṣmī in the Navadurgā dances of Bhaktapur (Gutschow & Basukala 1987: 137).
4. The heads of the buffaloes are not (as they often are) committed to the sacrificial fire but put in front of Bhadrakālī in the *pīṭha*. They are later to be divided as sī (shares in the head of the sacrifice) among eighteen members of the *dyo pyākhaṃ khalaḥ*, which includes the nine *sī guthi* members. As a rule, the *sī* of goat sacrifices are distributed only among the *sī guthi* members, but the goats sacrificed during the *pyākhaṃ* provide twelve parts of *sī* (by dividing the nose in two, the tongue in three parts) which are served to three members of the dancing team in addition to the *sī guthi* members.
5. For a general treatment of this and other aspects of fire sacrifice see Van den Hoek (1992).
6. In historical regard the paper by Linda Iltis (1990) on the Harisiddhi *pyākhaṃ* is most illuminating.
7. For the sword procession which the Bhadrakālī Jyāpu *guthi* brings out on the day of Vijayā Daśamī, see next chapter. For similar Bhairava procession (that has its own 12–year cycle) see Toffin (1993: 67-72).
8. For a general view of kingship and divinity in Nepal see Van den Hoek (1990b). See also Toffin (1993: esp. chapter 1-4).
9. The intermediate performance for Nāsaḥdyocheṃ (the second one) takes place at Pāhāṃ Carhe in March after the rejuvenation of the masks and the re-empowerment of the divine dancers.
10. In the cycle of Pacalī Bhairava dances the duck is released in the same way by a Rājopādhāya brahmin, who also supplies the *sī jā*.
11. The sequence is: 1. The Nāsaḥdyo *kalaśa* 2. The Mahālakṣmī mask carried on a stick 3. Siṃhinī 4. Vyāghinī 5. Indrāyaṇī 6. Pacalī Bhairava (Āju) 7. Bhadrakālī (Ajimā) 8. Vārāhī 9. Vaiṣṇavī 10. Kumārī 11. Brahmāyaṇī 12. Rudrāyaṇī 13. Gaṇeśa. In Kirtipur Gaṇeśa, also the last one in the sequence there, kindles the fire before dying himself. As the eldest son of Bhairava it is his duty to light his father's pyre.
12. Yak tails adorn the long decorated poles (*dhunyāmunyā*) with which acrobatic feats are performed and which on the way are swayed in front of the *dhimay* musicians.
13. See Van den Hoek & Shrestha (1992a: 60-62, 71); also above, p. 91.
14. The shifting of residence in keeping with the Bhadrakālī resp. the Pacalī *pyākhaṃ*, however, indicates an inner spatial distribution, as does the allotment of Bhadrakālī's panther skin to either the Vatu or the Tebāhāl *dyocheṃ*. If really pressed to the point, the Gathu may ascribe the Pacalī *pyākhaṃ* more to Kvane and the Bhadrakālī *pyākhaṃ* more to Thane, without however giving it any more significance than a mere shift of their sojourn. The dances themselves, in their view, transcend local divisions, and do both have the same range and power of

action. This view is supported by the fact that Indrāyaṇī, the sister and antagonist of Bhadrakālī, who belongs to Thane in the spatial distribution of the city and has a *yātrā* of her own, is, at the level of the Bhadrakālī *pyākhaṃ*, a member of the gaṇa embodied by the dancers.

Notes to Chapter 8

1. If a new Kumārī is to be installed, this happens during a ceremony whereby the small girl is first tested by making her walk amidst or across the severed buffalo heads (Allen 1975: 10).
2. In fact, warfare in Malla times appears to have no connection or resemblance at all to its ritual expression in Dasain. In the time of the three kingdoms war consisted of skirmishes and often surreptious raids. In D.R. Regmi's words 'the rabble played the major part in the operations', that is, up to the end of the sixteenth century when the rulers came to rely more on tribal (non-Newar) soldiers for their standing army. Yet it seems that actual warfare retained a sacrificial aspect. Regmi quotes derogatory remarks about Nepalese warfare from Father da Loro's letters (1740): 'When somebody has to sue for peace this is done when one man is killed. Whoever inflicts a loss of this type ultimately wins' and 'if you cut off the head of one of the enemies you win the battle' (Regmi 1966: 458-461, see also 1011). These eye-witness accounts resemble the descriptions of stone fights in the bed of the Viṣṇumati river which were aimed at making a victim for sacrifice (see chapter 1). They may hence indicate that warfare itself kept its sacrificial nature up to the time of the Śhāhī conquests when killing became functional.
3. It is in each family celebrated according to the *tithi*, the day of the lunar calendar on which the last deceased parent has passed away.

Notes to Chapter 9

1. The *rakṣābandhan*, the protective string which was tied around everybody's wrist at Gunhi punhi and which could before be offered to Indra during Indra yātrā (see above, chapter 4) can also and finally be attached to the tail of a cow during Tihār.
2. Manandhar's (1986: 264) complete definition is: 'a lamp pot with a receptacle for storing oil, an image of Gaṇeśa, images of serpents, an ornate handle, and a lamp'.
3. The same fruit was used in the *abhiṣeka*, the ritual bathing, of Pacalī Bhairava, see chapter 6, p. 67-68.

Bibliography

Acharya, Jayaraj

1992 *The Nepāla-Mahātmya of the Skandapurāṇa. Legends on the Sacred Places and Deities of Nepal*. Jaipur/New Delhi: Nirala Publications.

Allen, Michael R.

1975 *The Cult of Kumari: Virgin Worship in Nepal*. Kathmandu: Tribhuvan University, Institute of Nepal and Asian Studies (INAS). Republished Kathmandu: Madhab Lal Maharjan, Himalayan Book Sellers, 1980.

1994 (ed.) *Anthropology of Nepal: Peoples, Problems and Processes*. Kathmandu: Mandala Bookpoint.

Anderson, Mary M.

1975 *The Festivals of Nepal*. Delhi: Rupa & Co. Reprinted Calcutta: Rupa & Co. 1988. First published by George, Allen & Unwin in London, 1971.

Bendall, Cecil

1903 A History of Nepal and Surrounding Kingdoms (1000-1600) compiled chiefly from mss. lately discovered. *Journal of the Asiatic Society of Bengal* 72: 1-32.

1981 *Corpus Inscriptionum Indicarum* Vol. III. *Inscriptions of the Early Gupta Kings*. Revised from Fleet and edited by B. Chhabra & G.S. Gai. New Delhi: Archaeological Survey of India.

Biardeau, Madeleine

1981 L'arbre śamī et le buffle sacrificiel. In: M. Biardeau (ed.) *Autour de la déesse hindoue*. Paris: Éditions de l'École des Hautes Études et Sciences Sociales, pp. 215-243. English translation 1984.

1984 The Sami Tree and the Sacrificial Buffalo. *Contributions to Indian Sociology* (New Series) 18: 1-24.

1989 *Histoires de poteaux: Variations védiques autour de la Déesse hindoue*. Paris: Publications de l'EFEO, vol. 154.

Bista, Dor Bahadur

1976 *People of Nepal*. Kathmandu: Ratna Pustuk Bhandar. First published 1967.

Bodewitz, Hendrik Wilhelm

1973 *The Jaiminīya Brāhmaṇa I, 1-65*. Translation and commentary with a study: *Agnihotra and Pranagnihotra*. Leiden: E.J. Brill (Orientalia Rheno-Traiectina 17). Orig. PhD thesis University of Utrecht.

1976 *The Daily Evening and Morning Offering (Agnihotra) According to the Brahmanas*. Leiden: E.J. Brill (Orientalia Rheno-Traiectina 21).

Bosch, Frederik David Kan

1968 Indra's strijd met Vrta. *Bijdragen tot de Taal-, Land- en Volkenkunde* 124(2): 241-263.

Boullier, Véronique

1993 Une caste de Yogi Newar: Les Kusle-Kapali. *Bulletin de l'École française d'Extrême-Orient* 80(1): 75-106.

Bühler, George

1969 *The Laws of Manu*. New York: Dover Publications. First published 1886.

Buitenen, J.A.B. van

1931 (ed. and transl.) *The Mahābhārata*. I, The Book of the Beginning. Chicago: University of Chicago Press.

Burghart, Richard

1984 The Formation of the Concept of Nation-State in Nepal. *Journal of Asian Studies* 44(1): 101-125.

Caland, Willem

1896 *Die altindischen Todten-und Bestattungsgebräuche*. Amsterdam: Frederik Muller (Verhandelingen der Koninklijke Akademie van Wetenschappen te Amsterdam, Afdeeling Letterkunde, vol. 1, no. 6).

1931 (transl.) *The Pancavimsa Brahmana*. Calcutta.

Chattopadhyay, Kshitis Prasad

1980 *An Essay on the History of Newar Culture*. Kathmandu: Educational Enterprise. First published in *Journal and Proceedings of the Asiatic Society of Bengal*, New Series XIX (1923), No. 10, pp. 465-560.

Das, Veena

1997 *Structure and Cognition: Aspects of Hindu Rituals and Castes*. Delhi: Oxford University Press. First published 1977.

Deep, Dhurba Krishna

1978 *The Nepal Festivals*. Kathmandu: Ratna Pustak Bhandar.

Détienne, Marcel

1972 *Les jardins d'Adonis: La mythologie des aromates en Grèce*. Paris: Éditions Gallimard.

Doherty, Victor S.

1978 Notes on the Origins of the Newars of the Kathmandu Valley of Nepal. In: James F. Fisher (ed.) *Himalayan Anthropology: The Indo-Tibetan Interface*. La Haye/Paris: Mouton, pp. 433-445.

Dumont, Louis

1964 Marriage in India: The Present State of the Question. Postscript to Part One, Nayar and Newar. *Contributions to Indian Sociology* 7: 77-98.

1964 *La civilisation indienne et nous: Esquisse de sociologie comparée*. Paris: Armand Colin.

1966 *Homo Hierarchicus: Essai sur le système des castes*. Paris: Gallimard.

1970 *Homo Hierarchicus: Le Système des castes et ses implications*. 2nd edition. Paris: Gallimard. English translation 1970.

1970 *Homo Hierarchicus: The Caste System and its Implications*. London: Weidenfeld & Nicolson. Revised English edition: Chicago/London: University of Chicago Press, 1980.

Eggeling, Julius

1900 *The Śatapatha Brāhmaṇa* (transl.), Part V. Oxford: Clarendon Press (Sacred Books of the East). Repr. Delhi 1963.

Ellingson, Terry Jay

1990 Nasa: dya:. Newar God of Music, A Photo Essay. *Selected Reports in Ethnomusicology* 8: 22-227.

Fisher, James F.

1978 (ed.) *Himalayan Anthropology: The Indo-Tibetan Interface*. La Haye/Paris: Mouton.

Fürer-Haimendorf, Christoph von

1956 Elements of Newar Social Structure. *Journal of the Royal Anthropological Institute* 86(II): 15-38.

Gaborieau, Marc & Alice Thorner (eds.)

1979 *Asie du Sud: Traditions et changements*. Paris: Éditions du Centre National de la Recherche Scientifique (CNRS).

Gellner, David N.

1986 Language, Caste, Religion and Territory: Newar Identity Ancient and Modern. *European Journal of Sociology* 27: 102-148.

1992 *Monk, Householder and Tantric Priest: Newar Buddhism and its Hierarchy of Ritual*. Cambridge: Cambridge University Press. Repr. New Delhi: Cambridge University Press 1996.

Girard, René

1972 *La violence et le sacré*. Paris: Éditions Bernard Grasset.

Giuseppe, Father

1794 Account of the Kingdom of Nepal. *Asiatick Researches* II: 241-253. Repr.

New Delhi 1979, pp. 307-322.

Gonda, Jan

1967 The Indra Festival according to the Atharvavedins. *Journal of the American Oriental Society* 87: 414-429.

Greenwold, Stephen Michael

1974 Buddhist Brahmans. *European Journal of Sociology* 15: 101-123.

Gutschow, Niels

1982 *Stadtraum und Ritual der newarischen Städte im Kathmandu-Tal: Eine architecturanthropologische Untersuchung*. Stuttgart: Kohlhammer.

Gutschow, Niels & Ganesh Man Basukala

1987 The Navadurgā of Bhaktapur: Spatial Implications of an Urban Ritual. In: Niels Gutschow & Axel Michaels (eds.) *Heritage of the Kathmandu Valley*. Sankt Augustin: VGH Wissenschaftsverlag (Nepalica 4), pp. 137-165.

Gutschow, Niels & Manabajra Bajracharya

1977 Ritual as a Mediator of Space in Kathmandu. *Journal of the Nepal Research Centre* 1: 1-10.

Hamilton, Francis B.

1986 *An Account of the Kingdom of Nepal and of the Territories annexed to this Dominion by the House of Gorkha*. New Delhi: Asian Educational Services. First published 1819.

Hasrat, Bikrama Jit

1970 *History of Nepal: As Told by Its Own and Contemporary Chroniclers*. Hoshiarpur: V.V. Research Institute Book Agency.

Heesterman, Johannes Cornelis

1964 Brahmin, Ritual and Renouncer. *Wiener Zeitschrift für die Kunde Süd- und Ostasiens* 8: 1-31.

1978 The Conundrum of the King's Authority. In: J.F. Richards (ed.) *Kingship and Authority in South Asia*. Madison: University Press of Wisconsin.

1983 Other Folk's Fire. In: J. Frits Staal (ed.) *Agni: The Vedic Ritual of the Fire Altar*. Vol. 2. Berkeley: Asian Humanities Press, pp. 76-94.

1985 *The Inner Conflict of Tradition: Essays in Indian Ritual, Kingship and Society*. Chicago: University of Chicago Press.

1993 *The Broken World of Sacrifice: An Essay in Ancient Indian Ritual*. Chicago: University of Chicago Press.

Herdick, Reinhard

1986 Neue Kulte in Kirtipur. In: Bernhard Kölver (ed.) *Formen kulturellen Wandels und andere Beiträge zur Erforschung des Himālaya*. Sankt

Augustin: VGH Wissenschaftsverlag, pp. 249-282.

Hodgson, Brian Houghton

1971 *Essays on the Languages, Literature and Religion of Nepal and Tibet.* Varanasi: Bharat-Bharati. First published 1874.

1880 *Miscellaneous Essays Relating to Indian Subjects.* 2 vols. London: Trübner & Co.

Hoek, Albertus Wilhelmus (Bert) van den

1979 The Goddess of the Northern Gate: Cellattamman as the Divine Warrior of Madurai. In: Marc Gaborieau & Alice Thorner (eds.) *Asie du Sud: Traditions et changements.* Paris: Éditions du CNRS, pp. 119-129.

1990a Hindu ritueel en Westerse planning: Een Nepalees offerfestival in vergelijkend perspectief. [Hindu Ritual and Western Planning: A Nepalese Sacrificial Ritual in Comparative Perspective.] *Antropologische Verkenningen* 9(3): 16-31.

1990b Does Divinity Protect the King? Ritual and Politics in Nepal. *Contributions to Nepalese Studies* (CNAS, Tribuvan University) 17(2): 147-155.

1992 Fire Sacrifice in Nepal. In: A.W. van den Hoek, D.H.A. Kolff & M.S. Oort (eds.) *Ritual, State and History in South Asia: Essays in Honour of J.C. Heesterman.* Leiden/New York/Köln: E.J. Brill (Memoirs of the Kern Institute 5), pp. 532-555 + 7 ill.

1993 Kathmandu as a Sacrificial Arena. In: Peter J.M. Nas (ed.) *Urban Symbolism.* Leiden/New York/Köln: E.J. Brill (Studies in Human Society 8), pp. 360-377.

1994 The Death of the Divine Dancers: The Conclusion of the Bhadrakālī *pyākhaṃ* in Kathmandu. In: Michael Allen (ed.) *Anthropology of Nepal: Peoples, Problems and Processes.* Kathmandu: Mandala Bookpoint, pp. 374-404.

1996 Gender and Caste in the Perfect Buddhist Gift: The *Samyak Mahādāna* in Kathmandu, Nepal. *Contributions to Nepalese Studies* (CNAS, Tribuvan University) 23(1): 195-211.

Hoek, A.W. van den, D.H.A. Kolff & M.S. Oort (eds.)

1992 *Ritual, State and History in South Asia: Essays in Honour of J.C. Heesterman.* Leiden: E.J. Brill (Memoirs of the Kern Institute 5).

Hoek, Bert van den & Bal Gopal Shrestha

1992a The Sacrifice of Serpents: Exchange and Non-Exchange in the *sarpabali* of Indrāyaṇī, Kathmandu. *Bulletin de l'École française d'Extrême Orient* (BEFEO, n.s.) 79(1): 57-75.

1992b Guardians of the Royal Goddess: Daitya and Kumār as the Protectors of Taleju Bhavānī of Kathmandu. *Contributions to Nepalese Studies* (CNAS, Tribuvan University) 19(2): 191-222.

Höfer, András

1979 *The Caste Hierarchy and the State in Nepal: A Study of the Muluki Ain of 1854*. Innsbruck: Universitätsverlag Wagner (Khumbu Himal 13, 2).

Hollé, Annick, Gérard Toffin & Krishna Prasad Rimal

1993 The 32 Maharjan Tols of Kathmandu City. In: Gérard Toffin (ed.) *The Anthropology of Nepal: From Tradition to Modernity*. Kathmandu: French Cultural Centre, pp. 21-61.

Hoksen, Frans P.

1974 *The Valley and Towns: a Record of Life and Change in Nepal*. New York: Weatherhill, etc.

Hunter, William Wilson

1896 *Life of Brian Houghton Hodgson, British Resident at the Court of Nepal*. London: John Murray.

Iltis, Linda

1985 *The Swasthānī Vrata: Newar Women and Ritual in Nepal*. PhD thesis University of Wisconsin, UMI 8528426.

1990 The Jala *Pyākhaṃ* in the Historical and Cultural Perspective. In: Prem Santi Tulādhar (ed.) *Nepālabhāṣā va Thvayā Sāhitya Vibhāgiya Goṣthī*. [The Newar Language and Literature: A Departmental Seminar.] Kathmandu: Lacoul Publication, pp. 141-67.

Joshi, Bhuwan Lal & Leo Eugene Rose

1966 *Democratic Innovations in Nepal: A Case Study of Political Acculturation*. Berkeley: University of California Press.

Josselin de Jong, Patrick Edward de

1956 De visie der participanten op hun cultuur. *Bijdragen tot de Taal-, Land- en Volkenkunde* 112(2): 149-168. English translation 1977.

1977 The Participants' View of Their Culture. In: P.E. de Josselin de Jong (ed.) *Structural Anthropology in the Netherlands: A Reader*. The Hague: Martinus Nijhoff (KITLV Translation Series 17), pp. 231-252. 2nd ed. 1983.

Juju, Baldev & Surendra Man Shrestha

1985 *Nepāḥyā Tāntrik Dyaḥ va Tāntrik Pūjā*. [Tāntrik Gods and Goddesses in Nepal.] (In Nepālbhāṣā). Kathmandu: Privately published.

Kane, Pandurang Vaman

1968-75 *History of Dharmaśāstra: Ancient and Mediaeval Religious and Civil Law in India*. 5 vols. Poona: Bhandarkar Oriental Research Institute. First published 1930-62.

Kasā, Prem Bahadur

1965 *Nāsaḥdyoyā Mye*. [Songs of Nāsaḥdyo.] Kathmandu: Himancala Pustak Bhavan.

Kirkpatrick, William

1975 *An Account of the Kingdom of Nepaul, Being the Substance of Observations Made During a Mission to that Country in the Year 1793*. New Delhi: Asian Publication Services. First published 1811.

Krick, Hertha

1982 *Das Ritual der Feuergründung (Agnyādheya)*. Hrsg. von Gerhard Oberhammer. Wien: Verlag der Österreichischen Akademie der Wissenschaften (Veröffentlichungen der Kommission für Sprachen und Kulturen Südasiens 16).

Kuiper, Franciscus Bernardus Jacobus

1983 *Ancient Indian Cosmogony*. Delhi: Vikas.

Lamsāl, Devi Prasad (ed.)

1966 *Bhāṣā Vaṃśāvalī*, Part II. Kathmandu: Nepāla Rāṣtriya Pustakālaya.

Landon, Perceval

1928 *Nepal*. 2 vols. London: Constable and Co. Ltd.

Lévi, Sylvain

1898 *La doctrine du sacrifice dans les Brahmanas*. Paris. Repr. Paris: École Pratique des Hautes Études, 1966.

1905-08 *Le Népal: Étude historique d'un royaume Hindou*. 3 vols. Paris: Ernest Leroux (Annales du Musée Guimet, Bibliothèque d'Études, tome XVII-XIX).

Lévi-Strauss, Claude

1963 *Structural Anthropology*. Harmondsworth: Penguin.

1964-71 *Mythologiques*. 4 vols. Paris: Librairie Plon.

Levy, Robert I.

1987 How the Navadurgā Protect Bhaktapur: The Effective Meanings of a Symbolic Enactment. In: Niels Gutschow & Axel Michaels (eds.) *Heritage of the Kathmandu Valley*. Sankt Augustin: VGH Wissenschaftsverlag (Nepalica 4), pp. 105-134.

1990 *Mesocosm: Hinduism and the Organization of a Traditional Newar City in Nepal*. Berkeley: University of California Press.

Lewis, Todd Thornton

1984 *The Tulādhars of Kathmandu: A Study of Buddhist Tradition in a Newar Merchant Community*. PhD thesis Colombia University, Ann Arbor UMI 8506008.

1993 Contribution to the Study of Popular Buddhism: The Newar Buddhist Festival of Guṃlā Dharma. *Journal of the International Association of Buddhist Studies* 16(2): 309-354.

Lingat, Robert

1967 *Les sources du droit dans le système traditionel de L'Inde*. Paris: Mouton & Co.

Locke, John K., S.J.

1985 *Buddhist Monasteries of Nepal. A Survey of the Bāhās and Bahīs of the Kathmandu Valley*. Kathmandu: Sahayogi Press.

Löwdin, Per

1985 *Food, Ritual and Society among the Newars*. Uppsala: Uppsala Research Report in Cultural Anthropology 4.

Macdonald, Alexander W.

1983 *Essays on the Ethnology of Nepal and South Asia* I. Kathmandu: Ratna Rustak Bhandar (Bibliotheca Himalayica III, 3). First published 1970.

Majumdar, Ramesh Chandra

1971 *History of Ancient Bengal*. Calcutta: G. Bharadwaj.

Malla, Kamal P.

1980 *Purvaja Lumaṃkā*. [Remembering the Ancestors.] Kathmandu: Thahneya Thakujuju Khalaḥ. (Nepal Saṃvat 1100).

1981 Linguistic Archaeology of the Nepal Valley. *Kailash* 8(1-2): 5-23.

1982 *Classical Newari Literature: A Sketch*. Kathmandu: Educational Enterprise.

1983a River-Names of the Nepal Valley: A Study in Cultural Annexation. *Contributions to Nepalese Studies* 10(1-2): 57-68.

1983b The Limits of Surface Archaeology. Review of Mary S. Slusser, *Nepal Mandala* (1982). *Contributions to Nepalese Studies* 11(1): 125-133.

1989 (ed.) *Nepal: Perspectives on Continuity and Change*. Kathmandu: Centre for Nepal and Asian Studies (CNAS).

Manandhar, Thakur Lal

1986 *Newari-English Dictionary: Modern Language of Kathmandu Valley*. Edited by Anne Vergati. Delhi: Agam Kala Prakashan.

Monier-Williams, Monier

1988 *A Sanskrit-English Dictionary*. Delhi: Motilal Banarsidass. First published 1899.

Nepal, Nirish

1985 Gaṃthā mugaḥ. *Ināp*, a Nepālbhāṣā Weekly, Kathmandu, July 17.

Nepali, Gopal Singh

1965 *The Newars: An Ethno-Sociological Study of a Himalayan Community*. Bombay: United Asia Publications.

Nijland, Dirk J., Bal Gopal Shrestha and Bert van den Hoek

1997<av> *Sacrifice of Serpents: The Festival of Indrāyaṇī, Kathmandu 1992/94*. Leiden: Institute of Cultural and Social Studies. Pal Super VHS/Betacam SP, color, 108 minutes.

Oldfield, Henry Ambrose

1880 *Sketches from Nipal, Historical and Descriptive*. 2 vols. London: W.H. Allen and Co. Repr. Delhi: Cosmo Publications, 1974.

Ossenbruggen, Frederik David Eduard van

1977 Java's *monca-pat*: Origins of a Primitive Classification System. In: P.E. de Josselin de Jong (ed.) *Structural Anthropology in the Netherlands: A Reader*. The Hague: Martinus Nijhoff, pp. 32-60 (KITLV Translation Series 17).

Pal, Pratapaditya

1974a *The Arts of Nepal*. 3 parts. Leiden: E.J. Brill.

1974b *Buddhist Art in Licchavi Nepal*. Bombay: Marg Publications.

Parry, Jonathan I.

1981 Death and Cosmogony in Kashi. *Contributions to Indian Sociology* (New Series) 15: 88-11.

Paudyal, Nayanatha (ed.)

1963 *Bhāṣā Vaṃśāvalī*, Part I. Kathmandu: Nepāla Rāṣtriya Pustakālaya.

Petech, Luciano

1958 *Medieval History of Nepal (c. 750-1480)*. Roma: Istituto Italiano per il Medio e Estremo Oriente. 2nd revised edition 1984.

Platenkamp, Josephus D.M.

1988 *Tobelo: Ideas and Values of a North Moluccan Society*. PhD thesis University of Leiden.

Pradhan, Rajendra Pd.

1986 *Domestic and Cosmic Rituals among the Hindu Newars of Kathmandu, Nepal*. PhD thesis University of Delhi.

Raghavan, V.

1979 *Festivals, Sports and Pastimes in India*. Ahmedabad: B.J. Institute of Learning and Research.

Rājvaṃśī, Samkarman

1986 Jhīgū Nakhaḥyā suru Gathāṃmugaḥ. [Gathāṃmugaḥ: The Beginning of our Festivals.] *Ināp*, a Nepālbhāṣā Weekly, Kathmandu, August 6.

Regmi, Dilli Raman

1965-66 *Medieval Nepal*. 4 vols. Calcutta: K.L. Mukhopadhyay.

1969 *Ancient Nepal*. 3rd edition. Calcutta: K.L. Muhopadhyay.

Regmi, Mahesh C.

1976 *Landownership in Nepal*. Berkeley: University of California Press.

1978 *Land Tenure and Taxation in Nepal*. 4 vols. Kathmandu: Ratna Pustak Bhandar. First published 1963-68.

Rosser, Colin

1966 Social Mobility in the Newar Caste System. In: Christoph von Fürer-Haimendorf (ed.) *Caste and Kin in Nepal, India & Ceylon: Anthropological Studies in Hindu-Buddhist Contact Zones*. London/The Hague: East-West Publications, pp. 68-139. Repr. New Delhi 1979.

Sayami, Dhooswan

1980 *The Lotus and the Flame: An Account on Nepalese Culture*. 2nd revised and enlarged edition. Kathmandu: Ratna Pustak Bhandar. First published 1972.

Sharma, Prayag Raj

1977 Caste, Social Mobility and Sanskritization: A Study of Nepal's Old Legal Code. *Kailash* 5(4): 277-299.

1983 The Land System of the Licchavis in Nepal. *Kailash* 10(1-2): 11-62.

Shrestha, Bal Gopal

1996 Visible and Invisible Aspects of the Devī Dances in Sankhu, Nepal. *Contributions to Nepalese Studies* 23(1): 255-269. Reprinted in: Harald Tambs-Lyche (ed.) *The Feminine Sacred in South Asia*. New Delhi: Manohar, 1999: 100-113.

1999 The Newars: The Indigenous Population of the Kathmandu Valley in the Modern State of Nepal. *Contributions to Nepalese Studies* 26(1): 83-117.

2002 *The Ritual Composition of Sankhu: The Socio-Religious Anthropology of a Newar Town in Nepal*. PhD thesis University of Leiden. Commercial edition forthcoming at Kathmandu: Tribhuvan University, Centre for Nepal and Asian Studies (CNAS).

Shrestha, Narayan P.

1997 *Kathmandu: The Eternal Kumari*. Lalitpur: Saroj & Kauz.

Shrestha, Bal Gopal and Bert van den Hoek

1995 Education in the Mother Tongue: The Case of Nepālbhāṣā (Newari). *Contributions to Nepalese Studies* 22(1): 73-86.

Shrestha, Bal Gopal and Han F. Vermeulen

2001 In Memoriam Bert van den Hoek (1951-2001). *European Bulletin of Himalayan Research* 20-21: 151-163. Includes a bibliography of A.W. van den Hoek, which is slightly adapted and expanded in the bibliography at the end of this book.

Shrestha, Surendra Man & Baldev Juju

1980 *Nepāḥyā Tāntrik dyaḥ va Tāntrik Pūjā*. Kathmandu: Privately published.

Slusser, Mary Shepherd

1982 *Nepal Mandala: A Cultural Study of the Kathmandu Valley*. 2 vols. Princeton: Princeton University Press.

Snellgrove, David L.

1957 *Buddhist Himalaya*. Oxford: Bruno Cassirer.

1989 *The Cohesive Role of Sanskritization and Other Essays*. Delhi: Oxford University Press.

Southall, Aidan

1993 The Circle and the Square: Symbolic Form and Process in the City. In: P.J.M. Nas (ed.) *Urban Symbolism*. Leiden/New York/Köln: E.J. Brill, pp. 378-393.

Toffin, Gérard

1978 Intercaste Relations in a Newar Community. In: James F. Fisher (ed.) *Himalayan Anthropology: The Indo-Tibetan Interface*. La Haye/Paris: Mouton, pp. 461-481.

1979 Les aspects religieux de la Royauté Néwar au Népal. *Archives de Sciences Sociales des Religions* 48(1): 53-82.

1984 *Société et religion chez les Néwar du Népal*. Paris: Éditions du Centre National de la Recherche Scientifique (Cahiers Népalais).

1986 Dieux souverains et rois dévots dans l'ancienne royauté de la vallée du Népal. *L'Homme* no. 99: 71-94.

1992 The Indra jātrā of Kathmandu as a Royal Festival: Past and Present. *Contributions to Nepalese Studies* 19(1): 73-92.

1993 *Le Palais et le Temple: La fonction royale dans la vallée du Népal*. Paris: CNRS Ethnologie.

1993 (ed.) *The Anthropology of Nepal: From Tradition to Modernity*. Kathmandu: French Cultural Centre.

1994 The Farmers in the City: The Social and Territorial Organization of the

Maharjan of Kathmandu. *Anthropos* 89: 433-459.

Underhill, M.M.

1921 *The Hindu Religious Year*. London: Association Press/Oxford University Press.

Vajrācārya, Asakaji [Ganesh Raj]

1987 *Nepal Varṣa Kriyā Nakhāḥ Cakhaḥ Pustakam*. Pāṭan: Privately published. [Originally written in Sanskrit by the Pandit Kaṇhānanda Brāhmaṇa and translated into Newari with a commentary.]

Vajracarya, Dhanavajra

1968 Licchavikālika Basti. *Pūrṇimā* 18: 87-101. [Abridged as 'Licchavi Settlements' in *Regmi Research Series* 1(1), 1969: 7-9.]

1973 *Licchhavikālakā Abhilekha*. [The Inscriptions of the Licchavi Period.] Kathmandu: Institute of Nepal and Asian Studies. Republished with an English translation by D.R. Regmi 1983.

1989 Medieval Nepal. In: Kamal P. Malla (ed.) *Nepal: Perspectives on Continuity and Change*. Kathmandu: Centre for Nepal and Asian Studies, pp. 77-100.

Vajrācārya, Dhanavajra & Kamal P. Malla

1985 *The Gopālarājavaṃśāvalī*. Wiesbaden: Franz Steiner Verlag.

Vajrācārya, Gautam Vajra

1976 *Hanumāndhokā Rājdarbār*. Kathmandu: Tribhuvan University, Centre for Nepal and Asian Studies (CNAS).

Varya, Tank Vilas

1987 *Nepal: The Seat of Cultual Heritage*. Kathmandu: Educational Enterprise.

Vermeulen, Han F.

2002 A.W. van den Hoek (1951-2001): Nepal-kenner en antropoloog. *Samachar. ICFON Newsletter* 11(3): 15. International Council for Friends of Nepal (ICFON), The Netherlands.

Witzel, Michael

1980 On the Location of the Licchavi Capital of Nepal. In: Georg Buddruss & Albrecht Wezler (eds.) *Festschrift Paul Thieme. = Studien zur Indologie und Iranistik Heft 5/6*. Reinbek: Verlag für orientalistische Fachpublikationen, pp. 311-337.

1992 Meaningful Ritual: Vedic, Medieval and Contemporary Concepts in the Nepalese Agnihotra Ritual. In: A.W. van den Hoek, D.H.A. Kolff & M.S. Oort (eds.) *Ritual, State and History in South Asia. Essays in Honour of J.C. Heesterman*. Leiden/New York/Köln: E.J. Brill (Memoirs of the Kern Institute 5), pp. 774-825.

Wright, Daniel

1972 (ed.) *History of Nepal*. Translated from the Parvatīyā by Munshi Shew Shunker Singh and Pandit Shri Gunanand. Kathmandu: Nepal Antiquated Book Publishers. First published 1877.

Zanen, Sjoerd M.

1979 'Gardens of Adonis' in the Mediterranean area and in South India: A Comparison of their Structure. In: Marc Gaborieau & Alice Thorner (eds.) *Asie du Sud: Traditions et changements*. Paris: Éditions du CNRS, pp. 145-151.

1986 The Goddess Vajrayoginī and the Kingdom of Sankhu (Nepal). *Puruṣārtha* 10: 125-166.

Publications of A.W. (Bert) van den Hoek

Compiled by Han F. Vermeulen and Bal Gopal Shrestha

1971 'Antropologie is anders.' [Anthropology is Different.] *Antro* 3(6), 6 pp.

1971 'Hoe antropologen eruit zien.' [How Anthropologists Look Like.] *Antro* 3(7), 2 pp.

1976 'Een kanttekening bij de methode van het structuralisme.' [A Note on the Method of Structuralism.] *Antro* 6(5): 7-12.

1979 'The Goddess of the Northern Gate: Cellattamman as the 'Divine Warrior' of Madurai.' In: Marc Gaborieau and Alice Thorner (eds.) *Asie du Sud: Traditions et changements.* Paris: Éditions du CNRS, pp. 119-129.

1985 'De culturele dimensie van ontwikkeling: een sleutelbegrip in UNESCO's toekomstbeeld.' [The Cultural Dimension of Development: A Key Concept in UNESCO's Policy.] *IMWOO-Bulletin* 13 (3): 12-14.

1986 'The Cultural Dimension of the Jonglei Development Projects in South Sudan.' In: G.C. Uhlenbeck (ed.) *The Cultural Dimension of Development*, The Hague: Netherlands National Commission for UNESCO, pp. 77-87.

1988 *Cultural Diversity and the Ideology of Development: UNESCO's Role in the International Debate on the Cultural Dimension of Development.* Leiden: Faculty of Social Sciences, Leiden Institute of Development Studies and Consultancy Services (LIDESCO R-88/10). ix + 68 pp.

1990a 'Hindu ritueel en Westerse planning: een Nepalees offerritueel in vergelijkend perspectief.' [Hindu Ritual and Western Planning: A Nepalese Sacrificial Ritual in Comparative Perspective.] *Antropologische Verkenningen* 9(3): 16-31.

1990b 'Does Divinity Protect the King? Ritual and Politics in Nepal.' *Contributions to Nepalese Studies* (CNAS, Tribhuvan University) 17(2): 147-155.

1990c 'CNAS and CEDA: Two Centres of Asian Studies in Nepal.' *South Asia Newsletter* No. 5: 22-24.

1990d 'Report on the 11th Conference on Modern South Asian Studies.' *CNWS Newsletter* No. 3: 10-11.

1990e 'De afkondiging van de Nepalese grondwet 1990.' [The Proclamation of the Constitution of Nepal in 1990.] *Nepal Nieuws* No. 3: 2-7.

1990f 'Eindelijk een nieuwe grondwet.' [A New Constitution At Last.] *Nepal Nieuws* No. 4: 2-8.

1991a 'Report on the VIIIth World Sanskrit Conference.' *South Asia Newsletter* No. 7: 41-42.

1991b 'Nepalese verkiezingen brengen politieke duidelijkheid.' [Elections in Nepal Provide Political Clarity.] *Nepal Nieuws* No. 2: 2-9.

1991c 'Hongerstaking sterft een zachte dood.' [Hunger Strike Dies a Solemn Death.] *Nepal Nieuws* No. 3: 2-5.

1991d 'Een kijkje in het parlement.' [A Look in Parliament.] *Nepal Nieuws* No. 3: 6-7.

1992a 'Fire Sacrifice in Nepal'. In: van den Hoek, Kolff and Oort (eds.), pp. 532-555 + 7 ill.

1992b 'Locale verkiezingen locaal beschouwd.' [Local Elections Considered Locally.] *Nepal Nieuws* 3(3): 4-10.

1992c 'Nepali, Sanskrit en de etnische talen.' [Nepali, Sanskrit and the Ethnic Languages.] *Nepal Nieuws* 3(3): 11-18, ill.

1992d 'Sanskrit Education: An Outsider's View.' *The Independent Weekly* 2(28), September 2 p. 2.

1993a 'Kathmandu as a Sacrificial Arena.' In: Peter J.M. Nas (ed.) *Urban Symbolism*, Leiden/New York/Köln: E.J. Brill, pp. 360-377.

1993b 'Les Divinités protègent-elles le roi? Rituel et politique au Nepal.' *L'Ethnographie* 89(1): 19-28. Translated from the English (1990b) by Xavier Blaisel.

1993c 'Review of Paul Atkinson, *The Ethnographic Imagination: Textual Constructions of Reality* (London: Routledge 1990).' *Social Anthropology* 1(3): 356-357.

1994 'The Death of the Divine Dancers: The Conclusion of the Bhadrakālī pyākhaṃ in Kathmandu.' In: Michael Allen (ed.) *Anthropology of Nepal: Peoples, Problems and Processes.* Kathmandu: Mandala Bookpoint, pp. 374-404.

1996 'Gender and Caste in the Perfect Buddhist Gift: The *Samyak Mahādāna* in

Kathmandu, Nepal.' *Contributions to Nepalese Studies* (CNAS, Tribhuvan University) 23(1): 195-211.

1999a 'Gender and Caste in the Perfect Buddhist Gift: The *Samyak Mahādāna* in Kathmandu, Nepal.' In: Harald Tambs-Lyche (ed.) *The Feminine Sacred in South Asia*. New Delhi: Manohar, pp. 46-62. Originally published 1996.

1999b 'De IHI-ceremonie.' [The Ihi Ceremony.] *Samachar*, ICFON Newsletter 8(4): 2.

2000 'Gathammugah: de uitdrijving van de geesten in Kathmandu' [Gathāmugaḥ: Expulsion of the Ghosts in Kathmandu.] *Samachar*, ICFON Newsletter 9(3), May, pp. 1-3. Also on the International Council for Friends of Nepal, The Netherlands, homepage.

2002 'Gathammugah: de uitdrijving van de geesten.' [Gathāmugaḥ: Expulsion of the Ghosts.] *Chautari* No. 9, Summer, pp. 8-9. Abridged version of 2000.

Hoek, A.W. van den, D.H.A. Kolff & M.S. Oort (eds.)

1992 *Ritual, State and History in South Asia: Essays in Honour of J.C. Heesterman*. Leiden: E.J. Brill (Memoirs of the Kern Institute 5).

Hoek, Bert van den & Bal Gopal Shrestha

1992a 'The Sacrifice of Serpents: Exchange and Non-Exchange in the *sarpabali* of Indrāyaṇī, Kathmandu.' *Bulletin de l'École française d'Extrême Orient* (BEFEO, New Series) 79(1): 57-75.

1992b 'Guardians of the Royal Goddess: Daitya and Kumār as the Protectors of Taleju Bhavānī of Kathmandu.' *Contributions to Nepalese Studies* (CNAS, Tribuvan University) 19(2): 191-222.

1995 'Education in the Mother Tongue: The Case of Nepālbhāṣā (Newari).' *Contributions to Nepalese Studies* 22(1): 73-86.

Hoek, A.W. van den & Sjoerd Zanen

1976 *Netwerk en structuur: Theoretische studie van sociale verandering in een Libanees bergdorp.* [Network and Structure: Theoretical Study of Social Change in a Lebanese Mountain Village.] Leiden: Instituut voor Culturele Antropologie en Sociologie der Niet-Westerse Volken (ICA-Publicaties 14). 47 pp. ill.

1987 'Dinka Dualism and the Nilotic Hierarchy of Values.' In: Rob de Ridder and Jan A.J. Karremans (eds.) *The Leiden Tradition in Structural Anthropology. Essays in Honour of P.E. de Josselin de Jong*. Leiden: E.J. Brill, pp. 170-96.

Hoek, Bert van den, Sjoerd Zanen & Philip Leek Deng

1978 *Social-anthropological Aspects of the Jonglei Development Projects in South Sudan (field-work report)*. Leiden: Instituut voor Culturele Antropologie en Sociologie der Niet-Westerse Volken (ICA-Publicaties 67). 107 pp. maps, ill. Reissued with a new introduction 1985.

Nijland, Dirk J., Bal Gopal Shrestha and Bert van den Hoek

1997<av>*Sacrifice of Serpents: The Festival of Indrāyaṇī, Kathmandu 1992/94*. Leiden: Institute of Cultural and Social Studies. An ethnographic videofilm, Pal Super VHS/Betacam SP, color, 108 minutes.

Hoek, A.W. van den, Erik de Maaker, Dirk Nijland and Bal Gopal Shrestha

1998 'Film South Asia 1997.' *IIAS Newsletter* No. 16, p. 16.

Interview

1991 'Vikāsa va Saṃskṛti Rakṣyā Nitāṃ Nāpaṃ Juimā.' [Development and the Protection of Culture must be carried out simultaneously.] Interview by Bal Gopal Shrestha, conducted in English and translated into Nepālbhāṣā (Newari), published in *Ināp*, a Nepālbhāṣā Weekly, 9(44), November 20, pp. 3 and 7.

Forthcoming

Hoek, A.W. van den, Dirk J. Nijland and Bal Gopal Shrestha

2005 'Sacrifice of Serpents: Ethnographic Images and Anthropological Interpretation.' In: Metje Postma and Peter Crawford (eds.) *Evaluating Visual Ethnography: Research, Analysis, Representation, and Culture*. Aarhus: Intervention Press. Papers of the international conference held under the same title at Leiden, September 21-24, 1999.

<av> *Agnimatha: The Fire Temple in Pāṭan*. (Film, in preparation). Parts 1-4.

<av> *Pacalī Bhairava: The Festival of Liquor and Death*. (Film, in preparation).

Glossary

Compiled by Bal Gopal Shrestha

Ācāju: a Newar Hindu priest, karmācārya
abhiṣeka: consecration
abhiṣikta: consecrated
agnihotra: oblation to fire
Āju: ancestors
ākhāḥ (*ākhāḥcheṃ*): gymnasium
antyeṣṭi: the last rites
ārati: the showing of a light, an evening ritual
āsana: a seat
aṣṭamātṛkā: the eight mother goddesses (see also *mātṛkā*)
asura: a demon

babhū: a kind of cymbal
bāhāl (*bāhāḥ*): a Buddhist monastery (Skt. *vihāra*)
bahi: a smaller Buddhist monastery
baji: flattened or beaten rice daytime foods
balcā: a temporary hut
bali pūjā: the ritual offerings made to ward off evil spirits
bāsuri: a flute
bau: food offered to deceased ancestors, spirits and ghosts
baumata: the lights for the ancestors
baupāḥ: a bowl containing food offered to deceased ancestors, spirits and ghosts
betāl: ghost image associated with Pacalī a gentle kind of demon
Bhairava: the terrible form of Śiva also god of death
bhajan: the singing of devotional songs
Bhāṣāvaṃśāvalī: a nineteenth century chronicle of Nepal
bhegaḥ: an earthen pot
Bhikṣu: a celibate monk
Bhimsen: the Newar god of trade and second brother of Pāṇḍava in the Sanskrit epic Mahābhārata
bhūdyo: the ghost god

bhūt (bhūtpret): ghosts or goblins
bhuyuphasi: a pumpkin
bhvagatyā: a large green citrus fruit which is red within
bhvay: meals served during festivals or festive occasions such as marriage
bicāḥ pūjā: worship in the temple a few days after the completion of the deity's procession
bvaṃcā: small earthern pot with rice or other grains

caitya: a small Buddhist shrine
catāṃmari: pancakes made of rice flour
chali kathi: silver-ornamented stick
chusyā: a pair of small cymbals
cipa: remanants of food left by other person and hence polluted
cīrhaṃ: a small one
Citrakār (Puṃ): the painters
Cyāme: sweeper caste

dabū: a platform
daitya: a demon
dāgiṃ (Skt. *dākiṇī*): a demoness
dakṣiṇā: fees
dakṣiṇāyana (Skt.): the summer solstice
dāṃ: money
daṃga: two-headed drum
dāna: a gift
dāphā: a kind of music that uses one pair of two-sided large drums (*khiṃ*), a pair of cupped cymbals (*tiṃchu*) and traditional devotional songs
darśana: to pay respect
Dasain: Nepali name for the annual Hindu festival of the goddess Durgā (see also Mohanī)
devaṃ: a shroud
Devī: a female deity, a form of the goddess Durgā
dhākacā: a bamboo basket decorated with colourful cloths
dhāmi: a sorcerer
dāphā: type of music played with a set of instruments including drum, pipe and cymbals
dharma: religion, sense of discipline, right action
dharmayuddha: a battle between good and evil

dhau baji: yogurt served together with beaten rice
dhimay: large two headed drum
dhvaja: flag
dhukū: the treasure store in the house
dhunyāmunyā: a long pole decorated with yak tails and flags carried by *dhimay* players
digudyo: lineage deities
dīkṣā: a ritual initiation
dīkṣita: consecrated
dṛṣṭi kaṃkegu: ritual opening of the eyes of a god's image
dvārapāla: doorkeepers
dyo (*dyaḥ*): gods
dyo pyākhaṃ: divine dance
dyocheṃ: a god house
dyo lhāyegu: a kind of music for paying respect to gods and goddesses

gaṇa (*gaṃ*): a troupe of deities
Gaṇeśa: a Hindu god, a son of the Lord Śiva and the goddess Parvatī
Gathāṃmugaḥ: the ghost god
Gathu: the caste of gardeners
ghaṃgalā: anklet with a string of small bells
ghaḥsū: the house purification rite performed on eleventh or twelft day after a death
Ghaṇṭākarṇa: bell-eared, name of demon
ghāṭ: river banks for bathing
Ghaṭasthāpanā: the first of the ten days of Dasain
Gopālarājavaṃśāvalī: the 14th century chronicle of Nepal
Gorkhā: a district situated in the west of Nepal, the former kingdom of the ancestors of present royal dynasty of Nepal
Gorkhālī: inhabitants of Gorkhā, name of the language spoken by these people which is known now as Nepali, the official language of Nepal
grāma: the village
gubhāju (*guruju*): a Buddhist Vajrācārya priest
guṃgū: a kind of incense
guru: teacher
guthi (Skt.: *goṣṭhī*): socio-religious associations of the Newars
Guthi Saṃsthān (the Guthi Corporation): the government office in charge

of religious endowments
gvaḥjā: rice pastries made for ritual offerings
gvay: betel nuts
gvay dāṃ: offering of betel nuts and coins to a deity, king or a patron of rituals as a gesture of invitation
gvaysvāṃ: a nut-shaped flower

hāthudyo: the god of the spouting beer
hāthu hayegu: the spouting of beer
hiti: water spout, tap
homa: burnt offering

Indra: the king of the gods
ikāpaḥkā: a mixture of yellow and brown mustard seeds
itāḥ: wicks (see also *kheluitāḥ*)

jalpay luyegu: pouring liquor into the jar of Pacalī Bhairava
janai: the sacred thread that Brahmins wear
jā (Nep.: *bhāt*): boiled rice
jajmān: patron responsible for sacrifice (see also *yajamāna*)
jātrā (*yātrā*): processions of gods and goddesses or pilgrimages
jhāṃkri: faith-healers of mostly Tamang origin
jīva nyāsa: the ritual insertion of life into images of deities, masks and dancers
Jośī: the caste of astrologers
juju (*mahārāja*): the king (see also Thaku juju)
juju pūjā: king's worship
jutho: polluted (see also *cipa*)
Jyāpu: the caste of farmers
jyoti: a light

kāhāḥ: trumpet
kalaḥ: a basket or metal vessel with a handle used for carrying materials for worshipping
kalaśa: a holy jar
kaṃypvī: a disk struck to the beats of the drums
kanhāysvāṃ: the green leaves offered to Pacalī Bhairava during his yātrā
Karmācārya: a Hindu Newar priest (see also *Ācāju*)

Kāṣṭhamaṇḍapa: the great wooden resthouse on the Maru side of the palace square, from which Kathmandu derives its name
Katiṃ Punhi: the full moon day of the month of *Āśvina*
kavaṃcā: demon offering
khaḍga: a sword
khaḥ: scaffold, palanquin
khāisi: a bitter orange
khāsi: a cauldron
khalaḥ: a group, family
kheluitāḥ: long wicks used during the festival of Svanti (see also itāḥ)
Khicā pūjā: the worship of dogs
khiṃ: two-sided large drum
khuṃdyo: the stealing god
khyāḥ: a furry creature
Kijā pūjā: the worship of brothers by their sisters
kisali (*kisli*): a shallow earthen pot with a betel nut and a coin
koṭ: fort, place where buffaloes are sacrificed during the Dasain festival,
kotaḥ: a plate for worship
koṭhā: room
kṣemā: apology
kṣema pūjā: the 'worship of apology'
Kṣetrapāla: the guardian of a locality
kule: a measuring pot
Kumārī: the virgin goddess, a virgin girl representing the goddess
kvaṃ: a jar
kvane (*kone*): lower or southern part of the city or a town
kvāti: a soup made of nine kinds of grain

laḥ: water (see also *yachiṃ laḥ*, *nīlaḥ*)
lākhe: a demon
Lakṣmī pūjā: the worship of the goddess Lakṣmī
lasakusa: a welcoming worship
latyā: the first śrāddha after one and a half month of the death
lāykū: palace
līlā: a play
liṅga: phallus

Mahādev: great god or god of the gods, another name of Śiva
Mahākāl: Śiva in his fierce form, the god of death
Mahāṣṭamī: the eighth day of the Dasain festival
Mahānavamī: the ninth day of the Dasain festival
makaḥ: a fire pot
Mānandhar (Sāymi): the caste of oil pressers

mandaḥ (*maṇḍala*): a cosmic diagram
mantra: incantation, spell
maraḥjā: special food given in charity
matayāḥ: the procession of lights
mātṛkā: goddess mother (see also *aṣṭamātṛkā*)
Mha pūjā: the worship of the self or body
mhyāmasta: daughters and out married daughters
Mohanī: black soot mark, hence the Newar name of the Hindu festival of goddess Durgā (Nep.: *Dasain*)
mokṣa: release
mūrti: a statue or an image of a god or goddess
mvādyo: a living god

nāga, nāgin: divine serpents
nakhaḥ: major festivals
naḥlāsvāṃ: the holy sprouts grown in house shrines during the festival of Dasain
namaskāra: a homage
nānicāyāḥ: the procession of Kumārī through the centre of town on the last day of Indra yātrā
naraka: the hell
Nārāyaṇa: name of the Lord Viṣṇu (see also Viṣṇu)
Nāsaḥdyo: the god of dance and drama
nāstika: an atheist
Navarātri: the ninth nights dedicated to the goddess *Durgā*
Nāy: the butchers
nāyaḥ: leading elder, especially of a group of builders
nāykhiṃ: butchers' music
Nepal Saṃvat: the Nepal era, introduced on 20 October 879 AD
Nepali: people of Nepal, the official language of Nepal
Newar: the Newar people in Nepal, their language, which is more popularly known by the name Nepālbhāṣā among the Newars and Newārī among the western philologists)
nīlaḥ: clean water used in rituals
nimantraṇa: invitation
nitya pūjā: a morning worship
nvakū: the second eldest or deputy head
nyāsa: life

odana: a sacrificial porridge

Pacalī: the god Pacalī Bhairava, a legendary king of Pharping
padmāsana: sitting in lotus seat

pāḥ: a turn
pālācā: a shallow earthen bowl
pāḥlāmha: the person whose turn it is
pañcaibājā: music of the Damāi caste
pañcāmṛta: five sacred liquids
pañcāṅga (*pātro*): almanac, traditional calendar
pañcapatā: a small five-coloured flags
pañcarātri: another name designated to the festival of Tihār orYama pañcak
Parvatīyā (Parvate): people of the hills, non-newar Nepali speaking
pasūkā: five-coloured threads
pātāla: the underworld
pāṭī: a restplace, shelter
pipā: army recruit
pitṛ: (Skt.): deceased ancestors
pātra: a bowl
pātro: a printed almanac, traditional calendar
pāyāḥ: sword procession
phetā: a turban
phulpāṭī: bunch of flower on a bamboo stick (royal attribute brought from Dhāding, adjoining Gorkhā on 7th day of Dasain)
pigaṃdyo: a deity with a *pīṭha*
pikhālakhu: place of worhip in front of Newar houses
pīṭha (New: *pigaṃ*): usually open air shrine especially of the eight mother goddesses
Poḍe (*Dyolā*): fisherman caste, also cleaners or temple guardians
potāy: rice flour used in rituals
pradīpa: light
prasād (Skt.): remainder of sacrificial offering given to worshippers as a blessings
preta: spirit (see also *bhūtpret*)
pūjā: worship with (usually vegetal) offerings
Pūjā kothā: a place of worship
pulu: a reed mat
Punhi (Pūrṇimā): a full moon day
Putuvār (Duiṃ): the palanquin carriers and trumpeters's caste in Newar society
pvaṃgā: long pipe
pyākhaṃ: dance and drama
pyākhaṃ khalaḥ: dance team
pyākiṃ: a three-hooked nail

rājguru: royal teacher and priest
Rakshas (*rākṣasa*): a demon

Ranjitkār: the dyer caste in Newar society
ṛṣi: seers
ratha yātrā: chariot procession

sagaṃ: foods for blessing
sāit: the auspicious moment
śakti: divine power
saliṃcā: an earthen platter
samay baji: a festive food containing beaten and popped rice, black soyabeans, ginger, roast meat and liquor
saṃnyāsin: world renouncer
sanā: the funeral procession
sanāguthi: a funeral association in Newar society (see also *sī guthi*)
Sāpāru: the cow's first day of the dark half of Guṃlā month
sarpahoma: a sacrifice of serpents
sataḥ: a resthouse or shelter
selāunu (Nep.): to immerse
Śhāha: the ruling dynasty of present-day Nepal
Shrestha: the trader or administrator caste in Newar society
sīguthi: a funeral association in Newar society (see also *sanā guthi*)
sī kāḥ bhvay: a feast in which the parts of the head of a sacrificed animal is divided among the eldest members of a family or a socio-religious association
sī jā: the 'death-food'
Siṃhinī (Simbā): the Lion-faced guardian goddess
sinājyā: transplanting rice
siṃphaṃ: a wooden measuring pot
śmaśāna: the cremation ground
sohra śrāddha: the sixteen days dedicated to *śrāddha* rituals for the deceased
soma: the juice of Soma plant
śrāddha: ceremony in honour of deceased forebear
stupa: a Buddhist monument (see also caitya)
sukūlā: dried meat
sukundā: an oil lamp with an image of Gaṇeśa
svāṃ: a flower
svarga: heaven
Svayambhū: the self-emanated god, a famous Buddhist *caitya* in Nepal

tāḥ: cymbals
tāhāṃpha: pitcher
tāhāsā: a bamboo structure decorated with colourful cloths which is carried out in a procession on the day of the cow's procession

taḥsi: wild lime, common citron
Taleju: the tutelary goddess of the Malla kings of Nepal
tās: shiny cloths
Thakū juju: ritual king
thane: upper or northern part of a town or a city
thvaṃ: the local rice beer
ṭikā: coloured powder used for mark of blessing on the forehead of a person)
tīrtha: confluence, place of pilgrimage
tithi: lunar day
tisā: ornament
tulasī: the sacred plant *Ocimum basilicum*
tvāḥdevā: lamp stand
tvāḥ (*ṭol*): a quarter
tyāga: abandonment

upākhu vanegu: the festive circumambulation of the entire city in memory of the deceased of the past year by their relatives in Kahtmandu
utsava mūrti: statue taken out in procession (see also yātrā mūrti)

vāhana: vehicle (usually animal) of a god
Vajrācārya: a Buddhist priest
Vijayā Daśamī: the tenth day "of the victory" tenth day of the bright half of Āśvin month
vākijāki: a mixture of half-husked rice
vaṃśāvalī: chronicle
Viṣṇu: one among the three most important Hindu gods, also called Nārāyaṇa
vrātya: consecreted warrier (Vedic later reminescan t not fulgilling his sacred duties
Vyāghinī (Dhumbā): the Tiger-faced guardian goddess

yaciṃ laḥ: pure river water
yajamāna: patron responsible for sacrifice (see also *jajmān*)
yajña (Skt.): sacrifice
yaḥsiṃ: ceremonial poles
yātrā: processions of gods and goddesses (see also *jātrā*)
yātrā mūrti: procession image
yuddha: fight

Index